PLACES WHERE THEY SING

Conducting at Exeter Cathedral

Other books by Lionel Dakers

Church Music at the Crossroads (Marshall, Morgan and Scott, 1970)

A Handbook of Parish Music (Mowbray, 1976, revised 1982)

Making Church Music Work (Mowbray, 1978)

Music and the Alternative Service Book–Editor–(Addington Press, 1980)

The Psalms–Their Use and Performance Today–Editor (RSCM, 1980)

The Church Musician as Conductor (RSCM, 1982)

Church Music in a Changing World (Mowbray, 1984)

Choosing–and using–Hymns (Mowbray, 1985)

Parish Music (The Canterbury Press Norwich, 1991)

New Church Anthem Book–Editor–(Oxford, 1992)

The Church Anthem Handbook (Oxford, 1994)

Places Where They Sing

Memoirs of a Church Musician

LIONEL DAKERS

The Canterbury Press
Norwich

First published 1995 by The Canterbury Press Norwich
(a publishing imprint of Hymns Ancient & Modern Limited,
a registered charity)
St Mary's Works, St Mary's Plain,
Norwich, Norfolk NR3 3BH

British Library Cataloguing in Publication Data

A catalogue record for this book is available
from the British Library

ISBN 1-85311-122-8

Typeset by Chansitor Publications Limited, Beccles, Suffolk

*Printed and bound in Great Britain by
Biddles Ltd
Guildford and King's Lynn*

For my wife Elisabeth, my constant companion and supporter through so much of this story.

My grateful thanks to Anthony Rota for so meticulously scrutinising my literary efforts and, not least, for the invaluable suggestions and corrections he made.

Contents

Preface   *page* xi

1.   Starting Points   1
2.   The 1930s—A Kentish Boyhood   7
3.   Eton suits and Evensong   19
4.   Halcyon boyhood days—or were they?   28
5.   A less relaxed period   31
6.   14560967 Private Dakers   40
7.   York—the Army and music intertwined   43
8.   Music on the banks of the Nile   53
9.   Aspects of student life in London   64
10. Windsor and Eton—Castle and College   72
11. In Yorkshire once again   92
12. Exeter—the early years   103
13. Exeter—a continuing saga   119
14. Farewell West Country   127
15. A totally different existence   152
16. The joys of globe trotting   170
17. Gaining momentum   179
18. Keeping the airlines busy   188
19. Overseas postscript   201
20. Farewell to the Palace   206
21. Sarum—Close and City   212
22. Reflections on reaching 70   224
23. Towards the future?   230

Index   235

'When to the sessions of sweet silent thought I summon up remembrance of things past.'

Shakespeare: *Sonnet XXX*

'In my beginning is my end.'

T. S. Eliot: *East Coker*

'In my end is my beginning.'

Mary Stuart, just before she died.

'If I were asked to say what is the most important production of Art and the thing most longed for, I should answer, a Beautiful House; and if I were further asked to name the production next in importance and the thing next to be longed for, I should answer, a Beautiful Book. To enjoy good houses and good books in self respect and decent comfort seems to me to be the pleasurable end towards which all societies of human beings ought now to struggle.'

William Morris

Preface

Oh dear—yet another musician writing his memoirs and adding yet more, as someone recently commented—albeit in another context—to 'the word-drunk world we inhabit'.

Why then; am I being presumptuous?

Is it egotism, is it vanity to even suggest anyone would want to read what follows? After all, I am not a famous politician, a field marshal, a television personality, nor even a spy.

I hope I may therefore be forgiven if I pause to look back, to loiter and even linger over what James Lees-Milne once called 'the lengthening galleries of memory'. Perhaps my justification might even claim to re-echo Oscar Wilde's maxim that anything worth doing is worth doing badly.

Freed for the first time from many commitments and responsibilities, I felt that my late sixties were a convenient time to move on to new and, for the most part, rather different pastures. Retirement does not, or should not, surely, signal the end, or a total eclipse, merely the culmination of a particular chapter and with it the opening of a new one full of fresh pursuits and challenges. In this I have been particularly fortunate.

I now have more time than was ever available before to look back through my diaries which, during the war years and then through to my days at Exeter, invariably contain, somewhat to my surprise, often lengthy daily entries not only of happenings but also of thoughts and observations. At the time it never occurred to me what lengths I had sometimes gone to in this respect. Scrap books, programmes, press cuttings and letters have helped me to think back and have forwarded the urge, even the impulse, to put pen to paper. Some of the photographs I have come across are another matter, for they show many of us before the ravages of time have altered features—and waistlines.

I never cease to be grateful for having been able to lead an interesting, varied and full life. How fortunate I have been in this respect, for the humdrum hardly ever surfaced. No two people are, thank God, ever alike, and this is my only, and I hope valid, excuse—even justification—for setting out on this retrospective journey.

I have always possessed a consuming passion for reading and collecting biography. I have again and again been inspired by the particular tale each tells, though I am not so naive as to suggest this quality is evident in mine. That is altogether another matter. I merely relate some facts, together with my thoughts and reflections as much concerning the future as the past, for the future is what really matters, not the retrospective nostalgia, pleasurable though it may be, to dip into the past. It is ultimately surely a question of anticipating with confidence what that unknown enigma—the future—may have to offer.

As a young man I certainly saw visions, although now, as an old—or reasonably old—man, I happen to dream fewer dreams.

LD

CHAPTER ONE

Starting Points

'Heaven lies about us in our infancy'—Wordsworth

In reading other people's biographies, I invariably find the initial chapters are heavy going and not very interesting, simply because I want to read about the person concerned, and not his antecedents. For myself, I have never had any burning desire to research my pedigree. I am, quite frankly, not much interested in my precursors, nor suspect would anyone else be.

All I do know, and this only by family surmise, is that my forebears probably came over from France at the time of the Norman Conquest, as so many did, or that the family name first appeared in the Domesday Book. The former could well be true because the French name would almost certainly be the Dacre or Dacres variant which today is found more widely than the way we spell it.

In modern times much of the family seem to have lived, worked and multiplied in Kent in the Medway Towns, notably in Rochester or on the north side of the river Medway in Strood.

At the age of five or six, that is, around 1930, I was regularly taken to see my grandfather, William Henry Dakers. This elderly widower lived in Northcote Road, Strood, where he was cared for by a Mrs Richards and her daughter. It was, as I recall it, a typical late 19th century terrace house of fairly large proportions, especially in the back living room and kitchen area though, as with all things when you are young and small, it probably seemed larger then than it was in reality. There was a little back garden at the bottom of which was the main railway line from Victoria to the coast, where I would look out in eager anticipation for the then infrequent Continental Expresses, as they were romantically called, and which were unique in having 1st, 2nd and 3rd

1

class coaches all in the splendid green livery of the Southern
Railway.

I well remember my grandfather as a rather frightening
person, probably because he had a large beard and seldom smiled.
He seemed to be more or less permanently seated in a large
horsehair chair in one corner of his room which was at the front
of the house and where he could look out through the thick lace
and velvet curtains to the so called recreation ground on the
other side of the road, and where in the bandstand on Sunday
afternoons the local band would play Suppé, Sousa and the many
predictable marches, waltzes and selections so beloved in the
early 1930s. He fed me with Ovaltine rusks—I cannot think
why—though the taste of them I can recall to this day. These
formed the high point and invariable climax of my visits. Even
so, I still found him formidable, nor can I in any way recall what
sort of conversation we may have had.

In his working life he had been a resolute and fairly hard-
headed businessman building up a highly successful and much
respected estate agency firm, W. H. Dakers and Sons, which was
well known throughout the Medway Towns. His sons were my
Uncle Will and my father. Much of my grandfather's generally
doctrinaire attitude towards life was reflected to an extent in my
father's subsequent attitude towards me whenever I wanted to
embark on something not in line with his somewhat inflexible
notion of how things should be done, such as 'if you want to
educate your children privately at a boarding school, that is your
affair, but don't expect me to help you finance this', a maxim he
persisted in to his dying day. He would then go on to tell me that
if the local day schools were good enough for him, they were
good enough for his grandchildren. The idea of betterment in
succeeding generations never seemed to enter into his head,
though he mildly applauded his nephews being sent to Dover
College and even later contemplated the same for me at Sutton
Valence, though nothing ever came of it. In later years I was to
resent more and more being denied such an education even
though I seemed to make my way without it, but I realise what I
missed out on in so many ways and which I believe a public
school would have provided.

2

By one of those odd quirks of human nature, my father, while being over-generous to many people, which some took advantage of, was the very opposite where I was concerned. As time went on I grew more and more alienated from him, and he from me. As with so many parental relationships we completely failed then, as later, to understand each other, simply because we were diametrically opposed in much of our thinking. I suspect that in his latter years he felt that I did not much care for him. This was not true; it was merely that our ways of life grew increasingly apart and we had so few interests in common. When he died he did however leave virtually everything to me, his only child. This enabled my wife and me to live less precariously than in our early married life, for a church musician then, as now, was not exactly in the top income bracket. Through careful investment, his estate enabled us to provide not only for our future years but equally importantly to help our grandchildren educationally in ways previously denied me. It has also given us, and them, much pleasure.

My father never became reconciled to my opting for a musical career and, as a result, to my rejecting the family business and its comparatively rich pickings. 'You've made your bed and must therefore lie on it,' was his not very original conclusion, though I think that in his last years, when he saw me making some headway in my chosen career, his attitude was slightly modified. Even so, neither he nor my mother seldom showed little more than token interest in what I was doing, nor did they make much effort to be present at major events which later involved me.

It was in the early 1930s that my father jointly inherited with his brother, William, the family business which my grandfather had founded in 1880. Uncle Will had two sons, the eldest, Geoffrey, becoming a partner in a firm of Medway Towns solicitors rejoicing in the name of Bassett and Boucher, his abiding joy in life being that of playing 'goff'. The other son, Charles, could I suppose be described as the black sheep of the family. He embarked on an acting career and, much to the embarrassment of the locals, was found by the police in bed with a naval rating from Chatham Dockyard. This resulted in a court case which in those days caused something of a stir to all concerned other than Charles who, although something of a rebel and a misfit, was as a result as thoroughly ostracised as Oscar Wilde had been a generation earlier. He met with some success on the stage and appeared in productions at the Gate Theatre in Villiers Street, a small theatre in the arches under Charing Cross Station, renowned in pre-war years for short runs, no stars, and a very intimate atmosphere. Charles subsequently joined the French Foreign Legion, for which I should think he was highly unsuited, and he died ignominiously somewhere in North Africa.

There was also my cousin Dorothy who succumbed to consumption in her teens. All I can remember of her is that she languished mysteriously bedridden behind closed doors in the family home in Goddington Road, and that hardly anyone ever saw her.

While my Uncle Will was a dear and gentle soul to whom I was much attached, his wife Dora was a cold-hearted person involved more in local Conservative Party politics than in her family. She treated her husband in a very hard and insensitive way. Uncle Will was an amateur organist who from time to time deputised at Cobham Parish Church for Miss Woods, who for me was something of a goddess because she was an ARCO (Associate of the Royal College of Organists). Renowned for its brasses, this beautiful church was opposite The Leather Bottle Inn, immortalised by Dickens who spent his latter years at nearby Gadshill Place. At Cobham I would sit with my uncle on the organ bench, turn the pages of his music for him and sometimes even be allowed to pull out or push in stops, so I have to thank him for introducing me to the world of organs and church music. It was also at Cobham that I briefly met and obtained the autograph of Martin Shaw, then going round the country promoting his Folk Mass and other parish communion musical approaches considered in those days by many to be *avant garde* and therefore suspect.

My mother's family came from Hornsey in North London, an area I would later get to know well when I was 'trying out' London organs and regularly visited the nearby Alexandra Palace where I was permitted to play the organ for one shilling an hour. I would go by Underground to Wood Green and then, full of an excitement and anticipation which never waned on each successive visit, board the single-decker bus up the hill to the Palace.

My great grandfather was an unusually gifted chess player who in the 1860s invented and built Ajeeb, 'the Mysterious Chess Automaton'. A lifesize Moorish figure was seated, in the words of a report in *Lloyd's Weekly*, 'on a cushion, beneath which is a perfectly open table. In front is a small cabinet with doors, which are all opened, as well as the back and chest of the figure. Any stranger is at liberty to play a game with the Automaton, and on a recent occasion Prince Hassan, son of the Viceroy of Egypt, tried his skill'. Ajeeb was exhibited at the Crystal Palace where he played upwards of 100,000 games against all comers, winning on average 99% of the contests. The novelty of the invention spread as rapidly as the speed of the moves the automaton made. It is on record that many notable people visited Ajeeb, including the Shah of Persia, the Empress of Russia and the Sultan of Zanzibar. Ajeeb toured throughout Europe and eventually the United States.

As a small boy I was intrigued by the mystery of it all, though neither my grandparents nor parents ever divulged the secret behind this extraordinary phenomenon.

My mother's father worked all his life for Liberty's in Regent Street where he was a gifted furniture designer doing in a most artistic way what John Betjeman's father was doing in similarly related respects. We still have in our dining room a splendid full-length wall mirror he designed and made. My mother inherited his artistic gifts, delighting in painstakingly painting greetings cards, some of which I still have. When my grandfather died, his widow, always known as Grandma Hooper, came to live with us. I remember her as a distinctly fierce person who would periodically emerge from her bedroom wearing a hat that resembled a bee's nest, and would then proceed to chastise me for being naughty on any conceivable pretext. I would then take comfort in Boo-Boo, a woolly toy dog who was my inseparable companion, even though one of his glass eyes had long since fallen out, so I made him an eye-shield which I considered the right and proper thing to do.

Although I was never all that close to my father, who anyhow was something of a workaholic, my mother doted over me. Even so, I do not recall being the subject of great parental affection on her part. Later on, although I regetted having no brothers or sisters, our own children and then our grandchildren have brought so much compensatory joy.

My mother, through her fairly strict upbringing, was a disciplined person conditioned by routine. Every Saturday night she would unfailingly give me a spoonful of syrup of figs 'to keep the bowels open'. Even if I did not then know what bowels were I was fully aware of what usually resulted from my weekly dosage. I enjoyed the taste of syrup of figs much more than that of Scott's Emulsion, a filthy concoction which I loathed having to swallow, and to smell. While syrup of figs would invariably have its repercussions within hours, Scott's Emulsion never seemed to do anything other than leave a nasty taste in the mouth. For her part, my mother regularly took senna pods which, she would assure us, would alleviate her persistent bouts of constipation, though she was far too prim to refer to this as such.

CHAPTER TWO

The 1930s—A Kentish Boyhood

I was born in 1924 on February 24th, at 8 Gordon Road, Strood, a small, terraced Victorian house on the then sparsely populated hills above the Medway Towns. To be born north of the Medway made me by ancient custom a Man of Kent, whereas south of the river I would have been a Kentish Man. Next door at number 6 lived Mr & Mrs Clare and Mrs Clare's spinster sister, Miss Jarrett. To all of us she was Aunty Jarry, the dedicated part-time nanny to whom I was to become very attached.

When I was five my father built his dream home on the then London Road a couple of miles further out of the town and on even higher ground. Uplands, as it was named after the road in Hornsey where my mother had been brought up, and where she first met my father, was then one of only a handful of houses and was virtually in the country. My father, part of whose early training had been as a draughtsman at Aveling and Porter, a local firm who made steam-rollers and traction engines which I would later come across in remote parts of the British Empire, designed the house himself. Although it was on a fairly predictable, even unadventurous, plan, it was a child of its time and he was understandably proud of it when a local builder in Higham had completed the work for £1,000. As the house was situated in more than half an acre of ground, the immediate task was to create a garden.

Meanwhile, my links with Gordon Road continued, for when I was six I was sent to the infants' school there, where the headmistress was a Miss Butler. She always wore a brown habit and many years later was to end her days as a lay sister at the Community of St Mary the Virgin at West Ogwell in Devon, where I visited her during my time at Exeter. Miss Butler was assisted by Miss Hawkins who, even at that tender age, I

7

recognised as being a young, pretty and vivacious person. She gave us vivid pictures of The Holy Land which have always remained with me and which had an almost uncanny resemblance to reality when we visited Palestine fifty years later.

I can still all but smell, let alone feel, the plasticine which seemed to be an integral part of life in the school. How well I remember the floors of plain scrubbed board full of splinters only too ready to bury themselves into you when you slipped and fell. Next door was the larger senior school presided over by the heavily bearded Mr Marsh who lived a few houses up the road from Uplands and was known in the school as Bugswhiskers, a name even sometimes uttered by my father who normally was an inveterate stickler for etiquette and politeness.

To revert to 6 Gordon Road, this became something of a second home to which I would be despatched for the night when my parents were at a dance, at the then popular whist drives, or when they were occupied in one way or another working for Dr Barnardo's Homes, this last being something they were firmly dedicated to and did a lot for. I well remember the annual children's party at Chatham Town Hall, and later being told about the white-tie evening dance which followed it. The Aldershot Tattoo and the Chelsea Flower Show were other occasions on which I would find myself staying overnight at number 6. Even at this distance of time I vividly remember the zinc bath which would appear on Saturday nights and be placed in front of the open fire on which large heavy kettles covered with soot would heat the water in readiness for the ritual of my weekly immersion. I recall equally clearly the smell of laundry being aired in front of the open fire as well as remembering my pram, and can even recall looking up from its snug warmth at Aunty Jarry, who had the unenviable task of taking me on walks, whatever the weather.

My parents were keen musicians, my father being a violinist and my mother a pianist. They would regularly join forces with other string players, notably Violet Edmonds, an extrovert cellist, who with her sisters lived at nearby Rede Court, and whose brother George acted as chauffeur for his large Rolls Royce, a ride in which was for me a treat not to be missed. After

I had been banished to bed I would hear below me in the drawing room the musical evenings which were a regular feature of life at Uplands, as were the string trios and quartets led by my father and which featured prominently as background music to the annual church bazaar. As a small, and at that time thoroughly disinterested, child I was regularly taken to the Co-operative Society Hall and subjected to Grieg, Sullivan, Franz Lehar's Waltzes, Dvorak's Humoresque, Schumann's Traumerei, *et al*, part and parcel of for the most part long forgotten 'light' music. These remain as firmly in my memory as do the portable gramophone and the many '78' records my parents had amassed, not least 'White Horse Inn' which was one of the latest hits which my parents adored and saw a number of times at the Coliseum in St Martin's Lane. Liszt's 2nd Hungarian Rhapsody was a great favourite of my own for which, as with all records then, you had to feverishly wind up the motor, not forgetting to change the steel needle for each side of the record. A complete winding would just about last for one side of a 12 inch record which revolved at what seemed a fantastic speed and was the more interesting to watch if the record was slightly warped.

In childhood, as I mentioned earlier, everything seemed so much larger. (Is this because when you yourself are small anything you look up at seems so big?) Uplands, and especially the garden, which was fairly large by any reckoning, was no exception. My mother loved her garden and over the years spent more and more time in it. She took very much to heart the saying 'You are nearer God's heart in a garden than anywhere else on earth', a sentiment I am not sure I could fully echo any more than my father's fatalistic summing up of sudden death as 'Man proposes, God disposes'. Anyhow, she took it all most seriously and I can still see her kneeling to painstakingly weed the herbaceous borders. Trimming the lavender bushes with a pair of scissors was another favourite pastime, as was her making of lavender bags to sell for the church bazaar. She had a fetish for the edges of the lawns which she kept immaculate, and how annoyed she would be if someone trod too near the edge and broke it down, a propensity I inherited from her in later years when we were living at Addington Palace. How she loved feeding carefully cut crusts of bread to the sparrows, and how annoyed she became when the superior blackbirds swooped down and stole these offerings.

My main contribution to the garden was my delight, even passion, for mowing the lawns with the Qualcast mower, and especially for carefully maintaining straight lines on which I prided myself. In those days motor mowers were something of an innovation and when my father bought one he would never allow me to use it lest 'it might run away with me'. Less enjoyable was the rolling of the lawns for which we had a vast and heavy contraption filled with water but which was reasonably manoeuvrable when you eventually got it under way.

The far end of the garden was given over to vegetables, and it was here that the raspberries were my mother's especial pride and joy. During the season it would be a regular teatime ritual for people to be invited to the house for raspberries and cream topped with lots of sugar, while as a treat I would be allowed to scrape out what was left in the cream carton. In a similar way I would sometimes be allowed to lick the cream on the underside of the cardboard discs which in those days were used to seal glass milk bottles. Far less tasty was the raspberry vinegar which my mother regularly concocted because she firmly believed this helped to cure colds.

Another facet of gardening were the bonfires which I always enjoyed being responsible for, especially when everything was dry and burned easily. Sometimes these would continue simmering for some days, with my stoking them up each night and then seeing how much had burnt through by the next morning all being part of the ritual. Years later, when we were living at Addington Palace, bonfires conjured up instant memories of boyhood, their smell being so evocative and distinctive.

Thinking back to events that are now nearly sixty years ago, I often wonder why one remembers certain things so vividly. Perhaps it was the regularity of particular happenings such as the Monday morning saga at Uplands. Frank Cason, the local grocer, would arrive on his bicycle soon after breakfast, then be invited to seat himself at the kitchen table to take my mother's weekly order. The necessities, such as butter, sugar and tea, were always first on the list, followed by luxuries—crystallised peel, dried currants, sultanas and chocolate biscuits—which were not ordered every week. What was meticulously written down in Mr Cason's order book would then be delivered early next morning, this time by the errand boy whose bicycle had a large wicker basket which fitted into a metal frame in front of the handlebars.

Mr Cason's visit would be followed by another weekly ritual which my mother called 'washing day'! Kitchen mats would be rolled up and galvanised iron baths and tubs brought in, their contents soon to be emitting clouds of steam. What a performance it all was, the more so if it was raining and the drying of the laundry had to take place in the kitchen instead of the garden. The distinctive odour this created lingered to be the background to Monday lunch, or dinner as it was then called, for in those days we always ate in the kitchen unless there were visitors. There would be the inevitable cold meat left over from the Sunday roast, mashed potatoes and mushy cabbage, which sometimes would be fried together to produce 'bubble and squeak'. There was also Military pickle with its colourful label on the bottle depicting the Horseguards. Rice pudding would invariably follow—and how I detested the skin on its top—sometimes tapioca pudding or even, horror of horrors, bread and butter pudding which I could never then nor now abide, and which in my haste to be done with it I would eat as fast as I could and which would prompt my mother to recite her favourite maxim, 'Don't hurry your food, dear, or you'll get indigestion'. On the other hand, my mother made quite a speciality of tripe and onions which I greatly relished.

Another periodic event was the delivery of coal, with the coalmen sitting high up on their waggon, which was drawn by two old horses. We invariably ordered a ton at a time and my mother was assiduous in checking the delivery of the twenty sacks this comprised, though there was no mistaking each as the contents, carried high on head and shoulders, were tipped with a great noise into our coal cellar. My mother was equally assiduous in disappearing into the cupboard under the stairs whenever there was a thunderstorm. She dragged me in with her and consequently instilled in me a fear of lightning and thunder which lasted for some years.

But this was not my only fear or dislike, for I loathed then, as now, anything to do with camping or living rough, such as picnics on the beach accompanied by the smell of seaweed, and sand in the sandwiches. Above all else I hated swimming which was anathema to me, stemming from the time when, as a seven year old, I was deliberately pushed into a swimming bath by my headmaster who considered that a sure way of overcoming my reluctance to get into the water. Little did he realise how that put me off swimming for ever, with my long held penchant for creature comforts leading me towards the more rewarding substitute of total immersion in a hot bath.

My mother relied entirely on my father, something which in her later years developed into such an obsession that in the end she would virtually never allow him out of her sight. When she died we thought my father would take on a new lease of life but this was not to be, for he was so conditioned to being at my mother's beck and call that he could not in the few months left to him adjust to his new-found freedom.

My parents had periodic flirtations with the Church and for a while they joined The Oxford Group which was very much the in-thing in the 1930s. Fairly late in life my mother was baptised and confirmed but she fell out with the priest who had prepared her and this seemed to sour her attitude towards the church at large and especially towards the clergy. From an early age I experienced on and off a vague hankering in contemplating ordination, but it was the musical aspect of the Church to which I was becoming increasingly drawn. One of my childhood pre-occupations was the 'broadcasting' of Evensong at the piano in the drawing room. I would duly commence with the bells and the preliminary organ music. Aunty Jarry was frequently press-ganged into being the congregation though we seldom got much further than the psalms, mainly because at that time I had no idea about what to do with the canticles. I also devised a parish magazine for the Church of St Matthias, this because my birthday coincided with what was then his feast day. I gave up after three issues, each with a pastoral letter from me, the Vicar.

The task of providing the flowers was assigned each Sunday to my mother.

At this time I learned to use my father's typewriter. After my mother's death I found a number of letters from me to her dealing with a variety of 'business' matters such as insurance and invoices for what I believed she owed me. Although I suspect that much of their contents were taken from papers I had seen on my father's desk, perhaps they were sowing seeds for later administrative tasks which were to be mine.

Shopping in Strood with my mother was another ritual which I so well recall. In those days the shops stayed open until late in the evening on Saturdays and we would commence by visiting Budden and Biggs, the local wine merchants, presided over by the two elderly Woodward sisters. Here I would sit on the mahogany counter while my mother stocked up with Australian Emu wine which was her favourite tipple. Another port of call would be Hill, the fishmonger which, like Budden and Biggs, was demolished after the war, as was most of Strood High Street when it was widened. Frozen and refrigerated food being very much a thing of the future, fresh fish was stored in wooden boxes between which would be sandwiched large blocks of ice which were handled into position with great iron tongs. If you wanted cutlets of cod these were ceremoniously measured and then chopped, bones and all, from the whole fish, while fillets of plaice were sliced from the bone in a most expert way and then washed clean, after which the marble working area would be hosed down in readiness for the next customer. We would also assiduously visit Woolworth's every Saturday; in those days it proudly advertised 'nothing over sixpence'.

Sometimes we would venture into the grocer's shop majestically presided over by Mr Cason senior. Here I remember sugar in large hessian sacks from which one's order was weighed and put into a blue bag, the top of which was ceremoniously and expertly folded and tucked in. Mahogany canisters held tea and coffee while the floor was always covered with sawdust. A couple of wooden pats would extract what was needed from a large block of butter, then moulded into a brick-size shape which was neatly trimmed, added to or subtacted from, until the exact weight required was arrived at. While this was being done, and if I had been 'a good boy', I would invariably be given a small piece of crystallised peel, and how good it tasted!

It was at this time that my father became very keen about cars while they were still something of a novelty. Having learned to drive, he bought an Austin 7 which had a sort of mottled leather coachwork and a thermometer on the front of the bonnet which told you the all-crucial radiator temperature. Cars frequently boiled over in those days, so we all anxiously eyed the tell-tale red line which would rise ominously as we went up a steep hill, the more so as my father would never change down the gear until the car had almost shuddered to a standstill. Boughton Hill, on the way to Canterbury, was one such challenge which seemed very long and formidable, though today it seems far less forbidding. There was a silk curtain for the rear window which my father would lower on the rare occasions when he drove at nights and which would shield him from the lights of any following car.

Eventually he bought a Sunbeam Talbot, then considered to be something of a sports car and quite trendy, but as he seldom drove at more than 30 mph, even though many of the roads were virtually empty, much of the potential of this car was never explored. If he did go faster—and he would sometimes get venturesome and feel very proud perhaps to have exceeded 40 mph, he soon thought better of it and would severely recite his oft quoted 'It's better to be ten minutes late in this world than ten years too early in the next'. At one time he had an Austin 12, though I was envious of my uncle Will's larger Austin 16.

In those days AA Scouts, as they were called, drove motor cycles with side-cars full of tools and other things needed for breakdowns. When they saw the AA badge on your car they would always salute you.

Petrol cost one shilling (5p) a gallon. Goodsell and Frid, the local garage, had a single pump which was worked by hand. As whoever was serving you furiously pumped to and fro, you saw the fuel filling up a glass container on the pump, a gallon at a time. This would then empty itself into your tank. Although cars only held five or six gallons at the most, it was nevertheless a lengthy, but always for me an intriguing, process, and fun when the tank was full and petrol spilled without warning on to the ground.

Goodsell was as corpulent, brawny and good hearted as Frid was waspish and far less friendly. Although their personalities rubbed off on each other, they were a successful and efficient business partnership.

We went on many drives around the Kentish countryside, my mother always wearing a hat and sometimes my father, for whom driving gloves were *de rigueur*, the unfailing order of the day. Wednesday afternoons were mid-week early closing for shops and offices, so this was a favourite time for a drive, and then there were always Sundays. Canterbury was a favourite Wednesday haunt, with tinned salmon and salad for tea at Lefèvre's store with its resident quartet playing selections from Ivor Novello and Noel Coward, whose shows were then all the current rage.

Holidays took us further afield, to Gorleston-on-Sea, to Margate, and sometimes at Christmas to Folkestone where, as at Uplands, I would climb into my parents' bed early on Christmas Day morning for the exciting emptying of a pillowcase full of presents which often included additions for my Hornby railway or Meccano.

A favourite preoccupation was that of pretending to be a bus conductor, for which my mother made me a suitable cap and uniform. I would collect used tickets, sort them into their respective values, and I even had a board complete with springs into which they were clipped in a most authentic way. Maidstone and District were then, as now, the main operators and I obtained from one of my father's tenants who was a real conductor some of the waybills which they had to fully and meticulously fill in for each journey.

At an early age I had a tricycle, followed by a small bicycle which was eventually succeeded by a full size Raleigh complete with three-speed gear and which cost £3. 19. 6. By then I felt I had really arrived, even though my father would not allow a racing model with dropped handlebars as he felt this to be too radical, even dangerous. My rides, although maybe of only a dozen or so miles, were great adventures through which I was exploring a whole new world, not least in my discovering the remarkable beauties of the Kentish countryside, its villages and in particular its churches. On the lighter side was the venturesome holding on to the back of a lorry trundling up one of the many steep hills to be encountered in that part of the world. All would be well, and the ascent blissfully easy, until the driver of the lorry saw me and shouted at me to let go.

Yes—life was very different then, but it was after all fifty, even sixty, years ago, while today we inhabit a world now changed out of all recognition in so many respects. The 1930s were years of calm, with virtually no vestige of hurry, be it at the grocer's shop, motoring, or the general ambience of what then seemed to be carefree days undisturbed by the immediacy of worldwide news through what was then a very subdued media by contrast with today. On Sundays I was not allowed sweets or that then comparative rarity, the ice cream; as the shops were not generally open on Sundays that was a matter easily resolved. And life was so much less hazardous overall; it was perfectly safe to walk or cycle on your own, however remote and isolated a part of the countryside you chose. The fear of murder, rape, attack or burglary were all but non-existent, though my father persisted in his obsession for bolting doors and windows on the slightest pretext; consequently, even in the hottest weather, Uplands would frequently feel musty and airless. It never occurred to you to put a lock on your bicycle nor usually to lock your car.

Today, when the five day week and opportunities for holidays overseas abound, the pace seems to be the more hectic and urgent in all that we do, with our ever-restless thirst for rushing from one place, or country, to another possessing us at every turn and resulting in a breathless pursuit of more and more speed and immediacy.

Conversely, and by marked contrast, the elements seem to be much the same today as then in conditioning and effecting our lives. The sharp distinctions between the seasons were all too obvious to a small boy. If winters then seemed colder and summers hotter, perhaps they were, or perhaps one was the more exposed to them. Short trousers resulted in chapped legs and chilblains when, in East Kent, we were particularly prone to any

Siberian winds coming our way. Even in summer we were fairly fully clad with ties and jackets the invariable order of the day. All in all, however, we were far less cushioned than we are today. At Uplands there was no central heating: my mother laboured daily in making, and then next morning cleaning up the remains, of coal fires. She also tended oil stoves whose obnoxious paraffin gave off such unpleasant and clinging smells. Water for baths was heated by an old fashioned and potentially lethal copper geyser. There were no heaters in cars even in our Exeter days when as a family we were once so desperately cold in driving to Henley-on-Thames that our breath produced ice on the inside of the windscreen. Fog, and thick pea soupers at that, or in towns a black smog which emitted soot and smuts, often accompanied snowy winter days and especially the nights when outside all was uncannily quiet while we inside were in a warm sitting room which contrasted forcibly with the temperature in the bedroom and bathroom. But at Christmas, which I recollect was often a white one, all such matters were forgotten, for there were always the magic lantern and Blind Man's Buff at parties for which I had to wear my Eton suit.

How welcome then, as now, was the first real warmth of the spring sun and the garden awakening after winter. The first mowing of the lawn gave off a unique smell of grass cuttings as at no other time in the year, and then before we hardly realised it, it would be summer, with the evocative smell of newly clipped privet hedges, catmint, geranium, and my mother's ubiquitous lavender bushes. As it became hotter, so the green paint on the house would give off a distinctive smell which no other paint did: no less evocative was the smell of putty in the warm sun.

With autumn came the inevitable run down to winter, leaves everywhere and, as Osbert Sitwell once so poetically put it, 'the keen air of the dying year', though I am not at all sure that I thought of it quite so romantically as a small boy, for the inevitable coldness of an East Kent winter was at hand.

But when I reflect, as I seem to do more and more as I grow older, I remember so vividly, almost uncannily, everyday things which then seemed so integral a feature of life. The lamp-lighter unfailingly coming along the road each evening, and the long pole with which he mysteriously contrived to light the gas lamps in turn. I can hear even now the noisy double-decker trams slowly struggling up Strood Hill, which then seemed so steep, and today so gentle an incline. Then there was the added novelty of traffic lights just beginning to be in use in those days, with rubber pads in the road which the pressure of car wheels would change as you drove over them, and what fun we children would have in stamping on them to change them when no one was looking. There was the then ubiquitous wearing of braces and, *de rigueur*, waistcoats, whatever your age, and how I remember fumbling with shirts which you had to put on over your head, for unlike today they did not unbutton all the way down. And there was that never failing nostalgic element of smell, with Woolworth's for some reason as distinctive of carbolic as National Trust shops today are of Lavender, soap and pot-pourri.

When I was a small boy, every acquaintance seemed automatically to be called Uncle or Aunty—Uncle Smith or Aunty Ballard. Equally crucial to my young life were my much-loved Meccano and my Hornby railway, both of which were systematically added to at every Christmas and birthday.

What happy and carefree days they were—or so they seemed!

CHAPTER THREE

Eton suits and Evensong

In 1931, at the age of seven, I became a day boy in the then Rochester Cathedral Choir School in Minor Canon Row. It nestled under the shadow of the cathedral where the spirit of Dickens breathed at virtually every turn, with the Bull Hotel, Satis House and Jasper's Gateway all just round the corner. The row of houses opposite the Cathedral School was, in the estimation of Dickens, one of the finest in England.

The school had been in existence since the 7th century, later primarily to educate the twelve cathedral choristers, although there were twenty-five or more non-singers of whom I was one. It has always baffled me why my parents did not at least enter me for a choral scholarship, something I have always since regretted, even resented, as much as never having had the opportunity of a university education. Through odd snippets of conversation I gleaned that my parents probably felt such aspirations were beyond their station in life and therefore 'not quite us'. I suspect they also considered such moves rather élitist, though that was fifty years before that word and concept would assume the stigma it holds for many today.

The headmaster, the Revd Rupert Johnstone, was also Precentor of the Cathedral, and was known to all and sundry as Tim, his full-time staff being Miss Thornhill, who was responsible for Forms 1 and 2, with Tim teaching Forms 3 and 4. I never remember seeing Miss Thornhill smile, and she was even more formidable when she ceremoniously clipped pince-nez spectacles on to her nose before embarking on a lesson. When we arrived, soon after 8 o'clock on winter mornings, the caretaker was invariably coaxing—and not very satisfactorily—the coal fire in each of the classrooms, with clouds of smoke and little heat issuing into the room, though by mid-morning the fires would

19

be giving off abundant warmth. The school itself was as Dickensian as its surroundings, not least in the dark and invariably smelly underground loos.

Punishment, which Tim dispensed liberally, was at its best the writing of lines, but more often the cane or the strap which was inflicted on us in 'The Little Room' which, when you were sent there, invariably meant waiting for some minutes, probably to prolong the anticipatory agony, before Tim appeared, told you to drop your trousers and kneel on the table. The number of strokes you received were in proportion to what was considered to be the severity of the crime, and I suspect that Tim derived some sadistic pleasure from this routine.

Although understandably we feared Tim, we nevertheless respected him, for I believe he really was as genuinely concerned for our well-being as with our training for life. He certainly instilled into me a broadly based concept of personal discipline, of how to plan life and, by no means least, the importance of good manners, and for this last I have always been grateful, even if such matters are too often given scant priority in some schools today.

Scholastically, the curriculum took in the basics, and little more. There was plenty of Latin, and to this day I can still quote from memory much of Kennedy's Latin Primer, such as *'A, ab, absque, coram, de, palam, clam, cum, ex and e'*, or the even more colourful *'Ante, apud, ad, adversus, circum, circa, citra, cis'*, while I can still vividly see the drawings which illustrated *Latin for Today*. The fairly comprehensive grounding we received in Latin is something I have always valued, if only because when I am not sure of the meaning of a word, the Latin root invariably gives a clue to the answer.

Among the visiting staff was 'Cosher' Lee who taught us geography and who, as his nickname might suggest, had the reputation of being another fairly liberal dispenser of corporal punishment.

As a guide to progress—and a very useful one—there were weekly reports in which I featured prominently for neatness—something I obviously inherited from my mother. My ability was less evident in most other areas, especially mathematics, though my early prowess in spelling was a further bonus point. Tim meticulously entered our marks for tests into a large register and, knowing he kept this book in his classroom desk, I remember on more than one occasion surreptitiously altering my marks to advantage when no one was around, otherwise I knew I would be sent to 'The Little Room' at the end of the week.

Latterly, I played the hymn each day for morning prayers, using one of the old brown covered early editions of *English Hymnal*. I even took a humble part in my only ever excursion into acting, namely the annual school performances of Shakespeare.

Each Monday the non-singers attended Evensong in the Cathedral where, in the canticles, the choir sang the then fashionable pronunciation of 'Ar-brah-ham' and 'Eez-rye-el'. When my attention faltered, as it frequently did, I would study the coloured shields painted on the opposite wall over the names of past bishops or, when kneeling, I would rub my nose on the highly polished surface of the book rest in front of me, and be intrigued by the smell of the wax polish. We were also bidden to follow the lessons but, as our bibles were a different translation from the one on the lectern, I would delight in seeing how long I could follow my bible before it differed from the version being read from.

At Evensong one day I well remember smiling at something which had obviously amused me. I caught Tim's eye whose stony glare froze me, for I knew what that meant. Back at school I was summoned to his study. 'And what was it, Dakers, that amused you at Evensong?' My explanation failed to convince him for I was told to drop my trousers and bend over for a caning. Although he did not say so, I imagine his reaction probably was 'I'll teach you to enjoy religion'.

The Head Verger, who seemed perpetually to wear his black cassock and white bow tie in or out of the cathedral, was the father of Joe Levett, the assistant organist of the cathedral who would eventually be my teacher. He would measure with such split-second precision when to conduct the lesson reader from his stall to the lectern so that he arrived neither too soon nor too late. I also recall being told by him that the Last Supper was behind the high altar, and I longed to trespass there to see just what sort of food was on offer, for at that time I was unaware that he was of course referring to the carved stone reredos.

The minor canon who often sang the services was Henry Welch. I could never understand at that time why he paused when he got to 'that both—our hearts and minds . . .' in the second collect at Evensong, and was convinced that he must once have received some bad news at that particular moment which had subsequently prompted him ever since to pause, and perhaps reflect. Soon after I started at the school my father and I happened to pass Henry Welch in the street. As I raised my cap to him my father asked who he was, and I readily responded 'Oh, that's Jesus Christ'.

I also recall that in 1936, when King George V died, how intrigued we were to hear the clergy pray for 'Edward our King'. It reminds me of the story many years later of the Bishop of Crediton taking Evensong at Dartmoor Prison at the time of George VI's death. When he momentarily forgot and said 'O Lord, save the King—Queen', the inmates immediately responded with 'Jack, ten, nine, eight, seven, six . . .'.

There were no school dinners in those days, so I went home on the local Maidstone and District bus, sitting either on the open top deck or beside the driver on one of the ancient contraptions with solid tyres then in service. My mother would frequently give me a penny for sweets which would buy two ounces of most of what was displayed in neat rows of jars in the confectioner's shop just by the bus stop in Rochester High Street. And how well I recall Peter's chocolate wrapped in brown paper which, on receipt of one penny, was dispensed from a machine on railway stations.

On Sundays, even in summer, we had to wear thick Eton suits complete with tightly fitting waistcoat and straw boater. Sunday School, at which we stuck coloured stamps each week on to a card issued by the Madagascar Missions, preceded Evensong in the Cathedral. On weekdays, even after school had finished, we were expected to remain in school uniform, a grey suit and blue cap complete with the arms of St Andrew, the patron Saint of the Cathedral.

The recreational side of school life consisted in the summer of cricket in The Paddock, the nearby playing field of King's School, or at other times rugby on a more often than not cold and windswept field on the Borstal Road. Neither was any more appealing to me than the periodic paper chases or cross-country runs which would end with our having to wade through a stream at Upnor, all of which I would evade on the rare occasions when the headmaster was not around. But I loved lying on the grassy banks of The Paddock, lazily gazing up on summer days through the beech trees to the blue sky. By contrast, the annual sports day was repellent to me though I did find my level in the one mile walking race which I usually won, much to everyone's surprise, for it was quite obvious that I was no sportsman. Over the years I have grown less and less interested in sport and can never appreciate the excitement generated by getting a ball into a hole or a goal-mouth. The skill which I am told this entails has always left me quite unmoved.

I joined the Wolf Cubs, '9th Medway—Rochester Cathedral' being proudly displayed on our uniforms. The pack was run by Tim's eldest daughter, Joan. I enjoyed deer-stalking through the bracken in Upnor Woods, and I learned about the Bandelog, the Mowgli and Akela of Kipling's *Jungle Books*. In between whiles we would eat banana sandwiches, the smell of which, as well as that of the haversack they were carried in, remains as one of the less pleasant reminders of my life as a cub. I eventually progressed to being a scout and with it to more strenuous pursuits and expeditions, often in a long disused and overgrown brickworks hard by the Medway where we would see the flying boats which Short Brothers were then perfecting at their factory. In the 1930s the prototype Canopus, (or was it Casseopia?), piggy-backed an experimental sea-plane which, much to our delight, we would watch being released from its parent while in full flight. These big flying boats were later to play a prominent part in the second world war.

So much, then, for the cathedral and its school which, I have no doubt, is where my love of cathedrals and church music was born, though I was completely unaware of its influence at the time.

23

A favourite hobby was for me the absorbing one of stamp collecting which I confined strictly to England and the British Empire. For the Silver Jubilee of King George V in 1935 there was a wide variety of exciting issues throughout the Empire, many of them for small exotic islands in the Pacific. Stanley Gibbons' shop in The Strand was a favourite port of call for me, while in those days they would send you a weekly selection of what they termed 'approval sheets' from which you extracted what you wanted, or rather what you could afford. Although my father strongly disapproved of this scheme, my mother, unbeknown to my father, supported the system, even to the extent of sometimes providing me with the necessary funds to pay for the stamps I wanted.

During these years I spent quite a lot of time either in my father's office or accompanying him on his business calls, one of his favourite ploys being to get me to deliver letters by hand, thus saving the postage. In a boyish way I suppose I enjoyed all this and I suspect it may have led him to think that this was sowing seeds for my eventual entry into the business. As later events were to prove, this was not to be the case, especially when I was more forcibly recruited into the firm and when rent collecting meant my bicycling or walking for miles, and in all weathers, around the Medway Towns and the surrounding towns and villages, often for whole days at a time, while my father did it all by car. In the not too distant future my mind would be set on things musical, and my rebellion would cause much consternation and unhappiness for all concerned.

The office had white china letters on its plate glass front window which proudly spelt out what the firm specialised in, while inside there was a high old-fashioned sloping mahogany desk which ran the length of the office. It was fronted by a brass grill with holes in it through which tenants paid their rent. You worked either standing up or perched on a high stool; large leather bound ledgers were in use and, as I so well remember, round rulers which invariably slipped just when you were making a line at the end of a column of figures. Each morning my father would pay a visit to Barclay's Bank to deposit the previous day's takings, usually to be followed by 'morning coffee' in a local teashop, a ritual my father observed to the end of his working life.

One rent collecting expedition which I really did enjoy was the weekly one on Tuesdays in Rochester which would include Troy Town, then something of a slum area and where the corpulent Dorrie Dewsberry cheerfully reigned as sub-postmistress at the back of an ironmongery and hardware shop which permanently gave off a distinctive smell of carbolic. Pots, pans and brushes were in profusion everywhere, even hanging from the ceiling. If what you wanted was not to be found there, a trap door giving on to a vast cellar would be lifted, revealing an even larger storeroom of every conceivable object which was considered to be hardware or ironmongery. Nearby was a dairy where we would sometimes have, for the princely price of one penny, a glass of ice-cold milk. This part of Rochester had a Victorian character and, intriguing though I found it, was in poor shape and was eventually demolished, only to be replaced by featureless blocks of flats.

My father had two enormous safes in his office. The ritual of opening and closing their heavy doors, which demanded considerable determination, was a ceremonial which began and concluded each day's business, as did a similar ritual at Uplands where double locks, mortise locks and a variety of window safeguards were in operation, although the 1930s were so peaceful and law-abiding as compared with today.

As a boy I became hooked on the cinema and was allowed to go fairly regularly to afternoon matinees. Anna Neagle in *Victoria Regina* was one film particularly to my liking and which I saw on a number of occasions, having bought the piano score of the theme music which I regularly played while imagining I was the full orchestra in the film. There was also *The Man Who Made Diamonds* which was an X-rated film, which in those days meant for adults only, but somehow I got to see it although forbidden to do so by my parents lest it might give me nightmares. How mild it all was by comparison with the horror films of today.

My love for music was now slowly, but surely, developing. My father had me vetted by his own then elderly teacher who reported that I had 'a nice piano touch' though she seemed surprised that I could not sing some particularly awkward intervals. She was not amused when I retorted 'Nor, I bet, can you'. In the early years of the war I went whenever I could to cathedrals, asking the organist if I could 'try' the organ. I even had the temerity to ask Sir Walter Alcock if I could play the Salisbury Cathedral organ. Unbeknown to me, my father wrote to him asking his opinion as to my potential. In his reply he said that I should 'try for a university music degree and if possible go as assistant to a cathedral organist. But I would never advise a young man following my profession when, as in your son's case, he has a chance of following an excellent business career'. This, of course, was music to my father's ear.

Despite suggestions from a number of people that I might perhaps pursue a career in music, my father was adamant that he knew what was best for me, which was the family business. As my pangs for music grew, I became more and more restive and felt increasingly frustrated. This invariably resulted in some unpleasant family arguments, with my mother positioned in the middle and trying to be the peacemaker. Such was our *modus vivendi*.

I was now at least having regular organ lessons either with H. A. Bennett, the cathedral organist, or with Joe Levett, his assistant, who was also organist of Chatham Parish Church. It was here that I made my public début by playing the hymn 'Lord, thy word abideth' at Evensong one Sunday. Even in those now remote days I suspect I would not have personally chosen so dreary a tune as *Ravenshaw*, but maybe that is why Joe off-loaded it on to me. Later I was to play voluntaries, and finally whole services for him. Somewhat less rewarding for me was having to grapple with the five species of counterpoint, then a norm in one's musical studies.

A highlight of 1937 was my being taken by one of my cousins to the Queen's Hall to hear Toscanini conduct Brahms' *Requiem* at the Proms. Another 'event' that year was seeing the glow in the sky one night when, twenty miles away, the Crystal Palace went up in flames.

Meanwhile, life at home went on in a fairly predictable way, with me, the only child, being cosseted by my mother who continued to brew raspberry vinegar or, whether for church fêtes or Christmas presents, to make her far more attractive Turkish Delight and Crème de Menthe, which she poured into large soup bowls and which, when it had set, was cut up into squares and liberally doused with icing sugar.

CHAPTER FOUR

Halcyon boyhood days – or were they?

Looking back on 'the slow season of childhood' as Siegfried Sassoon called it, is in many respects intensely nostalgic, for it was such a different world from today. By comparison, everything seemed so quiet and leisurely. The halcyon summer days were so blissful; we invariably seemed to have almost endless sunbaked summers which, even to a small boy, were so peaceful and relaxed—but we also experienced some ferocious thunderstorms.

As always, smell instantly recalls a host of memories such as the summer heat on paintwork, creosote on railway sleepers or the particular odour given off by the heavy Venetian sunblinds outside the windows at Uplands—and the earwigs which fell out of them in such profusion when they were let down. Yes—smell can be an extraordinarily vivid, and immediate, reminder of so much of the past. Over the years it has never failed so distinctively to conjure up places and situations such as the many smells of Egypt during the war, though not all of them, such as lemonade made with limes, were by any means unsavoury, any more than the nightly burning of eucalyptus logs in the hill stations of India or, nearer home, that very distinctive combination of old oak, furniture polish and 'atmosphere' to be encountered in many a London church, something I have never come across in quite the same way anywhere else.

No less evocative, I suspect, would be my mother smoking de Reske or Turkish cigarettes or, years later, my embarking for a while on those exclusive gold-tipped, brown Balkan Sobranie cigarettes. A favourite, if somewhat naive, trick of my father's was to assure you that he could make cigarette smoke come out of his eyes. While you expectantly fixed your gaze on him he would surreptitiously touch your hand with his lighted cigarette and delight in seeing you jump.

Then there were the blue and white 'Stop me and buy one' tricycles selling Walls' ice cream, and how I loved those long triangular shaped water-ices which deposited their colour on your tongue and which, as my mother never failed to remind me, were 'bad for the teeth'.

The wireless, as it was called in those days, was as much a part of life as television is today, even though the British Broadcasting Company periodically succumbed to what the announcer would call 'a technical hitch' which would herald some minutes of silence before all was again in working order. Children's Hour was a daily delight not to be missed, especially when for a fee of sixpence your name would be read out on your birthday. There was Toytown, with Ernest the policeman and Mr Grouser, with Pip, Squeak and Wilfred, invariably followed by 'The Fat Stock Prices' and, after the news, The Foundations of Music which always seemed to me, and I suspect to others, to be an endlessly dreary nightly series of chamber music recitals.

Later in the evening there would be regular weekly features such as *In Town Tonight* on Saturdays, with Eric Coates' 'Knightsbridge March' as its signature tune, while on Mondays one of my favourite programmes began with

'It's Monday night at eight o'clock
Oh can't you hear the chimes!
They're telling you to take an easy chair,
To settle by the fireside, get out your Radio Times.
for Monday Night at Eight is on the air.'

During the war years we never failed to be amused and greatly cheered by Tommy Handley's ITMA (It's that man again) show, with personalities such as the hard-drinking Colonel Chinstrap ('I don't mind if I do, Sir'), Mrs Mopp, the resident charlady ('Can I do you now, Sir?'), and a whole host of colourful and distinctive personalities all projecting such good, clean, and witty, fun. I suppose that in many respects it was the forerunner of the Muppet Show of today.

I so well recall on Christmas Eves twiddling the knobs of my parents' primitive wireless set and hearing a multitude of atmospherics as I searched for Midnight Mass from France. Those were the days long before Vatican 2 when such services were marvellously redolent with bells, plainchant, and loud organ music. In my mind I could visualise the ceremonial, and the air thick with incense.

The quietness of the Medway Towns in those years was soon to be shattered, first by the Battle of Britain, then by the nightly bombing of London. The narrow High Street of old established family businesses such as Ogden, the men's outfitters presided over by a dapper little man with a large waxed moustache and stand-up collar, Leonard's, the smartest of the stores, and the newsagent whose name and number was painted above the shop as the perfect palindrome—111 MALLAM 111—have long since gone. Just behind the High Street were the Cathedral Precincts and my school, and how vigorously on the day of the cathedral's patronal festival we sang from *The English Hymnal* the hymn which told us 'As of old St Andrew heard it by the Galilean Lake', to be followed a few days later by those wonderful Advent hymns as the build-up to Christmas.

The Second World War was to see a large influx of the Forces and especially of naval personnel at Chatham Dockyard where in happier pre-war days Royal Navy ships of many sizes congregated each August for Navy Week. What a thrill that was, with virtually unrestricted liberty, having paid your sixpence, to clamber up and down hatchways, even to get inside a submarine. Those were the great days of the Navy with a profusion of ships of all shapes and sizes not only at Chatham but also at Portsmouth and Devonport.

Meanwhile my parents sought to make me conform; all in all they chose only to see their fairly vigorous viewpoint, perhaps hoping to mould me in the ways *they* saw fit but which did not coincide with *my* way of thinking. Because they invariably took me to grown-up things, I eventually came to be much more at home with older people, and have remained so. As a result, I now have few boyhood friends.

CHAPTER FIVE

A less relaxed period

The Cathedral School closed in 1937. It was too small to be viable and so became the first of the choir schools to be axed. Since then the choristers have been educated at the nearby King's School. At that time I was 13 and my parents elected to send me to Gravesend County School, their choice again being that I should be a day boy. This was a large and impersonal school some twelve miles or so from my home, and was in such sharp contrast to the cosiness of the small and intimate school I had known for six years.

I was not at all happy at Gravesend and consequently had an undistinguished record, though with some success in Latin, Greek and French. I did however enjoy a new pursuit, that of ordnance survey maps which I found fascinating, and the ability I gained in reading them has been most useful to me over the years. Although my father provided much needed extra coaching in mathematics, my overall School Certificate results were abysmal. I prefer to think of my real education as a much later process realised through reading, travel, and life as such. The one worthwhile event I remember in those years was a school visit to France where we stayed in Grenoble and where we bought Green and Yellow Chartreuse from the famous nearby monastery and which we drank like lemonade in the hotel bedroom. The Gravesend days were by no means my happiest schooldays.

I was 15 when war came in September 1939. As in 1914, this heralded the end of a whole way of life. Obviously we did not realise this at the time or feel its full effect until the post-war years, when many of the hopes and aspirations for the brave new world we all anticipated, and were led to visualise, were not in the event realised. Whatever else, it would never be the old order again.

My father's immediate preoccupation was that of having an air-raid shelter built in the orchard at the far end of the garden. It was an elaborate reinforced concrete affair ten feet below ground with a further six feet of excavated soil on top. It always smelt damp inside, and it was! Bunks were installed for what was later to become the ritual of regularly sleeping in what my father called 'the dug out' and which no doubt recalled for him the Western Front where he served during the First World War. Later on the nightly bombing of London began and although we suffered little damage as such, the Medway Towns were very much in the flight path of the waves of German bombers being intercepted by our fighter planes on their way to London and, not least the incessant thunder of anti-aircraft fire, some of it from a battery of ack-ack guns less than a mile away from us.

During the autumn of 1939 it had been something of a ghost war; while much was anticipated, little materialised. During those weeks of warm late summer and early autumn we regularly slept in deck chairs outside the shelter, having usually munched Woolworth's Devon Cream toffees as a nightcap. More often than not we would wake early and then, as ever since, I never failed to be moved by the dawn chorus and the beauty of sunrise.

1940 saw the Battle of Britain, much of which took place in the skies above us. Almost every day of that glorious summer we would watch formations of fifty, sixty, or more German heavy bombers, mere dots in the sky, making their way towards London, their precision formation soon to be broken up and, hopefully, many of them to be shot down by our Spitfires and Hurricanes.

By this time a repertoire of war songs was in evidence. 'Wish me luck as you wave me goodbye' and 'There'll be blue birds over the white cliffs of Dover' are as memorable and singable today as all those years ago, nor are they any less nostalgic tear-jerkers. As a nation we were so confident; despite the all too recent trauma of Dunkirk we were so buoyed up by Churchill, and certainly never remotely realised how near we were to invasion by the Germans. If we had known then what we learned at the end of the war about concentration camps, I suspect our confidence and relatively carefree attitudes would have been rather differently coloured.

The bombing attacks gradually intensified to such an extent that my parents took up the school's offer to evacuate its pupils to Beccles in Suffolk where I was billeted with a motherly widow, Mrs Foyster, who was responsible for looking after three of us and who fed us almost exclusively with baked beans on toast (which I anyhow loved), though food was already beginning to be in short supply prior to full-scale rationing. The winter of 1940 was an exceptionally harsh one, so much so that each day we had to plod our way on foot through the snow three or four miles each way to Shipmeadow for lessons in a rambling, cold, and disused workhouse which was our school. I was soon motivated towards the splendid parish church in Beccles where the elderly organist not only allowed me to practise but constantly warned me of the privations of a musical career, regularly showing me his down-at-heel shoes and telling me that because he was an organist his poverty extended to his being unable to afford having them repaired.

Eventually this interlude came to an end. I returned home and left school. Having thrown off the shackles of what had been a fairly miserable ending to my school life, I feared that my father then presumed I would not now be deterred from pursuing a career in the family business. Nothing could have been further from my aspirations, though for the present I had as a prelude to succumb to being sent as a trainee to my father's accountants in Rochester. The firm rejoiced in the name of 'Tribe, Clarke, Darton and Pollock, incorporating Bull, Darton and Pollock, and G. Pepper and Son'. There, under the shadow of the cathedral, I learned to add up columns of figures, the one fruit of my accountancy flirtation I have always been grateful for. It stood me in good stead, unlike those who today seem unable to work out anything without the aid of a pocket calculator. Eventually I was moved on to auditing the books of a mushroom farm, but here I met my Waterloo for I was completely out of my depth and falsified the trial balance which the partner, to whom I had been allocated, quickly exposed.

My salary was all of £4 a month which would be ceremoniously handed over to me by the senior partner, Mr Pollock, who always seemed to sit at an empty desk and would guardedly enquire how I was getting on. Back at home, £3 of this was immediately handed over to my mother for my keep.

My father, to whom business skills were second nature, failed to understand how my business acumen could be so stupid, some of which I have to admit was contrived, but I suspect he had no intention of understanding because he was adamant that I go into the family business as he had a generation previously. As a businessman, his over-riding objection to a musical career was the poor money I would earn, for he knew the sort of salary I would have received had I been in his firm, as I was to realise later when he died and I learned how relatively wealthy he was. For him there was also the added sadness that there seemed to be no one else in the family to inherit the business.

Sooner, rather than later, my training in accountancy came to an end and I was sent to work for my father. He provided driving lessons which I feigned I could not cope with as I knew this would lead to my being more extensively involved, so he made me bicycle, walk, or go everywhere by bus. This was the beginning in earnest of the cleavage which continued on and off until the Army claimed and in many ways saved me in 1943.

All this time I was working hard at the organ, disappearing from the office whenever I could on the pretext of having outside work to do, which was usually a half truth as I would proceed to practise the organ. I thought that I was being rather clever and that my real motives went undetected, but everyone in the office apparently knew and turned a blind eye including on occasion, I think, my father. Anyhow, I was seldom called to account, for some of the staff actually acquiesced, or even encouraged me.

My mother meanwhile continued with her gardening and secretly took my side, which was at least some consolation, for the frustration I was experiencing in realising my ambitions and aspirations, was very real, with my constant prayers being that I might one day become a cathedral organist.

During this time I became organist of All Saints' Church, Findsbury, a fine old building perched high on a hill above the Medway, its spire an unmistakable landmark. The Vicar, John Lloyd, was a great encourager whose support I valued and responded to. He loved music and we would spend many an evening together at the Vicarage listening to his gramophone records, something I relished because he opened doors to orchestral music, at that time a relatively unknown field to me, such was my obsession with church and organ music. Those evenings later became a much anticipated part of each leave from the Army, not least for the mountains of ham sandwiches with which his wife plied me.

I was now working for my Associateship of the Royal College of Organists. The Findsbury organ was then hand-blown and as I could seldom find people to come and pump the organ with any degree of regularity, I found that by filling the bellows myself and then using the softest stop on the organ, I could get through the transposing of a hymn into another key before the wind supply ran out. Spurred on by my success, I then graduated to sight reading and score reading, having been rightly advised that the only road to success was daily practise at these tests. I passed the practical part of the examination without a lot of trouble, although it took three attempts before I was successful with the paperwork. After the second attempt and while waiting for the result, I was collecting rents in Snodland where I chanced to see a Wayside Pulpit poster outside a church which said 'Put your trust in the Lord and all will be well'. Next day the result came: I had failed!

In between whiles I pursued my near obsession for trying organs. Virtually no instrument within a radius of twenty miles, be it of real worth or not, escaped my attention, which must have made me a nuisance to clergy and organists alike. I invariably bicycled to each church and kept full records of specifications, together with comments and photographs. Alas, I have mislaid the three loose leaf books in which these youthful typewritten observations were meticulously housed.

Further afield, H. A. James, who was the London representative of Harrison and Harrison, the organ builders, let me loose from time to time on the organ in the Royal Albert Hall, Westminster Abbey and other London churches, as well as cathedrals in different parts of the country, this often in return for my holding down the notes as he tuned the instrument. How exciting it was, especially to play 'full organ' at the Royal Albert Hall. Looking back, the strange thing was that no one seemed to complain about the noise I revelled in making: perhaps it was put down to youthful enthusiasm which ought if anything to perhaps be encouraged.

A special and much valued treat was my father allowing me to be absent from the office from time to time for a day visit to London. I would travel on the 'workman's train', for which a special cheap ticket, price one shilling and eight pence, was valid so long as you arrived at Charing Cross Station before 8 am. I would have breakfast at Lyons Corner House next door to the station, which cost me ten old pence, after which the regular pattern would be to saunter down Whitehall to Westminster Abbey. I well remember discovering Little Cloister and the organist's house which was then at No. 7, and had been named Lytlyngton Tower by Sir Sydney Nicholson when he was the Abbey organist. I would never cease to revel in the beauty of the Abbey itself, saying my prayers there and asking that one day I might become a cathedral organist or a priest, but never an estate agent. Many years later, when I was on the short list for the Directorship of the Royal School of Church Music, I was again saying my prayers in the Abbey after being interviewed by the RSCM Council in Jerusalem Chamber, and on this occasion my prayers were answered.

I would then walk to St Luke's, Chelsea, a handsome early 19th century Georgian-Gothic church which had a fine Compton organ. It had for me the added aura of a detached console with luminous stop knobs. Having paid my now customary shilling to the verger, I would be let loose on the organ for an hour. During the day other churches would be taken on board, mostly after having studied *The Organ*, back numbers of which I was then collecting as and when I could afford them, and as they were available, from *Musical Opinion*'s pokey old and long since demolished premises in Chichester Rents, just off Chancery

Lane. At that time Gilbert Benham was regularly contributing his articles on 'Interesting London Organs', and these were an invaluable source material for me.

In this way I really got to know London, and I especially loved exploring some of the back streets, the mews, and the splendid squares of Chelsea and Kensington, some of which were already being heavily damaged by bombing. The second-hand music department of Foyle's shop in Charing Cross Road was another happy hunting ground.

These excursions would invariably be rounded off by going to a cinema. In those days most cinema shows consisted of a main film, and a 'supporting' one, with Gaumont British or British Movietone News separating them. Those were the days long before daily television newscasts but even if what was reported was anything up to a week old, it still seemed very up to date, especially if it had come from abroad. During the inevitable interval for ice creams I well remember on one occasion hearing some wonderfully majestic background music which I enquired about at the box office. This was the first time that I had heard the great tune which begins Elgar's 1st Symphony and which opened up for me a whole new world of orchestral sound and led on to so much more Elgar, then to Brahms, Mahler and Wagner. Despite the fact that I was but sixteen and highly impressionable, that noble tune clothed in such rich and equally noble orchestration spoke to me with an impact as nothing else previously had, and seldom has to the same degree since, though much has emerged and grown from that initial encounter. It was, in a word, a turning point in that I had quite by chance discovered romantic music—and what a revelation it was. Later on, though in a rather different way, much of my musical life would be moulded by Bach.

The train back to Strood ended the day. Those were times of black-out with only a solitary, and usually dim, blue light in each compartment. There would be frequent anti-aircraft gunfire and sometimes the line would be blocked by a bomb, but in those days it was all taken in one's stride, as was the two mile walk home from the railway station, often late at night.

My abiding love of London was certainly born in those days. Years later the post-Christmas choir holiday at Exeter often saw

37

me making similar expeditions, though then with the accent on exploring second-hand bookshops. London was relatively quiet at that time of the year. Even in the much later years living at Addington Palace, and when I was so often in London, it continued to exert its excitement and anticipation for me whenever the train crossed the Thames and entered Victoria Station.

Thinking back to those wartime days, there seemed to be very little apparent fear of the potential dangers that were all around us, perhaps because we were all in it together and caught up in events from which there was no escape for any of us. Much of my organ practising continued to be done in the evenings at St Mary's Chatham, after which I would bicycle home, often on pitch black nights—and with the blackout in operation they really were dark nights. There would frequently be anti-aircraft gunfire and from time to time the sound of a bomb whistling down. But I pedalled on, wearing my steel helmet as the only protection, to join my parents who were already settled down for the night in the garden shelter. I certainly do not recall having any great fears in those days, rather a sense of adventure, for what mattered most to me then was my organ practice.

I had to work very hard at my music because, although I may have had certain talents, things did not come all that easily to me either then or later, and anything I achieved was through dint of sheer hard work more than anything else. Although I was inevitably looked on as the local boy with musical gifts, I desperately needed incentive and encouragement, and this was not always forthcoming. Despite my parents' eventually coming round to a tacit acceptance that I genuinely wanted to make music my career, my father never really encouraged me as such, simply because it was no more in his interests than he believed it was in mine.

To a certain extent I can understand his reluctance to come to terms with the situation, for his consuming concern was the survival of the family business and his hope that I might see what he construed as sense, albeit at the eleventh hour. But I was hurt by my parents seemingly being so uninterested, even when I had achieved the Exeter Cathedral organ loft and with it a certain prominence, for when they visited us they would seldom attend a service or hear the choir. Nor, in the Rochester days did I receive all that encouragement or real incentive from my teachers as I would do later from Sir Edward Bairstow. Perhaps in their estimation I was not all that exceptional, which was probably true. But, how essential encouragement is, as I realised later when it became my task to encourage talent and hopefully influence for good those who came under my wing.

By the time I was eighteen, I was due to join the Forces. This was deferred for a short while on the rather slender grounds that I was working for my ARCO, but early in 1943, having done some fitful part-time service in the Home Guard, I was called up and found myself in the Army for the next four and a half years.

CHAPTER SIX

14560967 Private Dakers

I had by this time begun to keep a diary and would continue to do so for nearly twenty years. During my army life I used for this purpose a series of War Office notebooks. I frequently wrote at some length, often with fulsome comments and thoughts, some of them oh so youthful in the sureness that I had all the right answers. These have nevertheless been a useful source for material for these memoirs, often helping to remind me of people and events I had otherwise long since forgotten.

On 18 March 1943 I obeyed the summons, though with considerable reluctance, and certainly with a trepidation born of speculation as to what an entirely different and unknown future would hold for me. I duly arrived at Beverley Station in East Yorkshire and for the first time climbed into an army truck, something I never subsequently found all that easy. For the next six weeks at Victoria Barracks I was subjected to a thoroughly alien routine of incessant parade ground marching, rifle drill and endless 'spit and polish'.

One particularly futile occupation was that of having to dig slit trenches in the West Woods and then being told to fill them in again. How bitterly cold East Yorkshire could be at that time of the year when the wind drove in from the nearby North Sea. At virtually every turn there would be the repetitive monologue of the Cockney sergeant-major who constantly threatened us that 'by the time I've finished with you lot, I'll make you wish you never 'ad a mother'. Comforting sentiments such as these, plus the cumbersome, heavy, and ill-fitting combat kit we wore for hours on end, while running at the double, and my highly unsuccessful rifle range practice when I seldom came within an ace of the target, made me realise that I was not really cut out to be a soldier.

Worse still were the practice sessions with hand grenades. Even if they were dummies, they were soon followed by the real thing, as when I jumped into a trench with the sergeant, was told to pull out the pin and lob the thing at an imaginary target. With my uncertain sense of direction, and never having been anything approaching a good over-arm bowler, I threw the grenade more or less straight up into the air. 'Run, you bloody fool' yelled the sergeant and, as we both scrambled out of the trench and dived for cover, the grenade exploded more or less on the spot where a few seconds earlier we had been standing. My punishment for this misdemeanour was to be confined to barracks for seven days and to peel mountains of potatoes each evening after duties.

We lived in huts, sleeping on two-tier wooden bunks, with what was called a biscuit for a mattress and thick army blankets which were so rough, sheets being unheard of. I invariably seemed to land up on the top bunk, this because I was not quick enough in the rush to claim one of the lower ones. I repeatedly thought of the psalmist's injunction that 'If I climb up into heaven thou art there also', for sleep in these circumstances was a blessed interlude of peace.

Life in the huts was a combination of noise and smell, the former reminiscent of the babel of sound to be heard at one of those sherry parties where everyone talks at the top of their voices, though in the hut much of the language was more basic and continually spiced with repetitive adjectives not normally heard in a drawing room. As far as smell was concerned this emanated from eighteen bodies cooped up in a small and airless hut, coupled with the distinctive odour of uniforms which were often damp. No one in those circumstances had the opportunity, nor usually the inclination, to take a daily bath. The equally unpleasant smell of the Blanco and Brasso which we used on our equipment, buttons and cap badges, all added to what might be called the novelty of the new life. Here, as in any barrack room, there was the incessant singing and whistling of wartime hit songs, with 'Run, rabbit, run' and 'We're gonna hang out the washing on the Seigfried Line' being currently in vogue in 1943. Later on, and in less salubrious circumstances, it would be the more soothing and romantic sounding 'A nightingale sang in

41

Berkeley Square'. Even so, the more bawdy songs were fairly tame compared with some of the lyrics we were later to hear in Egypt and which were often pertinent to the well being, or otherwise, of King Farouk.

Although I seemed to have little in common with most of my colleagues, for their interests and mine were poles apart, there were nevertheless some kindred spirits, and how blissful were the shared, if infrequent, moments of respite. These I would usually spend in exploring the cathedral-like spaciousness and the unique architectural charm of Beverley Minster, surely one of the most beautiful and perfect of parish churches anywhere. I got to know the acting organist who allowed me to practise and to play voluntaries. On Saturday afternoons we were usually allowed out of barracks and would go to one of those long since defunct grocer's shops which in Yorkshire boasted a restaurant where we would devour baked beans on toast, cake and wartime ersatz coffee. Even in this restricted existence, I quickly realised the beauty of the East Riding, a part of the world I was later to know well.

Towards the end of my time at Beverley, the sergeant-major announced some cultural lectures we were to attend, 'the first of which will be on the subject of Keats, and I doubt if there's one of you higgorant men who knows what a Keat is'!

As on so many subsequent occasions when life seemed bleak, good fortune—and not least the good God—came to my rescue. All that unaccustomed marching in army boots had played havoc with my feet and, after medical examination, I was down-graded to 'Medical Category B7' which, in a word, meant I had flat feet. This proved my saving grace for, at the end of the six weeks' initial training, I was posted to the Royal Army Pay Corps in York where for the next two and a half years much of my life was to prove so happy and unexpectedly fruitful.

CHAPTER SEVEN

York –
the Army and music intertwined

The Pay Corps offices were scattered around the city in requisitioned schools and commercial property, while for accommodation we were billeted in private houses. I found myself with a dear old Yorkshire widow, Mrs Petler, who not only looked after me like a second mother but welcomed me into the warm and caring hospitality of a humble Yorkshire home and, in many respects, a unique way of life. I was initiated into eating Yorkshire pudding the Yorkshire way, I learned what it meant to 'side the pots' and at the New Year to experience the ritual of 'first footing'. This was the beginning of my subsequent affection and regard for Yorkshire and its people, something to be experienced to the full in married life at Ripon.

Within hours of arriving in York I was in the Minster and quickly came under the spell of the largest Gothic church north of the Alps, even though its medieval glass had been removed to safety during the war. It was to be some years before I would be able to revel in its full beauty, but I wandered into the Minster whenever I could to bask in its glorious architecture, and of course to hear the music. It was not long before I met Sir Edward Bairstow who had been the organist since 1913 and who, when he was offered Westminster Abbey, was reputed to have said that he would rather reign in hell than serve in heaven, such was his position and eminence in the North. I soon came under the spell of this remarkable musician who encouraged me to sit with him in the organ loft for services. How much I learned in the process, not least in the way he improvised before services, making up miniature snippets taken from the psalm chants. And how wonderfully he accompanied the psalms, weaving all sorts of independent tunes as additional counterpoints, and colouring

43

the words in a highly original and always excitingly romantic way. I never failed to be thrilled by his own highly individual set of chants for Psalm 114 and how at the end, on the words 'and the flintstone into a springing well' he would add the 32ft pedal reed for the final bottom C. The Minster's considerable echo added to the thrill as the sound rolled round the vastness of the building.

No less exciting were his improvisations at the end of the Sunday Eucharist when he would unfailingly build up to a most impressive full organ climax leading to the choir recessing while singing Psalm 150 unaccompanied, this a then unique York tradition. And then on Easter Day in the hymn 'Jesus Christ is risen today' the expectation of climax and the broadening out at the words 'Now above the skies he's King'. His playing of Bach would shock the purist of today whose style is frequently so fast, brittle and monochrome, whereas ECB, as he was always familiarly referred to, would produce ever-changing colours in works such as the Fantasia and Fugue in G Minor which revealed to me an uncanny perception and originality.

Such sounds, and more, came as something of a bombshell, and certainly as a revelation to my unashamedly romantic leanings, for I had never before heard music such as this. The experience was profound and unforgettable, as later when hearing and getting to know his church music with its intensely original line of thought which disclosed his innate sense of knowing how to explore to the full, through the vehicle of music, the inner depth and meaning of the many fine texts he elected to set.

After a while, when he conducted an unaccompanied anthem, I was allowed to play the chord for the choir, then to play voluntaries and finally entire services, for his assistant was also away in the Forces.

Bairstow had the well-earned reputation of being an inspiring teacher as I found when I commenced organ and paper-work lessons with him. He encouraged me as I had never been encouraged before, his charisma both infecting and inspiring me to the extent that I frequently worked at my studies into the small hours, sustained as often as not by fish and chips from the nearby fishmonger, while my Monday lunchtime lessons at 1 Minster Court were exciting occasions followed by sandwiches at the WVS canteen then to be found on No. 8 platform at York Station.

I was consequently greatly impressed by this musician who was so utterly professional and caring, but who also had the reputation of being difficult. Like all true Yorkshiremen, he often spoke his mind bluntly, without hesitation and, despite the home truths he was never afraid to utter, did not always for that very reason endear himself to everyone. In his time he was much sought after as an adjudicator but, because of his outspoken comments, it was said that he had adjudicated *once* at every festival. He was also credited with having said that when God gave a man a tenor voice he took away his brains.

All in all, the Minster, its music and ECB became a consuming passion for me, and such an incentive, the more so I suppose because life for me at that time was under constraint. In addition to my musical studies I seemed to find time for so many other pursuits which now began to emerge. All around me were new arenas and new interests, with people to help me explore those to the full. The army allowed me considerable flexibility, much of it through the expedient of turning the blind eye, as others had done in my father's office, realising that I was probably more cut out to be a musician than an accountant. So they let me go my own way as far as was possible. I became a willing messenger, running errands between the offices in the city which allowed me to sneak in and out of the Minster. I recall my Captain sending me to change his library book just before Evensong and telling me not to hurry back, so this errand took me well over an hour. Even so, there were times when I felt guilty, for it reminded me of occasions when I was out of school, however legitimately, during school hours, and of the sense of uneasy freedom this invoked.

My growing love of books came next to music and bore considerable fruit at this time, though serious book collecting and a widening of my interests were for the future. I roamed round the bookshops, not least Godfrey's in Stonegate with its second-hand department full of things I could not afford but nevertheless coveted. Night by night I read into the small hours and then, when Mrs Petler complained of my using so much electricity, I would resort to a torch under the bedclothes. In this way I came to terms with Milton's *L'Allegro*, while most of Walter Scott's *Kenilworth* was read in the loo at the office, usually in twenty minute sessions, in excess of which I would risk being missed. Shakespeare's *Sonnets*, Richard Jefferies and Henry Williamson were all discovered at this time. '*Tarka the Otter* is the most beautiful book I have ever read' I wrote in my diary. I even read while walking the mile or so to and from the office four times a day, a pursuit I copied from one of the actors at the York Rep. who was probably learning his lines.

Stimulating discussion was generated with like-minded friends, not least Philip and Margaret Turner, he a chartered accountant serving as a corporal in the Pay Corps. They fostered in me a youthful enthusiasm for much that was novel and exciting, and as much a revelation as was in other ways the Minster and its music. I suppose I was just at the right age to be impressed, and was living under some pressure, which contributed towards the overall impact. Aldous Huxley and C. E. M. Joad, the latter being all the rage in the 1940s, not only through his books but through the BBC Brains Trust programmes, led me on to explore the fringes of spiritualism and even Christian Science. Christina Rossetti, William Cowper and Rupert Brooke—in retrospect a strange trio of bedfellows—all came within my orbit, and in everything there was a youthful enthusiasm for many areas of literary interest, much of it documented in the diary with equal enthusiasm, though seldom with any hint of criticism.

As with books, so with music it was for me an age of great discovery. While the Minster disclosed so much that was new to me in church music, it was through the radio, records and concerts that I was to become a willing explorer of secular music. Wagner, Walton, Ravel, Rachmaninoff, and the Bax violin concerto, were but some of what headed my list at this time, with the diary full of comments, most of them I imagine little removed from the reactions I would probably make now, fifty years later. But it was English music on which I was particularly hooked, such as the then new 5th Symphony of Vaughan Williams with its hauntingly beautiful—and, oh, so English—*Romanza*, the *Serenade to Music*, *Job* and *On Wenlock Edge*, of which a friend had a pre-electric recording sung by Gervase Elwes. I so well remember the impact of my first encounter with Elgar's *Enigma Variations*, for I was already at heart a willing romantic. But even more vividly I remember a never to be forgotten *Dream of Gerontius* which Bairstow conducted at Leeds Town Hall, with the contralto a beautiful tall young girl dressed in white. This was the début of Kathleen Ferrier who sang from memory.

There was a lot of music taking place in York, with regular recitals in the Tempest Anderson Hall, while the London Philharmonic Orchestra often included York in its wartime tours to the provinces. Richard Tauber, the singer turned conductor, gave us sizeable chunks of Richard Strauss' *Der Rosenkavalier* which impressed me because he conducted from memory. Charles Munch and Sir Thomas Beecham appeared with the LPO at one of the York cinemas, the latter beginning one concert with the Berlioz overture *Le Carnival Romain* which, when he felt the strings were not bowing with enough vigour, prompted him to shout 'Tally-ho' which produced the desired effect.

Cycle rides, mostly on an ancient ladies' model which belonged to Mrs Petler's daughter, and had seen better days, allowed me to explore the Vale of York, with excursions to Ampleforth and Castle Howard, and magic views of York Minster in the distance as seen from the top of the Wolds. These journeys would often take in some of the Yorkshire rivers where I would lie on the bank, listen to the sound of water and bird song while looking up into the blue sky and the clouds, for in those days, as earlier in childhood, it seemed to be perpetual summer. Having arrived back in York I would, as often as not, read and revel in Richard Jefferies and Henry Williamson, both of whom encapsulated in such beautiful prose what I had been experiencing in terms of the English countryside.

In those days there was of course no television. If there had been, I doubt if I would have read and studied to the extent I did. But there was the cinema, and the one at Clifton had an organ and a very bad organist whom we had perforce to suffer as we were subjected to a ten minute interlude between the two main films. I went regularly to one or other of the York cinemas, perhaps once or twice a week, or else there was the excellent York Repertory Theatre which put on a new production each week. Enjoyable though the cinema might be, it had its drawbacks, as the diary reminds me: 'Took one of the ATS to the cinema. It was pouring with rain when we came out and I had to walk home with her. That's the disadvantage of taking a girl to the cinema'. Such was my unromantic lack of chivalry.

Every three months I was due for seven or ten days' leave and I would invariably get the overnight train to King's Cross so as to arrive south at the earliest possible moment, for there was always so much I wanted to pack in to the available time. Not least in this was London where my firmly entrenched ritual continued, though in a London now sadly disfigured by so much bomb damage and destruction. Even so, I was systematically exploring more and more parts in considerable detail and increasingly in the less central areas. High tea at Stewart's close by Marble Arch would invariably lead on by the No. 73 bus to the Royal Albert Hall which, after bombs had devastated the Queen's Hall, would for some years be the central venue for most orchestral concerts.

A new area of interest for me was ballet. I was introduced to Edward Dent who had by then retired as Professor of Music at Cambridge. He took me when on leave to Sadlers Wells and the Ballet Joos. He proved a kind friend not only in revealing to me more musical opportunities but also in sharing with me his interest in good food. He took me to some of the best of the Soho restaurants at that time, such as Kettner's and Le Petit Savoyard in Frith Street, or at his flat in Cromwell Place, Kensington, and this despite the rationing of food which by that time was becoming more rigorous.

These 'firsts' were not confined to music and eating but extended to my first glass of beer, in a public house in York, after which I had violent diarrhoea. I also at that time experienced my first, and only, ride on a tandem which I found strange in that I was not in sole control of the machine.

On one leave I recall being at home during the worst air raid of the war when the noise of the anti-aircraft guns, with bombs whining down and exploding all around us, was a really frightening experience. After that particular raid I went with my father to the top of nearby Broom Hill and saw a whole succession of large fires raging in the Medway Towns below.

When VE Day came in May 1945 and then, with the capitulation of Japan months later, the end of all hostilities, there were great services of thanksgiving in the Minster, stirring speeches by Winston Churchill, and national holidays when I dashed down to London to join in the festivities. These were most exciting and reflected the enormous relief in that the war had ended. The most pertinent comment in my diary at this time was that on May 6, 1945 there were thirty-five of us in the compartment on the train to London. This was obviously youthful exaggeration, for this was long before the days of open seating carriages, and when even a corridor coach was usually encountered only on long distance trains.

Particularly memorable in the York days were the friendships which emerged. Although people in uniform were invariably treated to generous hospitality by the civilian population, one encountered so many whose friendship continued long after the war had ended. Even so, it is sad that others have inevitably disappeared from the scene without trace, although some have suddenly emerged again after a gap of many years.

There was Bill Gibson, a blind bass songman in the Minster choir who, with his wife Ethel, threw open their home to me. She was also a singer and I often accompanied them on the piano and in doing so got to know and greatly admire much of the 20th century English song repertoire—Butterworth, Ivor Gurney, Vaughan Williams, Warlock and Quilter—though some of the accompaniments, like Frank Bridge's *Love went a-riding* defeated me through their sheer technical difficulty. There was also Dennis Laughton, a kindly though shy and lonely bachelor who later sadly took his own life. He sometimes invited me for weekends to his home in Fulford, and through him I was introduced to some of the many interesting people he knew.

49

At this time the army sent me to Cuerdon Hall, Preston, for a music instructor's course promoted by the Royal Army Education Corps. The person in charge was Eric Fenby whose association with Delius is now legendary, and with whom, despite he being a major and me a private, I struck up a friendship which has lasted over the years. As with me, he was longing to resume his musical career, so we had much in common and we spent most evenings at a local hostelry talking not only about Delius but music generally. Both of us were becoming more and more disillusioned with the army and its red tape, even more so now that the war had ended, and I was restive to take up the place Sir Stanley Marchant had, through Bairstow's good offices, offered me at the Royal Academy of Music where he was Principal.

A significantly happy occasion was my twenty-first birthday, for which my parents came to York and gave a dinner for a sizeable gathering of my new-found friends. I was extremely well remembered, but the gift which gave me the most pleasure was from ECB who presented me with three volumes of Bach's organ works duly inscribed by him. On that day I was at the Minster and took comfort from the words of the office hymn 'Come, Holy Ghost, our souls inspire'. Much of that hymn seemed so apt, not only in my having arrived at where I was, musically and in my majority, but equally in my aspirations for the future.

Pre-eminent in those days were the unexpected musical riches which came my way and which were so contrary to my expectations, for I was convinced that my having to join the Army would signal the enforced curtailment, at least until after the war, of any musical progress I had made up till then. In the event I was now making more music than ever before, and central to this was the Minster and ECB. How often I then uttered, as since, a fervent *Deo gracias*.

The York interlude allowed me, under the guidance of Bairstow, to complete my Associateship of the Royal College of Organists and then a year later to become a Fellow of the College. How well I recall saying to ECB that I hoped any nervousness in the practical examination would not spell disaster. 'Nerves?' he said, 'perfect love casteth out fear'. And it worked. Also in 1945

I completed the first part of the Bachelor of Music degree at Durham University where, under the then existing regulations, ECB was Visiting Professor of Music, and where the degree could be taken externally. But first I had to have Matriculation as an entrance qualification, having failed dismally in this while at school. So I took a correspondence course with Wolsey Hall, Oxford, while having tuition in Latin from an old priest in York who extracted from me all of five shillings a lesson, a sizeable sum in those days.

I also did a lot of organ practice in the Minster or in local churches, and in this way built up my repertoire, while I was always popular by volunteering to do fire-watching duty at the Pay Corps offices, this in case of any incendiary bombs being dropped by the Germans. While relieving my colleagues of unwanted overnight duties, this allowed me to pursue my studies in peace.

I was in and out of the Minster so much, and eventually seldom missed being in the organ loft for a choral service, to the extent that ECB once said he was fearful lest I should be 'confined to barracks' as a punishment for absenting myself so much from the office. 'You're always coming to Evensong when you shouldn't't', he said. 'Anyhow, you have a good precedent because old J. S. Bach ran off to hear Buxtehude, and let everything else go to blazes'.

I was asked to give a number of recitals while in York, sometimes on my own, at other times with singers like Bill Gibson, or combined piano and organ recitals, in this way coming to terms on the organ with the orchestral part of some of the Bach and Mozart concertos. Reginald Rose, who was organist at St Olave's Church in Gillygate, was music critic of *The Yorkshire Evening Post*, and he not only befriended me but greatly encouraged me, and taught me a lot through his erudite press notices after each recital I gave. I also continued to give recitals at Frindsbury when on leave. I even flirted with composition, mainly in song settings of poems by Sappho and A. E. Housman.

So, all in all, it was for me an easy war. Although I was not feeling complacent in my security, it nevertheless came as a great shock in the summer of 1945 to be suddenly told that I was to be posted overseas to Egypt. It was the more depressing, even at the time devastating, in that it came at the very moment I was hoping to be demobilised, something which in the event was not to be my lot, as with many others of my age group, until more than two years after the war had ended.

Having said my farewells in York, my embarkation leave was spent at home and in London, the last night of it in a Forces' Hostel in Cadogan Gardens where I realised with some nostalgia how lovely London squares can look in the autumn. For this next uncertain stage of my existence I armed myself with Housman's *A Shropshire Lad* and a phial of London soil taken from the Green Park. These would at least be some link with what I so valued, no matter what the future might hold in store for me.

CHAPTER EIGHT

Music on the banks of the Nile

'The light that never was upon the land or sea of his home strikes now for the first time upon his eyes. The swift and colourful daylight sinks as if by magic to a softly luminous afterglow, and then to the unearthly peace and remoteness of the desert night. An imagination that is awake and receptive may catch from that vision an infection that will last a lifetime.' – Lord Lloyd: *Egypt since Cromer.*

My last night in England was spent at a dreadfully primitive transit camp high on the Sussex Downs above Newhaven. Underfoot everything was wet and boggy chalk, and the loos so basic that I began to think that come what may, life could hardly be worse in Egypt. Typical of army life, reveille was at 4.15 the next morning, though there would be many hours of waiting until we would be on the boat for Dieppe before the slow trek by train down through France to Toulon.

My diary recorded an almost station by station account, for we stopped at every opportunity, generally to barter with the locals whose main need seemed to be for cigarettes and soap, for they were desperately deprived of so many basic essentials. It was more or less a case of only when the buying and selling was concluded would we trundle on to the next station where the process would be repeated. From our old LNER coaches, complete with bucket seats, we had plenty of opportunity to see the countryside and the enormous amount of damage which the war had wrought, especially to the bridges, many of which were only partially repaired and over which we crept at a snail's pace, for it was only a few months since the end of the war in Europe.

We eventually arrived in Toulon where, after a couple of days respite lazing in the Mediterranean sun we boarded a Polish ship, the SS Batory, which took us via Malta to Alexandria. The near animal existence on board for other ranks was to an extent alleviated by two of us with like minded interests finding a quiet corner where we could read and sun ourselves to our hearts' content. At Alexandria we boarded a train for Cairo, crossing the Nile for the first time. 'He who drinks the waters of the Nile returns to drink again' was neither uppermost in my mind, nor to be fulfilled for some years. Anyhow, at this particular juncture in my life I had no particular wish to see the Nile either then or ever again.

After some days at Abbassia, a vast colonial-style British barracks, I was posted to the Command Pay Office in the centre of downtown Cairo and which I quickly found to be so different from life in York. We lived in requisitioned flats just off Sharia Soliman Pasha as it then was, and where, when on so-called guard duty one night, I went to bed, as I gathered was the accepted practice. Unfortunately for me, on this occasion an Egyptian fellahin stole a sack of sugar and next morning I found myself on a charge. Fearing that I might be sent to an army detention centre or, worse still, to Aden which, because of its intense heat and discomfort, was the ultimate penalty transgressors were threatened with, I waited with some trepidation before being marched in to my Commanding Officer. My marching apparently did not please him so I was sent out and in three times, all no doubt intended to intensify the foreboding he must have seen in my eyes, before he sentenced me to forfeit three days' pay which, he said with a slight twinkle in his eye, would roughly be the equivalent of the fee for playing at three weddings.

My first impressions of Cairo were, I imagine, little different from those of the thousands of troops who found themselves there during the war. Forty or more years later, they are as vivid as ever, especially the smell of the body odour of horses and camels sweating in the heat, with the equally distinctive smell of the urine and manure they freely deposited anywhere and everywhere. There were the ancient black gharries, horse-drawn carriages which in those days vied for custom with equally ancient taxis, though the gharries were less likely to break down. Before the overthrow of King Farouk most lower class Egyptians wore the flowing ghalabiya, the more opulent perhaps sporting a tarbush. The noise, then as now, was as incessant as it was loud, while car horns and tram bells cheerfully competed with each other, the muezzins on the top of the minarets called the faithful to prayer and seemed to vie with each other to see who could shout the loudest. Traffic signals were ignored with gay abandon and all was chaos *in excelsis*. Even the Forces guide to Cairo warned one that on the trams there was 'limited seating accommodation, less limited standing, but unlimited hanging on'. And everywhere were people, hordes and hordes of them, talking, shouting, jostling and, more often than not, running.

For much of the year the heat was considerable and consequently the afternoons were given over to siesta; then the city would be uncannily empty and quiet, suddenly to spring to life again around five o'clock when shops and offices would open until well into the evening.

How strange, and certainly alien, it all seemed in those early days, and yet somehow it was all rather exciting, for this great cosmopolitan city with hundreds of miles of desert on its doorstep embraced East and West in a strangely extraordinary, almost bizarre, way. It had a vitality and a vibrance which grew on you the more you got to know it and the people of many nationalities who inhabited it. It seemed no less strange to find yourself transported from an England still very much in immediate post-war austerity to a land literally flowing with milk and honey, plus a lot more, for Cairo was a kaleidoscopic blaze of neon signs, shops full of almost everything still in short supply at home and, not least for me, the bookshops full of so much which was unobtainable in England. In those days Cairo abounded in wonderful French, Italian, Greek and Turkish restaurants, a cosmopolitan internationalism then virtually unknown in England and something I was soon to revel in.

Then there was for me the *real* Cairo which one could explore in those days in relative peace, usually with the help of the colourful Mrs Devonshire whose well patronised tours of historic Cairo catered primarily for the Forces. My first, and never to be forgotten, sight of the immensity of the Giza pyramids was with the vivid red evening sun sharply silhouetting them for all too short a while before its swift descent and with it the relief of the cool evening breeze.

I explored old Cairo with its churches and monuments going back so many centuries, as well as the endless labyrinth of passageways in the Mouski where every conceivable type of merchant had his shop. Most of all perhaps I never failed then, as now, to come under the spell of those ancient and splendid mosques, their grandeur and, perhaps most of all, their utter sense of peace in the very centre of the never-ending noise of the city, and their amazing aura of spirituality.

Virtually days after arriving in Cairo I went down with sinusitis and was sent to an army hospital in Helmiah. Every three hours a nurse would proclaim 'Bottoms up, boys' for her to inject penicillin with a four-inch needle into each buttock alternately. That year, although I spent Christmas in hospital, I was still able to hear the Festival of Nine Lessons and Carols from King's College, Cambridge on the radio, even if some of it was somewhat distant and subject to atmospherics.

One significant oasis in the teeming life of the city was Music for All, a Forces Club founded by Lady Dorothea Russell as her war effort. Her husband, Sir Thomas Russell to the English, and Russell Pasha to the Egyptians, had founded the Cairo police force some years before the war. Lady Russell lavished much effort and money on transforming an old cinema and its outhouses in Sharia Marouff into something akin to a London club. Central to the life of the club were two concerts each evening, ranging from gramophone record recitals to live concerts by the Palestine Symphony Orchestra. Poetry readings and plays also featured in an enviable atmosphere, complete with an extensive library, London newspapers and a restaurant run by Groppi, the world famed hotelier then in Cairo. Because it was an all ranks club it gathered round it those who were deprived of 'gracious' living but shared in common a love of the arts. Hardly a day passed without my being in the club, often for hours at a time when duties permitted.

I was still leading a relatively easy existence and I often contemplated then, as now, how different life could have been, and in all probability would have been, had my feet not been flat. Even so, there were many moments when I felt as depressed and deprived as at other times I was elated. Such was the variability of my moods, for at the root of it all was my pining for England. I had been so happy in York where life was productive and rewarding in many ways, though I did realise, as I commented in the diary, that 'changes, often in themselves unwarranted, have opened up new scope for development and progress', though I had no inkling then that this would soon underpin my life in Cairo. For the present, listening to music—and I now had many opportunities to do this—always helped blot out any restlessness or homesickness, and this despite the ever present army routine and discipline, much of which seemed at best petty, and at worst illogical. On balance, I felt rather like the proverbial fish out of water, and it would be some time before I would come to appreciate Egypt to the full.

A change for the better came with my being sent to work at the Semiramis Hotel which was on the banks of the Nile, next door to the British Embassy. The hotel had been requisitioned by the Army, and from my office high up in the building I had an uninterrupted view across the city to the distant Giza pyramids. This elegant old imperial-style hotel was full of character and it survived until some years after the war when it was torn down. In its place rose a new hotel, one of those faceless and predictable concrete jungles to be found in such monotonous profusion the world over. In its garden were army huts in one of which I was to live. Every morning after breakfast there was a routine inspection parade which I often managed to escape through the simple expedient of closeting myself in the loo, though I cannot imagine how it was that I was never missed.

A further improvement in my fortunes came with my being asked to become organist both of the Presbyterian Church and of All Saints' Cathedral. I never regretted opting for the latter which was a most beautiful and spacious stone church built just before the war to the designs of Adrian Gilbert Scott. On either side of the west door were carved the inscriptions 'Out of Egypt have I brought my son' and 'Egypt my firstborn'. The entire complex, which was a miniature of an English Cathedral Close, complete with immaculately kept lawns and flower beds, was set on the banks of the Nile and included houses for the Bishop and the Archdeacon, together with the Diocesan

Offices and accommodation for British Army Chaplains serving in Egypt.

The largish choir was made up of men and women from the Services, together with civilian residents, some of whom had been in Cairo for many years. Inevitable postings meant that the choir personnel changed from week to week, with a sense of impermanence and instability resulting. The consequent lack of continuity could be frustrating, the one unfailingly predictable factor being S. S. Wesley's short anthem *Lead me, Lord*, which by tradition was sung *ad nauseam* before every service and became as repetitive as the aged Bishop Gwynne bringing into virtually every sermon the quote 'It's a poor heart that never rejoices'. There were many weddings, for each of which I received the then handsome fee of one Egyptian pound, which usually went either on books or in restaurants. I also broadcast a half-hour organ recital every Sunday on the local Forces Programme. Looking through the diary I see numerous scathing comments on women in general, such as 'choir practice went fairly well except that the women, as per usual, looked—and sang—like a lot of dying fish.'

Being able to practise on the cathedral organ before breakfast was something I much valued as an antidote to whatever problems the day might, and invariably did, produce in the office, where I continued to struggle, mostly unsuccessfully, with accountancy.

The cathedral clergy were sometimes difficult, for even in those days they were constantly wanting a larger congregational participation in the music. I, for my part, had to keep the choir well occupied, and the resulting pull between the opposing parties created the sort of problems it still creates as much today as then. I imagine I was also difficult, although I sensed from some of the comments which found their way back to me that the concerts I promoted in the cathedral, such as the 'Music in the Cathedral' series, were to some extent resented by the clergy because they drew in so many more people than some of the services. On my first Good Friday at the cathedral the diary reminds me that I read 140 pages of T. E. Lawrence's *Seven Pillars of Wisdom* during the three-hour service, which was followed by hot cross buns at the Archdeacon's house, a tea-time tradition which had gone on for all of 23 years.

By now the Pay Corps must have despaired of my lack of accountancy skills for I suddenly found myself transferred without warning or reason to the Royal Army Education Corps, and with the rank of sergeant, although merely because this was then the lowest rank in the Corps. This was certainly a move in the right direction, and it was much more to my liking to be working in a library and to have recourse to many books.

Before long, Lady Russell, who was something of a martinet, especially when she was dealing with the upper echelons of the military or with the British Ambassador, had me seconded from the Army to become Director of Music for All. Although she proved to be a frightening person who ruled her staff, myself included, with a rod of iron, we all respected her businesslike attitudes, even though she tended to ride roughshod over all and sundry when it suited her. The result was a most efficient and dedicated team over which I presided. My main tasks were the planning of a highly varied weekly menu of events, the printing of programmes and the publicity involved. I was also responsible for looking after, and entertaining, the artistes. All this was certainly much to my liking and, although I did not realise it at the time, a valuable introduction to much of the administrative work I was to do years later at the Royal School of Church Music. Musica Viva, an early music group directed by Hans Hickman, frequently featured at the club as they did in Cairo's musical life generally, while latterly an orchestra formed by Hans Hoerner from fellow German prisoners of war housed in the Canal Zone, gave regular and much appreciated concerts.

I enjoyed presenting programmes of recorded music, accompanying singers, and even playing the 'harpsichord'—an old upright piano with drawing pins stuck into the hammers—for performances such as Purcell's *Dido and Aeneas* organised by the British Council. I had for a long time been interested in the concept of linking poetry and music, so used Music for All as the opportunity for devising and trying out such projects, even presuming to call myself the producer of the programmes. There were some excellent professional actors and readers in

Cairo, most of them in the Forces or ENSA, and they, inter-spersed with gramophone recordings, provided me with the material for 'The Coloured Counties' (after A. E. Housman), 'This England' and 'In Praise of London', for which the British Council loaned me effects records of Underground trains and London traffic noises. These programmes proved popular, probably because of the nostalgia they generated for those of us temporarily exiled from England.

I certainly worked hard and at all hours in those days, not least in copying out orchestral parts, for there were then no photocopiers. The main satisfaction was that I was now doing some of the things I felt more qualified to do—and hopefully do well—than when I was in the Pay Corps.

Even so, there was time for a fairly full social life. Cairo had some splendid restaurants, La Taverne Française, the Savile, St James's, the Pickwick Bar, and especially Groppi, the *crème de la crème*, all of which I regularly frequented, often in the company of Francis Stonor, then working as a liaison officer attached to the British Embassy. As he knew many people, this added to the interest and to my getting to know so many, not least those expatriates who lived permanently in Cairo.

And there was always the Astra, a coffee shop known affec-tionately for some reason as the pudding shop, just round the corner from the club in the Midan Kasr el Nil, where we would indulge in endless late-night discussion, though I now have no idea what we talked about, but talk we certainly did, not least with WAAF Olive Hill, then the latest in a succession of girl friends. There were highlights such as Gielgud in *Hamlet* at the Opera House, seeing the Sphinx by moonlight, and excursions to the desert, often with Patrick Fedden, a young priest who had recently come out from England to join the cathedral staff. One such excursion to the Pyramids prompted me to confide to the diary 'I had read of this with great excitement in an H. V. Morton book, yet it was only last night that I savoured this to the full. An unforgettably beautiful full moon shone down in a cloudless, starlit sky, bathing the desert in a wonderful blue haze and making the Pyramids and Sphinx look so large. The contrast of light and shade on the sides of the Pyramids was unforgettable.

A local Egyptian burned some magnesium ribbon for us under-
neath the Sphinx and in its light the face almost assumed a smile.
The desert seemed, and was, so quiet except for the barking
of dogs in distant Bedouin villages while the gentle, almost
imperceptible awareness of a faint and warm night breeze blew
across one's face.'

All in all, Cairo seemed so exciting at the time, certainly
compared with my visit there forty years later when so much had
inevitably changed, and by no means all to the good, for the city
had by then virtually trebled in size and was so much dirtier.
Large and opulent hotels are now to be found on Gezira Island
and in Zamalek, but virtually no trace remains of those splendid
restaurants or of the then equally elegant shops, many of them
French.

I now lived at Music for All in a comfortable little bed-sitter,
surrounded by my books and with a picture of Peter Warlock on
the wall. I was again able to indulge freely in reading until late
into the night, with Siegfried Sassoon, Henry Williamson, and
poetry my front runners. I virtually never wore uniform.

As Lady Russell paid me all of four pounds a week, with my
food thrown in for good measure, I had no need of my army pay,
though GHQ eventually suggested I should collect what had
accumulated. I accordingly donned my uniform but forgot that
my hair was now rather longer than the Army would have
tolerated. As I was bending down to sign for my pay the sergeant
major was aghast, and spluttered 'Get that hair cut, man, you
look like a bloody musician'!

Even with all these unforeseen privileges and opportunities,
I still experienced pangs of nostalgia and depression. Good
though life now was, I still wanted to get on with the serious
business of full-time study, and the slow pace of demobilisation
for people of my age group was frustrating. I had now served for
well over four years, the war having ended eighteen months
previously, and many of us were yearning to get on with our
careers. It was suggested that by voting Labour at the imminent
General Election the process of demobilisation would be speeded
up. Consequently many of us voted Labour, and did so solely for
this very reason, but to no avail.

Despite this temporary setback, I counted so many blessings which had come my way over the past few years and which on balance had far outweighed all the irritants. York and Cairo had opened so many unexpected doors for which I frequently uttered yet again a fervent *Deo gracias*, for my whole existence in Cairo was now absorbed in music.

From the autumn of 1946 onwards, the British Forces were gradually being run down in Cairo, either through demobilisation or the policy of evacuating, as it was called, to the Canal Zone, a large desert area south of Ismailia on the Egyptian side of the Suez Canal. Because of this the cathedral choir became increasingly depleted, as did the attendance at Music for All which eventually closed its doors in February 1947, having been in continuous daily use for over five years. We went out with a flourish, the final concert, given by the German POW Orchestra, ending with Beethoven's 5th symphony.

Everything was now changing, so I was more than glad when the time came for a month's leave in the UK. I left Egypt on my 23rd birthday and as we sailed up the Mediterranean I spent most of the days reading with, as I vividly recall, a wonderful view of Crete by moonlight. Since I was now a sergeant, the accommodation was marginally more comfortable than on the outward journey, and certainly far less crowded. We disembarked at Toulon and then by train crossed a France now rather different from sixteen months earlier. What better thrill could one have had than the train journey from Dover to London, through the Weald of Kent, Paddock Wood, and the Sassoon country I had by now got to know so well from his early autobiographical books?

Back at home I embarked on the now familiar round of visiting, with London concerts, bookshops and restaurants being savoured to the full. I went to Canterbury to see Gerald Knight, the cathedral organist, who had by now forgiven me for wanting to study at the Royal Academy of Music rather than at the Royal School of Church Music. Peacetime London was somehow not the same, for 'so much of the electric, and exciting, wartime atmosphere had gone'—so the diary concluded.

At the end of my leave, and because I had been seconded away from the Army, my papers had been lost, so once again, and for the last time, I was subjected to illogical red tape and was accordingly sent back to Egypt, although it was known that my release from the Army was due in six weeks' time. This unforeseen journey down the Mediterranean did at least produce some wonderful sunrises and sunsets while, reading the ship's noticeboard one day, I saw that 'Holy Communion 8 am' featured among the Sunday entertainments.

At Fayid, on the shores of the Bitter Lakes, I looked across to the Sinai Desert and the distant hills. I found some of my Cairo friends but, as with post-war London, it was not the same and hardly could be, for here there was no Music for All or cathedral, only the Army's little St Martin-in-the-Sands with its wheezy harmonium.

I was on my way home again in June 1947, this time stopping in Algiers and then Cuxhaven where we off-loaded German prisoners of war returning home. We docked at Hull and I turned full circle by going through Beverley before being 'demobbed' at Fulford Barracks in York where I was kitted out with civilian clothes, including an ill-fitting suit I subsequently sold to the Clerk of the Royal College of Organists.

At last I was really free, and how I revelled in euphoria at the English countryside. Life was now as Cardinal Newman expressed it, albeit in a different context, in *The Dream of Gerontius*—'that strange, inexpressible feeling, never felt before'. Years later when I read V. M. Yeates' *Winged Victory*, a gripping account of first world war pilots on the Western Front, I found similar emotions. 'All his other feelings appeared shallow and meretricious in the shock of discovering how unquenchable, how real was his love of England'.

CHAPTER NINE

Aspects of student life in London

One of the first things I did was to explore fully the Siegfried Sassoon country, for I had been much impressed by his writings not least, probably, because I had been distanced for some time from England and I wanted now to see the places of his youth in the Weald of Kent which he had so intriguingly described. As my parents loved driving in their car through Kent and Sussex, they willingly co-operated in this. I spent a few days staying at the local pub in Hever and did a lot of walking, sixteen miles in one day.

In July I bought my first limited and signed edition, Geraint Goodwin's *Conversations with George Moore*, this from Martin Secker's long since demolished little shop in Charles II Street off St James' Square. I found him not all that communicative which was a pity, because although I was somewhat reticent, I longed to ask him about the literary giants he had known, such as D. H. Lawrence, Norman Douglas and James Joyce. By then I was also in frequent contact with Gilbert Fabes, whose renowned bookshop I had visited in Rye. Fired in York by Philip Turner, I was now avidly collecting Henry Williamson in first editions, and in the course of time Fabes provided a lot of material for me.

My reading then, as now, was inclined to be haphazard and often revolved around current interests and discoveries which I would then explore to the full. I was constantly finding new outlets to pursue and, as with music, there was always something new on the stocks.

Despite an enjoyable holiday exploring Scotland with Pat Knox, an ATS sergeant I had known in York, I was still inclined to be unsettled and impatient for London, my studies, and then hopefully in the fullness of time my own cathedral organ loft. Then, as since, I tended to always believe that the grass must inevitably be greener on the other side. When I eventually got to the other side it was reassuring to find that this was true. I was also far from happy at the prospect of going back to live with my parents at Uplands. As with many of my contemporaries, army life had removed me far from my parents sedentary mode of existence. My own growing up process had been greatly accelerated by the broadening experience of life in the Forces, and living overseas. In the event, though I am not sure I realised it at the time, there was the business of having to adjust to life on one's own after the servitude of over four years in the Army.

I also now found the Medway Towns so run down, not only through the visible scars they bore from the wartime bombing, but equally, conditioned by the national malaise which had come over much of the nation as a reaction to so much put in to the war effort and its resultant tensions. The Medway Towns were fast becoming something of a depressed area, with the people I knew seeming so inhibited and parochial that I felt I was now no longer a part of that scene, even to the extent of being an intruder, and that I must at all costs break away from it. This was probably also due to my own state of mind, for I was going through a reaction though, more importantly as I rather naively commented in my diary, 'Anything ugly makes me unhappy'. This, nevertheless, is something which has always nagged at me, and especially then, for I was becoming engulfed in and much possessed with the lure of the pursuit of beauty, whether in music or in the revelation of just how beautiful so much of nature is, be it the Weald of Kent, those Mediterranean sunsets, or the beauty and allure of Egypt which, now that I was far removed from it, I realised, and not without a pang of nostalgia, to be something as beautiful and unique as it is historic. Consequently I recoiled from anything that savoured of being tawdry or lacking in beauty, which the Medway Towns then were.

In the autumn of 1947 I commenced my studies at the Royal Academy of Music, having found myself a bedsitter in Inverness Gardens, just off Kensington Church Street. Here I experienced that freedom from home I so wanted, and probably needed, a home from which in the course of time I was to become more and more estranged and even uncomfortable in, as my way of life and that of my parents diverged, they understanding me no more than I understood them.

Even some of the long anticipated expectation and high hopes of what life at the Academy would yield were not fully realised, mainly because I found Sir William McKie, the organist of Westminster Abbey, so disappointing a teacher compared with Bairstow. McKie's approach, that of technique primarily, and with little mention of interpretation or artistry, utterly failed to connect with me in any way, and was in such sharp contrast to ECB who, although a teacher of relatively few words, led one to a realisation of the inner meaning of music. He was no less an encourager than he was an inspirational force, and with him my technique somehow seemed with only a little guidance to more or less look after itself, provided I practised enough.

In the event, much of my first year at the Academy proved in many respects to be a disastrous anti-climax. Perhaps I had dreamed too many dreams while waiting in the Army and had expected too much, for the reality was by no means the fulfilling experience I had anticipated. My new tutors emphasised not what to do so much as what not to do. What a contrast. As a result, I was confused, even feeling uncertain of myself, and consequently I was fundamentally insecure. With it I became moody and often depressed for days on end, a state of mind which persisted over many years. In the long-term future, and whatever the situation, I was seldom to be fully content with my lot for long; I was frequently restless, dissatisfied with what I was doing and, despite my wife's entreaties to me to see sense and count my blessings, I was ready on the slightest provocation to want to throw in the sponge and seek new pastures. When I eventually came to my senses I realised how unrealistic I had been, especially when my own parental responsibility increased. It was not until after I became Director of the Royal School of Church Music in 1973 that I felt really fulfilled and contented. Maybe it was that by then I felt more confident, had more faith in myself, even proved myself, was more secure and was able to react more rationally and logically. This was especially so when a situation presented problems and challenges which I could not shed or sweep under the carpet for, at the RSCM, I had responsibility for a large organisation, something entirely different from what would have been demanded of me as a cathedral organist.

I now realise that my restlessness was in part the birth pangs of the impatience which has repeatedly dogged me and which, if anything, has got worse over the years. I cannot abide being late for anything; unpunctual trains and even more so aircraft, or being imprisoned in a traffic jam, get me worked up as much as those who do not promptly reply to letters or, even more so, the late arrival of the morning's mail. All these, and more, I acknowledge to be deficiencies in my make-up which are perhaps linked with a recurring nightmare dream of frustration at never getting to a station on time for a train, the anxiety of which is so real that I regularly wake up puffing and panting. No doubt a psychiatrist would have a ready explanation for this.

But, to revert to the Academy; I did so miss cathedrals. Although I would frequently be at St Paul's for Evensong, I longed for my own church and choir, a situation soon to be remedied. More immediately, there were concerts to enjoy at the Royal Albert Hall where I was often in Francis Stonor's box, while Edward Dent took me to Covent Garden and Sadler's Wells. The Academy years did at least give me the chance to hear many of the post-war procession of visiting conductors such as Furtwängler, Bruno Walter, de Sabata and Beecham, while Boult gave revealing readings of some of the then more out of the way works of Elgar and Vaughan Williams. And then there was all the excitement surrounding Richard Strauss conducting his own works at Drury Lane Theatre and treating us to some of his less familiar works such as the Alpine and Domestic symphonies. I particularly remember an unusual concert at Chelsea Town Hall with Norman del Mar conducting the freelance Chelsea Symphony Orchestra with the Australian pianist Noel Mewton Wood playing Busoni's Piano Concerto. I have never heard the work again although I see it has now been recorded. It is certainly an unorthodox piece with, as I recall it, an offstage male voice chorus incanting in German to Buddha in the last movement.

On my first day at the Academy I met John Sanderson, also a new student. He had served in Royal Navy submarines during the war and, as I was later to learn, had a bad time. Having found we had both been pupils of ECB created a bond between us which was to grow into a continuing friendship, especially in our shared love of books and book collecting. When I introduced him to Norman Douglas' *South Wind* I had no inkling of what I had set in motion, for when John died in Canada in the 1980s he had amassed one of the largest and most comprehensive collections of Douglas in private hands, while I was later to concentrate in a similar way on T. E. Lawrence. John and I also shared other interests which ranged from films, food, and exploring English cathedrals and their music, to what would grow into an obsessive love of France.

Early in 1948, Sir Stanley Marchant, the Principal of RAM, suggested me as organist of the parish church in the North London suburb of Finchley, and I was duly despatched to the Athenaeum to meet the Rector, Michael Ridley, who was a member of the Club. Entering its impressive portals for the first time it never even remotely occurred to me that thirty years later I would myself be a member and would come to regard the Club as something of a second home. Nor did I then foresee how well I would get to know his wife Betty in the years ahead.

St Mary-at-Finchley was a fine old church set in a surprisingly rural churchyard. I inherited a large and loyal choir of men and boys, though I found discipline something I had yet to master when dealing with the boys. Apart from Cairo, my experience of actually training a choir was limited, and where boys were concerned it was practically nil. I therefore had to learn the hard way through the experience of the inevitable mistakes I made, which in those early days were many, and considerable.

Even when I became a cathedral organist and constantly worked with boys I always felt I perhaps related better to adult sopranos and would often get better results from them. Virtually every Sunday I would be invited to lunch, usually with choir members and I regularly visited George and Polly Johnson to whose home in Whetstone I would travel by trolleybus. George was a chartered accountant in the City and also choir secretary. He possessed a remarkably good alto voice for someone in his sixties. Over the years the links with the Johnsons and their family would grow into a deep and lasting friendship which I greatly valued.

At Christmas, the men of the choir would give me what in those days was a handsome cheque—usually around £30—which was gratefully received by a fairly penurious student, although John Sanderson and I embarked far too extravagantly on books and good food. Pleas for help to my father fell on mainly deaf ears. I, having embarked on my chosen career against his wishes, must lie on the bed I had made, and fend for myself, sentiments he had frequently uttered before. He would constantly remind me that his father had not helped him, so he saw no reason to help me, and anyhow had not the Ministry of Education given me, as an ex-serviceman, a student grant? I well remember that on one occasion John and I were literally starving, so we quite unabashedly borrowed money from a young lady student who we knew was fairly well heeled. From time to time my father relented and would send me a cheque to keep me going, though I suspect this was at the behest of my mother, who tended to be more understanding and who viewed my financial state more benevolently.

I directed the 16th Century Singers, a study group I formed to give recitals at Finchley and elsewhere, while at the Academy I attended conducting and choir training classes, especially enjoying the latter where I worked with Douglas Hopkins. He taught me the psychological approach to the subject, such as how to relate to one's forces so that they respond positively, and how, when directing a choir, to look relaxed and confident, even to smile at your singers when they come to a passage which has always caused problems at rehearsal and of which they were nervous. How I wish I always heeded his words of wisdom, especially at Exeter when I was frequently bad tempered and impatient, and knew I was not getting the best out of my choir by cursing, and probably frightening, them.

At the Academy I was fortunate in winning prizes for my organ playing and even for composition, though I have never considered myself to be an instinctive, or even remotely inspired, composer, so I have always fought shy of putting pen to paper. I also played the organ for student performances conducted by Ernest Read of the Bach *B minor Mass* and the Fauré *Requiem*.

Paul Steinitz, whom I had got to know in York, was now teaching at the Academy and I was sent to him to study for the remaining part of the Durham Bachelor of Music degree. About that time he founded the South London Bach Society with which he achieved considerable fame, as he did for his Bach scholarship. He sometimes asked me to play the organ for concerts with his infant choir, and I particularly recall doing so in Chichester Cathedral for a performance of Britten's *Rejoice in the Lamb*.

There always seemed to be extra-musical pursuits claiming much of my spare time, with the theatre, ballet, and two particularly interesting exhibitions of Chagall and Paul Nash during my first year as a student. The London cinema in those days was particularly prolific in showing French films, some of which, like Cocteau's *La Belle et la Bête* and *Les enfants du Paradis*, John and I saw again and again. There was also a particularly attractive French actress called Anouk whom we both fell for. We sampled many restaurants but generally settled for the Petit Savoyard, Kettner's and the Café Royal. When funds were low, as they often were, we frequented Rupert's in Rupert Street where we were initiated into Greek wine, then virtually unknown in England.

Despite all this, I somehow never seemed to fully settle down. I was a restless creature and, not least, even though York had inevitably changed since Bairstow's death in 1945, I pined for it, seeing it in retrospect as having satisfied so many needs to the full as compared with my current musical studies. 'Perhaps I am passing through a phase of shedding the old life and finding a new one' was my diary assessment of the then current situation.

The love of France, its art, architecture and not least its food and wine spurred John and me to visit Paris for the first time in the spring of 1949, an invitation to give a recital at the British Embassy Church being the convenient excuse. This was the first time either of us had flown. Our insatiable appetite encouraged us in those few days to take in Chartres and Versailles, while in Paris we explored endless nooks and crannies on the Left Bank, saw Lalo's *Le Roi d'Ys* at the Opéra, visited the Louvre *in extenso*, the Folies Bergères and Oscar Wilde's grave in Père Lachaise. Through this somewhat indigestible though exciting introduction we came back to England as ardent Francophiles, determined to return at the earliest opportunity.

It was at this time that I met Roger Quilter, who befriended me at his elegant Acacia Road house in St John's Wood; he would often take me to the opera and ballet or to dine in choice Soho restaurants. He was most kind and encouraging to me, a young student, for he was then all of eighty years old. From him I heard first-hand accounts of his contemporaries in that rather special enclave of song writers, such as Frank Bridge, Peter Warlock and George Butterworth, who intrigued and fascinated me as much then as they had done when I first came into contact with their work through Bill Gibson in the York days. This was music towards which I felt an especial affinity.

I also regularly acted as page turner and general helper to those sitting the practical examinations for the diplomas of the Royal College of Organists. But pride of place in these London years went again and again to France, not only Paris but eventually to the South West in particular, with visits to Montauban, Carcassonne and Arles, and areas of France now very different from when I first passed through them on my way to Egypt only weeks after the war had ended. My delight in first experiencing Champignons à la Provençal was but one of the many revelations of France, as were visits to Marseilles and to Bandol with its D. H. Lawrence connections.

Perhaps this full and often exciting period, for on balance this is what it was, is best summed up by the diary entry 'I've come to the conclusion that if one wants to live, and not just exist, then the process is highly complex and difficult'. It was a mixture of this and the sheer revelation of so much which was now unfolding and the opportunities in so many fields which were becoming mine for the asking.

71

CHAPTER TEN

Windsor and Eton –
Castle and College

Life in a Royal Peculiar

In January 1950 I became assistant organist of St George's Chapel, Windsor Castle. When I went for my interview I was immediately and deeply affected by the sheer beauty of the chapel, its fan vaulted ceiling and the vivid blaze of colour in the Garter banners ranged high above the choir stalls. Nor was its history lost on me. For centuries it has been the Chapel of Knights of the Garter, the oldest and most illustrious order of chivalry in the world. I swiftly responded to such beauty and its setting within a castle, or more correctly a royal fortress, equally soaked in history, the skyline of which, whether seen from the Long Walk, or from the M4 motorway, never fails to thrill me as much now as when I saw it for the first time from the train. I could hardly believe my good fortune when I was appointed.

But it was the long and uniquely distinguished line of organists from Merbecke onward, with the equally unique tradition this succession of musicians had forged, which would both motivate and inspire me during my four years there. Sir William Harris had been organist since 1933, having previously been at Oxford as organist of New College and then at Christ Church. As a friend and contemporary of Stanford, Parry and Vaughan Williams, he would sometimes reminisce to me about them, what he had to say being enthusiastically noted by young ears only too eager to be impressed. Harris himself was a not inconsiderable composer of distinction who contributed significantly in his generation to the church and organ music repertoire.

Billy, as he was affectionately called by his friends, and referred to behind his back by the likes of such as me, was in some respects a person of marked contrasts. He was as original and at times venturesome in much of his composition as he was instinctively traditional in his organ playing. To him the then fashionable and relatively new pursuit of Baroque interpretation was anathema and was facetitiously summed up by him and others as 'tinkle, tinkle' or 'bubble and squeak' sounds. He was an avid performer of the organ music of Bach, invariably commencing a fugue using the diapasons. Feeling skittish one day he suddenly pulled out the 4ft Principal as well and chucklingly proclaimed 'Aha—Baroque!' as he set off.

He was inspired in his accompanying of the psalms and was almost on a par with Bairstow in this respect. He also kept a miniature score of Haydn's *Seven Last Words* string quartets on the organ console and would delight in playing one of the movements for the voluntary after Evensong. Here, as in Brahms' *Requiem*, he would 'orchestrate' in a colourful way, even to the extent of including soft sustained chords for the horn parts, so well did he know the full score. It was in matters such as these that I learned so much from him. After I had spent much effort learning the organ accompaniment to music like this, he would invariably disarm me by saying 'Too many notes. It's not what you play but what you leave out that really matters.'

In those days assistants did a lot of page-turning for the organist, running errands and being a general factotum. As we did only a fraction of the playing demanded of assistants today, it became something of an event when WHH conducted an accompanied anthem which I would play for. This was made the more difficult for me as I could not see him in those pre-closed circuit camera days. If the anthem was a loud one you heard a lot of yourself and little, if anything, of the choir. Add to that your having to play well ahead of the choir sound to counteract the time lag and you had all the ingredients of what initially was daunting. At the end of my time at Windsor I felt, and was, much more confident, and for ever after at Ripon and Exeter automatically played ahead of the beat and the sound, although at Windsor WHH frequently called up to me at rehearsals 'You're behind the beat'.

Mondays were my red letter days for he then taught at the Royal College of Music and I was left to play for both Mattins and Evensong, although he tended to put down on the music list non-demanding and somewhat unadventurous 18th and 19th century settings such as Kempton in B flat, Nares in F or Elvey in A. He expected me as part of my musicianship to play from the old open score books, which included the C clefs for the alto and tenor lines, and without a short score accompaniment. I also had to acquire the invaluable asset of being able to play from a figured bass, all of which was very good training.

Every term WHH would be away for a week examining for the Associated Board of the Royal Schools of Music. I was then left fully in charge and rejoiced at the prospect, for this meant my taking the morning and afternoon rehearsals of the choristers which would include my preparing the following Sunday's music, when WHH would be back to take over again. There were also two rehearsals each week of the full choir, which I initially found somewhat intimidating, for the lay clerks were fairly elderly, set in their ways, very much 'the old school' and notoriously cantankerous. If I suggested they might sing a certain passage a different way, the invariable retort would be 'Why, young man? What's wrong with the way we've always sung it?' For those weeks WHH put down a more representative and interesting choice of music than for solitary Mondays, and latterly would even ask me what I would like to have, though if I had the temerity to suggest something too ambitious I noticed it was invariably, and rightly, omitted from the music list.

In my earlier days Doc H, as generations of choristers called him, was not averse to testing me out. Having said he would not be at Evensong, there were occasions when, if I looked down the Nave from the organ loft, I would catch sight of him in the distance listening to my efforts, the sort of thing I would later do when I myself had an assistant. It was, I suppose, good training, with the subsequent observations he would make being useful criticism. Of such was my apprenticeship.

Soon after my arrival in Windsor the choir was invited by Columbia Records, who were working with the British Council, to take part in a recorded anthology of English church music for which E. H. Fellowes was the artistic director. Fellowes had been a minor canon at Windsor for many years and lived in what had in the 16th century been Merbecke's house. It was there that much of his monumental editing of Tudor Church Music was done for Oxford University Press. He also had the rare distinction of being present when the tomb of King Charles I was opened and he saw the beard crudely stitched on to what had been his skull.

Fellowes intoned the services in a quiet and dignified way, with every word, including his beloved '*know*-ledge' (a logical enough pronunciation) crystal clear. I had to play the organ for these recordings and among the anthems was Harwood's *O how glorious is the Kingdom*, something of a marathon for any organist to have to cope with. Night after night I would lock myself into the deserted chapel and as a result became so fluent that years later in Exeter I could still play this difficult assignment with relatively little rehearsal. I was soon to be put to the test again when the first ever choral evensong broadcast I had to play for included Stanford's *For lo! I raise up*. This was for me even more demanding as, being a live broadcast, there was no question, as with a recording, of doing it again if anything went wrong. I am sure WHH knew how invaluable an experience this would be for me, and seemingly he had faith in my ability to produce what was needed, though on some occasions I felt disappointed when, having asked me to prepare something fairly demanding, he would suddenly elect at the last moment to play it himself.

When WHH went to the West Indies for three months to examine for the Associated Board of the Royal Schools of Music, Henry Ley came up from Devon, where he had retired, to be responsible for the chapel music. He was something of a legendary figure, and had been ever since he was appointed organist of Christ Church, Oxford, by Bishop Strong while still an undergraduate. The stories about him during his years as Precentor, or Director of Music, at Eton are legion and endeared him to boys and staff alike, despite the eccentricities of this lovable person which at times exasperated his colleagues. It was said that boys flocked to his congregational choir practices in College Chapel because they were such fun, even if for the wrong reasons such as the chaos caused by his habit of invariably blowing his noise as he was announcing the number of the next hymn to be rehearsed. On another occasion, this time in Lower College Chapel, the singing got worse and worse: this prompted him to repeatedly call up to the organist, 'More organ, Beswick', a command which was duly obeyed. After four or five such entreaties, with the organ playing getting louder and louder, and the singing worse and worse, Beswick's bald head appeared through one of the porthole openings in the organ loft, and his plaintive voice was heard to say 'Please, Doctor, there isn't any more organ'.

Henry was a delightful character with one leg shorter than the other and a generously corpulent stomach. He rejoiced in taking friends to explore the countryside in an ancient Austin 7, its gearbox making ominous noises and smoke invariably coming up through the floorboards. At Windsor he particularly loved bicycling and I recall excursions with him and Sydney Watson, his successor at Eton, to country churches in the Thames Valley. On one occasion these two, wearing dirty old raincoats, were found by the lady caretaker on their hands and knees inspecting brasses. She was convinced they were carpet thieves!

At his advanced age his organ playing at St George's tended to be unpredictable, but he still accompanied the psalms in a memorably colourful way. One day at Evensong he excelled himself in Psalm 136 until he came to the verse about 'Og, the King of Basan' which he left unaccompanied, telling us 'I don't have a stop for Og'. On another occasion he suddenly opted at the end of Evensong for a piece by Basil Harwood which he admitted he had not played for about forty years. Although his performance was embarrassingly full of wrong notes, he was not in the least disconcerted. When it was over he turned to those of us in the organ loft, scratched his arms, as was his wont when telling a story, and said 'They gathered up the wrong notes—five basketfuls of them'.

Apart from golf—and he was a most erratic player with a self-confessed handicap of well over fifty—his abiding passion was trains. He personally knew many of the drivers of the splendid steam locomotives then in use and he would sometimes be allowed to travel on the footplate, the then General Manager of the Great Western Railway having been one of his pupils at

Eton. He would drive miles to a bridge or a level crossing to see a certain train pass. As he knew most of the timetable from memory he would invariably wave to the driver and tell him if he was on time or not. Henry even died in a train, on the long since defunct Sidmouth Junction branch line and quite near Ottery St Mary where he lived with his wife Mary and his many cats in an idyllic old thatched cottage with a stream running through the garden.

I felt that too much of my time at Windsor was spent in St George's School teaching choristers the piano. At one time I was giving as many as 53 lessons each week, this including non-choristers who were known as 'supers'. This would sometimes have its lighter moments when the inevitable tedium would be relieved by some of their delightful comments, such as the chorister who when asked to quote the seventh commandment said 'Thou shalt not *omit* adultery'. I also taught at Scaitcliffe, the prep school at Englefield Green, though this was a mixed blessing as the work was far from rewarding. The class singing I was responsible for imprisoned my victims immediately after lunch when the rest of the school were at games; the resulting discipline left much to be desired, but it did help to implement my meagre chapel salary of £100 a year.

I initially lived in sombre rooms in a house in Alma Road which had on the wall of the dining room one of those dreadful sepia prints of a shaggy-haired cow standing in a fog-shrouded Scottish Loch. Before long one of the minor canons rented me an attractive garret in his house in The Cloisters, with views across Windsor and Eton with the Thames Valley in the distance.

Before long I was befriended by May Ford who lived in a grace and favour house in the Castle. Her husband, Lionel Ford, had been Headmaster of Harrow and then Dean of York. Because of my York connection this delightfully eccentric character immediately befriended me. One evening she invited me to dinner, adding 'I want you to meet the Rector of Slough's daughter; she's very musical'. The girl we dined with seemed distinctly unmusical and, as we concluded the meal, May suddenly said 'Oh dear, I've just realised—I've invited the wrong girl. Come next week and I'll get the right one', and that was how, next week, I met my future wife Elisabeth.

Over the years I had a succession of girl friends and generally flirted with the opposite sex in a fairly sensuous way, but with Elisabeth I quickly knew this to be the real thing. Her unspoilt simplicity, her enormous strength of character and her resilience, which would reveal itself in the years ahead and would repeatedly put me to shame. I have never ceased to marvel at her instinctive feminine intuition in assessing as dubious characters those who seemed to me to be *bona fide*, so much so that one of her self-styled 'hunches' would immediately alert me in this respect. I have continually envied her discipline and willpower, and her thrift, which has caused much amusement in the family, though our fairly scant income in the early years justified this. And then there was of course our love of music and of the Church which were later to develop and flower so much.

For the immediate, life was so blissful. We foresaw no problems that were not surmountable and all was full of the excitement and hope of what was novel for both of us. We were obviously on our best behaviour for after all we were in love. Our relationship matured as the family increased, and what a remarkable example of motherhood she has been, though I took little part in the responsibilities of the children's growing-up process. In those days most fathers were far less involved than now in the day to day family chores. Elisabeth did not go out to work and was relieved of some responsibility by our having a succession of *au pair* girls from the continent who lived with us and helped with the children.

As the years passed by, we realised that even the happiest of marriages cannot escape some friction at times. Both of us have forceful personalities and consequently some clashes were—and still are—inevitable, but I believe these to be a valid part of a growing together process. My parents claimed that they never had a 'cross word', as my mother called it, in all their many years of married life. Although I do not recall ever seeing evidence of their falling out with each other, I am sure they must have had inevitable differences of opinion.

Elisabeth encouraged me to think more deeply about my religion, and do something about my prayer life. Previously, this had to an extent been somewhat lukewarm and without all that much commitment.

What I do know is that we have had to work at our marriage, and just as much now in retirement which creates an entirely new situation and with it, although relatively late in life, a new *modus vivendi*. But, we persevered and did not cave in and give up as so many couples do today. The moods and depressions which beset me in our early years of marriage tried Elisabeth's patience for, in a nutshell, I could be a difficult person to cope with, and I knew it, but I was not allowed to get away with it on the pretext of being a temperamental musician.

But for the moment to revert to May Ford about whom, as with Henry Ley, many stories were related. She was one of a large and distinguished family clan of Fords, Lyttletons and Alingtons who, when they periodically met for a celebration, were reputed to number in excess of eighty. According to one story the Dean and Mrs Ford giving a dinner party at the York Deanery, excused themselves over coffee to say goodnight to the children. When they had been absent for over an hour, the guests made discreet enquiries which revealed that the Fords had forgotten all about them and had themselves retired to bed. On another occasion a sherry party, soon after one of her many children had been born, coincided with the publishing of a book she had written about the Church of England. When someone congratulated her on the birth of the child she, in her vague way, thought she was being congratulated on the book. In the deep voice for which she was famous, she loudly retorted to the assembled guests 'Oh yes, my dear, and I did it all by myself, except for a little help from the Bishop of London'.

Although Elisabeth was during our courtship on the music staff of West Heath School in Sevenoaks, having previously studied at the Royal College of Music, or 'the other place' as we termed it, we frequently contrived to meet, often at the top of the escalators at Piccadilly Circus Underground, a most unromantic, if convenient, rendezvous. At Slough Rectory we often played music for two pianos, sometimes with Elisabeth's father who was himself no mean musician. Claude Williams was a somewhat formidable Anglo-Catholic priest of the old school with whom

I initially never felt entirely at ease, though I think he liked the idea of having a church musician son-in-law. He had been a chorister, undergraduate, and then Precentor of Christ Church, Oxford, and a member of Vincent's, the prestigious varsity club. Later he became a Minor Canon of Westminster Abbey where Elisabeth was born, then Vicar of St Saviour's, Eastbourne, before coming to Slough. This was a great change in every way after being in charge of a well-heeled parish on the Sussex coast. John Betjeman was scathing about Slough in one of his wartime poems, while some would deliberately misquote 'Can any good thing come out of Nazareth?' by substituting Slough. The answer is 'Yes, yes—my Elisabeth'!

In August of 1950, Elisabeth and I were given parental permission to go on holiday together, something almost unheard of in those days, first to Oberammergau to see the Passion Play, then on to Mayrhofen in the Austrian Zillertal where Elisabeth's parents joined us and where, having said Evensong together one evening in the little village church, I asked Elisabeth's father if I could marry her. That was on 20th August, so Psalm 104, the psalm set for the 20th evening, has always had a special connection. Next month, back in England, I passed the second part of my Bachelor of Music degree, so we had cause for a double celebration party.

In those days the Dean and Chapter of Windsor had never remotely contemplated the prospect of a married assistant organist and were in no way prepared to deviate in helping us either financially or in providing any accommodation. They even hinted, and almost suggested, that I look elsewhere for a job, such was the long-standing policy of having a bachelor assistant. Eventually, we were allowed by the Governor of the Castle to rent temporarily 18 Lower Ward. General Norton, the Military Knight whose house it was, had, because of his health, been given special dispensation by the King to live with his daughter at Binfield. Internally, the house was in bad shape and we spent much spare time getting it into habitable order and, because our finances were so slender, we did all the redecorating ourselves.

On 21st April, 1951, we were married in St Mary's, Slough by Elisabeth's father, with the Dean of Windsor giving the address. The Dean and Chapter marked the occasion by increasing my salary by 50%, making it now all of £150 a year. John Sanderson was my best man, with William Harris and Henry Ley playing before and after the service. We spent the first two nights of our honeymoon at Shelley's Hotel in Lewes, travelling 1st class on the train for the first time ever. During the weekend we explored the Sussex Downs before spending ten days in Paris and Fontainebleau.

Back in Windsor life went on in much the same way, including fairly frequent afternoon walks with Doc H in the Home Park. That summer I played the organ for the first of a number of Sunday afternoon performances of oratorios in the chapel at Royal Lodge. These were arranged and conducted by Lawrence West, the organist of the chapel, for the entertainment of the Queen, Princess Elizabeth and Princess Margaret, and not surprisingly he had little difficulty in persuading soloists such as Isobel Baillie and Kathleen Ferrier to take part. That summer included my first experience of a Garter Service with its colourful ceremonial and ritual which I revelled in to the full, also my first annual summer festival of church music which involved the chapel choirs of St George's and Eton.

Sydney Watson, the Precentor of Eton, asked me to become a part-time member of his staff, teaching piano and organ at the College. This was a task I thoroughly enjoyed and where I was to meet so many interesting people, and where the average age was distinctly lower than in the Castle community. The traditions of Eton, the dress of the staff and the boys, calling a term a Half, a chaplain a Conduct, and examinations Trials, all combined to appeal to me, unashamed romantic that I realised I was fast developing into. I felt proud, and privileged, to be associated in this way with so historic and unique a school.

As the work at Scaitcliffe became less and less enjoyable, with Eton more and more fulfilling, Elisabeth valiantly took on Scaitcliffe, for we needed the money. She dealt in no uncertain way with any miscreants, of whom there were many, and which prompted Doc H to hold Elisabeth's hands and remark 'To think these are the hands which spanked the Scaitcliffe boys'.

During the next year Sydney Watson invited me to become his assistant, Anthony Caesar having been appointed Precentor of Radley. I was in many ways tempted, not least by what would have been a vastly improved salary, although there was no house with the job. Another factor was that I found WHH could, as I saw it, be somewhat difficult and unpredictable on occasion, though I was sensitive to his criticisms, valid and just as I knew them to be. I also felt I was not being stretched to the full and was spending too much time observing him at rehearsals and in services, though I learned so much from this as I later realised when I became a cathedral organist and was able to put so much of what he taught me into practice. Add to this the sheer volume of routine day by day piano teaching at the choir school, gifted though many of the boys were, especially when they could be persuaded to practise regularly, and I saw the Eton prospect as a port of convenience, if nothing else.

More importantly, it would have taken me away from the cathedral circuit, and once outside it I realised it would be difficult to switch back again. Over the years I have seen too many people frustrated, and consequently imprisoned, because they did this very thing.

Although in the end I declined, as I did when he later wanted to put my name forward for the Directorship of Music at Ardingly, Sydney was generous in asking me to do things at Eton, such as playing the organ for the school concerts at the end of each Half, and which included the school song and the Eton Boating Song. To accompany all of a thousand young voices singing 'Lovely boating weather' was always for me a moving experience. I also became organist for the Windsor and Eton Choral Society which Sydney conducted with such enthusiasm and not a little humour, no doubt coined from his Oxford days with Sir Hugh Allen. It was certainly a great thrill to sing in the chorus for the rehearsals and then to be part of the orchestra as organist in works such as Elgar's *Dream of Gerontius*, Vaughan Williams' *A Sea Symphony* and Bach's *Christmas Oratorio*, all of which, and more, were an invaluable introduction and experience for what would lie ahead of me at Exeter.

Sydney, six feet tall, and thin, was as much a character as was Henry Ley who was short and rotund. Sydney's stutter was proverbial though it never seemed to worry or deter him. If in conversation you provided the word which was proving difficult for him, he would nevertheless persist until he was able to come out with it. Many are the stories told of his stutter, apocryphal or otherwise. One of the best was when he was at Oxford, where after Eton he became organist of Christ Church, and where he met one of his pupils in The High who was understandably anxious to know the result of his Finals. He related his concern to Sydney who said in a fairly prolonged way 'I've just seen the results, and you fe-fe-fe-fe- PASSED'.

It was while I was having my hair cut one morning at Thomas's, the delightfully Dickensian barber shop in Eton High Street, that the news came through of the sudden death of King George VI. The Castle immediately went into Court mourning so Elisabeth, who by that time was noticeably pregnant, had quickly to find suitable clothing. For the first and probably only time we heard the Sebastopol Bell in the Round Tower which is tolled only on the death of the Sovereign. St George's Chapel was immediately closed to the public and feverish work commenced on completely transforming it by building tiered seating to accommodate the many who would attend the funeral in a few days' time. Those of us living in the Castle were issued with passes without which we could not get out or back in again, and I well remember being impressed by the fact that even the London theatres closed until after the funeral.

The night before the funeral the BBC put out a radio programme with different parts of the Commonwealth paying their tribute. It ended with Wynford Vaughan Thomas setting the scene in St George's Chapel as a quiet prelude to the events of the morrow. The choir then sang Byrd's *Justorum animae*. This is an unaccompanied anthem for which I gave the choir their chord on the organ. This was not broadcast but it earned me a handsome fee because the programme was repeated on a number of subsequent occasions.

Next day I well recall WHH playing the hauntingly beautiful Prelude to Stanford's opera *The Travelling Companion* before the service, after which there was silence until we heard through the open West Door of the Chapel the distant sound of bagpipes playing the Lament *The Flowers of the Forest* as the cortège was slowly escorted into the castle. From the organ loft we saw the head of the procession arrive at the foot of the steps leading up to the Chapel and then the gun carriage bearing the coffin. There were a few words of restrained command as the coffin was lifted from the carriage and then the uncanny sound of the bosuns' pipes as the procession moved up the steps piping the dead King on board and into the Chapel. The choir then sang Croft's Burial Sentences.

Later that afternoon, well after the service was over and as dusk was beginning to fall, we went back into the Chapel and joined a small group of residents slowly filing past the open vault to pay their last respects. After all that had happened, the ceremony, the crowds and the like, it was an unforgettable privilege to do this in the now quiet and otherwise empty building.

1952 brought a number of significant events for Elisabeth and me. I was by this time becoming more restless and frustrated than ever before and, rightly or wrongly, felt I was marking time. As Sir William became older he seemed to rely more and more on me for all sorts of things, musical and otherwise, which more than ever reinforced my sense of duty towards him. I sensed, and I think with some justification, that I had now served my apprenticeship in various ways and so was excited when I learned early in May that Alfred Wilcock, the organist of Exeter Cathedral, was about to retire and, moreover, that the Dean and Chapter of Exeter had asked Doc H if he could recommend someone as a possible successor. It was to be months before Exeter finally made any further move, and I had begun to despair of ever hearing anything more. This was not helped by Henry Ley who was against my going there because as he, a Devonian, so strangely argued, 'Exeter is so remote'. It was not until September that Exeter called me for interview together with four others. I was subsequently told that I was placed second and not appointed because 'you are rather young and inexperienced'.

Not long after, Ely Cathedral became vacant, but although I applied and was backed by Sir William and others, there was no shortlist or interviews. In hindsight I did not regret this as much as I did Exeter which seemed to offer so much. Ely was by no means my favourite cathedral and, because I have always felt the cold, Cambridgeshire did not appeal to me. Being in the musical shadow of Cambridge, the small city of Ely really did seem remote.

Previously, on 30th May I duly noted in my diary 'Elisabeth bore me a daughter'. Rachel, the first of our four daughters, was born at 18 Lower Ward. As the family grew, my father despaired of us ever producing a son who would at least carry on the family name, even if not the family business. Years later at Exeter when Elisabeth produced our fourth daughter, Michael Dykes Bower, as inveterate a bachelor as were his three similarly distinguished brothers, was heard to remark 'The Dakers—ah, yes—they will go on having daughters', which prompted Elisabeth to wonder what possible evidence or inside information this convinced bachelor could have for thinking this.

That summer Doc H gave me a whole month's leave from duties, so we shared with Elisabeth's parents a bungalow at Swanage from which we explored so much of Dorset, a glorious and to this day largely unspoilt county with its superb landscape and coastline, Swanage itself excepted. My interest in T. E. Lawrence had grown apace since the Cairo days, so this was an opportune moment to visit his home at Cloud's Hill and see his grave in Moreton churchyard, even though a coachload of American visitors were swarming all over the place and being subjected to a loud running commentary. I also wandered over the Egdon Heath of Thomas Hardy, visited Dorchester and walked to Stinsford to see the church which featured in *Under the Greenwood Tree* and where Hardy's heart is buried in the churchyard.

During August my father took me to Holland for a few days, my having been there the previous year at the invitation of the British Council to take part in one of the first of the international organ improvising contests at St Bavo's Church in Haarlem, a frightening experience in which I was rightly placed last of the five contestants. Although I was flattered to be asked to represent Britain, only in hindsight did I realise the extent of what was expected of me in competition with far more experienced European organists trained so thoroughly in an art which in those days was something of a hit and miss affair in England.

As the average age of the inhabitants in Windsor Castle was fairly high, we tended to team up with the family of Sir Owen Morshead, the Librarian of the Castle. Their children were contemporary with us, and especially Mary who later became godmother to our Mary. Her sister Phoebe was married while we were still at Windsor and it was at the reception in the Castle Library that an agitated flunky announced Canon and Mrs Venables as 'the Venerable and Mrs Cannibals'. This delightful faux-pas not surprisingly became something of a Windsor classic, the more so as the Venables were not renowned for having a sense of humour. Alec Vidler was also a Canon of St George's at that time, he and Venables being known as V1 and V2. He ran a small theological college in his house, mainly for retired men from the Colonial Service and Indian Army seeking late ordination. These men were known as The Doves, or privately as 'Vydler's Idlers'. Alec Vidler also had a dog who rejoiced in the Old Testament name of Zimrah, while in Lower Ward, Major Clough, one of the Military Knights, would loudly summon to heel his dog Blimey, much to the amusement of visitors.

The Dean, although he took part in our wedding and was an old friend of Elisabeth's father, was remote, even to the extent of being quite unconcerned over our housing problem, while on the occasions when he wrote to me, although by now I knew him quite well, would sign himself '+ Eric Hamilton, Bp'.

The kindest of the canons was Duncan Armytage who really tried to help us over housing but, I suspect, cut little ice with his colleagues. It was at this time that General Norton died and we were given two weeks notice to find alternative accommodation. It so happened that another Military Knight's house in Lower Ward (No 9) was vacant and we were allowed to move there, though under the same stringent conditions. Being only a few yards away we moved ourselves, baby Rachel and all, on trolleys and wheelbarrows borrowed from the Clerk of Works. We were far too impecunious to hire a removal firm and anyhow the distance did not merit it. We had been in this house only two or three months before its rightful occupant died and we found ourselves in the same dilemma all over again. It was only then that the Dean and Chapter took pity on us and allocated us No 25 The Cloisters which had recently been carved out of No 24 where May Ford lived, and which had been the home of Walford Davies during his time as organist of St George's. No 25 was by far the largest house we have ever lived in, with its spacious drawing room part of the Castle Wall high above the High Street below, with an unforgettable view to the Thames and Eton. There we stayed until we moved to Ripon in the autumn of 1954.

At this time I began book collecting in a fairly serious way, the main obstacle being lack of funds, though in hindsight I regret the many attractive opportunities I had to miss simply because they were beyond my pocket. I also now had not only a wife to support but a daughter as well. Even so, I did sometimes save up and launch out, paying all of £5 for the T. E. Lawrence Golden Cockerel Press *Secret Despatches from Arabia* which I found in Hatchards, who in those days had a very good rare book department on the top floor of their Piccadilly shop. I also picked up a first edition of the first Penguin, Andre Maurois' *Ariel,* a rarity I found in nearly mint condition for one shilling. Through my interest in Lawrence I was introduced to the legendary J. G. Wilson who ran Bumpus's bookshop in Oxford Street. He had been a friend of Lawrence and showed John Sanderson and me the book Lawrence carried with him through his desert campaigns in the 1914-18 war, and in which he had copied out his favourite poems. This was later published as *Minorities.* Wilson also possessed one of only fifty copies of *The Mint* printed in the United States to safeguard copyright. We also saw proof sheets of the original (1922) edition of *Seven Pillars.* Little did I think that one day I myself would own three such sheets. Wilson also had some of Lawrence's Clouds Hill Library for sale, though how these came onto the open market is a mystery. I bought three of these now considerable rarities for the handsome sum of £6.

Looking through my diaries I see I made a note of each book I read. I think I must then have read considerably faster than nowadays, for in the second half of 1953 alone are listed twenty-eight titles, of which only three were on music. My interests were widening all the time, sometimes spurred on by John Sanderson or simply because I happened to discover an author or new subject. At this time I was devouring a lot about travel in the Middle East, being fascinated in particular by Robert Byron and Gertrude Bell.

We would sometimes spend some days after Christmas at Eastbourne where friends of the Williams lived. We stayed in considerable comfort in Lushington Road, I exploring the interesting second-hand bookshops then to be found in Eastbourne, while in the evenings we would sometimes dine at Chez Maurice, a splendid French restaurant in the Seaside district of the town.

After the choristers had gone on holiday on Boxing Day, post-Christmas services in the Chapel were sung by the lay clerks. For these there were some strange, though intriguingly original, chants for the psalms, most of them specially written for men's voices by Walford Davies. Doc H invariably left me in charge to play for most of these services for, as he confided in me, he was not particularly attracted to the sound of men's voices. On one such day I noted in the diary 'The lay clerks, by and large, are a proud and irreligious bunch. They sang badly all day, with nearly everything unaccompanied dropping a semitone in pitch. They certainly are a queer and awkward bunch and quite unaccountable', the definition 'queer' then having a rather different connotation from nowadays.

One of my tasks before services was to deliver any messages the Doctor might have for the choir. He had a strange dislike of Christmas and would send me round to the choir vestry before Mattins on Christmas Day to give 'my love to the boys and my greetings to the men'. The lay clerks were not renowned for being particularly friendly among themselves, and the story was related of one of their number, suddenly imbued with goodwill and wishing a colleague a happy Christmas, ventured to enquire how his wife was, which prompted the tart reply 'If it comes to that, how's yours?'.

Queen Mary died in March 1953 and was buried beside King George V in the nave of St George's. Although the funeral service was as impressive as that of George VI, it was more low key by comparison and a generally much smaller occasion. Her death caused the temporary postponement of the 70th birthday dinner I had arranged for the Doctor who on occasion was not without a quick wit. Having duly drunk his health the distinguished gathering sang 'Happy birthday to you'. When he rose to reply his first comment was 'Thank you—but I think you could have made a bit more of the climax'. On another occasion when one of the Anglo-Catholic minor canons was making his preparation at the altar prior to celebrating the Sung Eucharist, Doc H, watching him from the organ loft, was somewhat bemused and intrigued by the accompanying antics this entailed. 'You know', he said, 'one of these days he's going to produce a rabbit out of his surplice'.

In June of that year Queen Elizabeth II was duly crowned in Westminster Abbey. St George's Chapel being a royal foundation, the complete choir took part as by ancient custom. As this also included me, much of the early part of the summer was taken up with preliminary rehearsals either in Windsor or latterly in St Margaret's, Westminster. We then transferred into the Abbey for the final full dress rehearsals which included the many processions and ceremonial. The choir, consisting of some 400 singers, was drawn from many different sources, including eminent solo singers. In order to ensure adequate rehearsal and efficiency, our proof of attendance was a stamp we collected after each practice and which we solemnly stuck on to something reminiscent of a Sunday school card. Without a full complement of stamps no one, however distinguished he might be, was allowed to sing on the great day.

On June 2nd we were up at 4 am in order to be at Westminster by 6.30 am. It was a memorable and historic occasion despite the length of the day, though there was much to see during the three hours before the service began. My seat was in the back row of the platform constructed for the choir on either side of the choir stalls, but high above in the triforium which gave one a magnificent panoramic view. During the longish wait before the service began, groups of people were allowed to stretch their legs at certain times, and it caused us amusement when on the loud-speaker system we heard 'All Bishops in Block B may now depart for ten minutes', followed by a mass exodus of scarlet robes waddling off to the toilets in the Cloisters. Back at Windsor in the evening we climbed to the top of the Round Tower for the fireworks display and the bonfire in the Home Park, but it was so rainy that we saw little. For my humble contribution I received one of the specially struck coronation medals, while Elisabeth and I, together with her parents, were invited for the first time to a Buckingham Palace Garden Party.

Earlier in the year I was asked to go back to the Royal Academy of Music as a temporary professor while one of the organ staff was in Canada for a term. I subsequently did a second stint, this time teaching harmony and counterpoint among professors who seemed to spend all their working life on the top floor of the building which was given over to these subjects.

Elisabeth and I had planned to go to Spain for our holiday that summer but, as the Inspector of Taxes informed me that I owed him £24 more than anticipated, (and that was a large sum of money in those days), we opted for a less expensive visit to Belgium.

1954 saw no let up in my longing to be running my own ship, and it therefore came as a great thrill when I was invited to become organist of Ripon Cathedral. I think that in the event I was more regretful at leaving Eton than St George's, for on the other side of the river we had made so many special friends among both staff and pupils, and we much enjoyed the frequent round of sherry and dinner parties. There was also a lot of music making, from Nora Byron's madrigal groups to Harry Babington Smith's *ad hoc* performances of Bach cantatas in which we sang, while latterly I had been responsible for the music at the Lower Chapel Christmas carol service which Hugh Howarth had inaugurated and to which we all greatly looked forward.

Another reason I suppose was that I foresaw Ripon as the fulfilment of my apprenticeship and the consequent opportunity to put all that I had learned into practice, though I did not quite anticipate that the challenge I knew would be mine would prove quite so formidable. I also realised that this would probably be the parting of the ways in terms of school teaching, and certainly in terms of the uniqueness of Eton, for I relished the self assurance and bearing for which Etonians are renowned, such as on the occasion when a recently ordained Conduct was interviewing boys. When he had the temerity to ask a burly soccer player of seventeen if he was ever troubled by impure thoughts, the quick response was 'No, sir, to the contrary, I rather enjoy them'.

That summer also saw the last Garter Service I would be involved in. Perhaps because of this I was more moved than ever. 'The splendour, pageantry, and sense of history becoming alive, never ceases to thrill me, almost beyond words' is how the diary summed it up. That was the occasion when Winston Churchill was installed as a Knight.

CHAPTER ELEVEN

In Yorkshire once again

'Ee, by goom, so you've cum oop Nawth to Yorkshire, lad'.

Our arriving in Ripon brought us, as we anticipated it would, to an entirely different situation from the somewhat rarified, and certainly privileged, life of living in Windsor Castle. We were given a first floor flat in High Saint Agnesgate, a quiet little lane on the south side of the cathedral. It had large rooms and a garden which went down to the river. Any feeling of being out on a limb after Windsor was quickly dispelled by the legendary down to earth kindness and hospitality which the Yorkshire folk so freely dispensed towards us and who, as I had learned from living in York, speak their mind in no uncertain way. You certainly know where you are with them. But equally, if they take to you—and we were most fortunate in this respect—their sincerity and warmth of friendship is such that you readily become one of them—and for life.

To this day we cherish our long-standing Yorkshire friends as much now as we initially did all those years ago, and we always enjoy our visits 'oop Nawth' with the friendly shops, pubs, pork pies and Yorkshire puddings, and not least the glorious ever-changing scenery of the dales and moors.

No less legendary is the accompanying fund of stories, real or apocryphal, and invariably spiced with a sting in the tail which makes them quite unique. Among the many I have collected, one of the best is that of the Yorkshireman who gave his friend a live pig. Wondering where to keep it as he had no garden or back yard, he concluded that the only possible place would be the bedroom. 'But think of the smell' said his friend, to which came the quick reply 'Pig'll 'ave to poot oop with that, won't it?'.

Some years later, on revisiting Ripon, I met up with someone I had not seen for a long time. When I suggested a drink at the Black Bull in the Market Square, he said in his broad Yorkshire accent, 'Now that you've coom oop in't world, I 'ope you're not all stook oop. If you are, you'll have to buy own blewdy drink, so I 'ope you've got yer brass with yer'.

In those days the cathedral had no choir school. That was to come after my time and was made possible by a far sighted Dean and Chapter who sold to America two of their valuable Caxtons from the cathedral library. With the proceeds they bought St Olave's, a local prep school which has since become a most successful resident choir school. In my time we sang daily services but drew on local boys whom you either kept, or lost, through the way you related to them, for children in Yorkshire can be as outspoken as the adults—and equally as loyal. The situation was compounded by the fact that Ripon then was a smallish market town of around 10,000 people, so the possible recruits were not all that thick on the ground.

Charles Moody, my predecessor as organist, had reigned as such for all of fifty-two years, though I suspect he never got the chance of serving 'in heaven' as did Bairstow. He was a Dickensian martinet of the old school who ran his choir on feudal lines. I was told that when the boys sang out of tune his favourite reaction would be to go along the line clouting each chorister on the ear. If the victim ducked, Moody would kick his shins and bellow 'That will teach you to sing out of tune'. One old chorister I knew suffered from permanent deafness as a result. Moody was even once known to chase a similarly out of tune and unpopular minor canon round the cathedral churchyard while cheering choristers urged him on.

When I arrived, Moody had been on his so-called death bed for many months, though when he retired he revived and lived on for some years. I found the choir and the cathedral musical scene at a low ebb and, more crucial, that the choristers had dwindled to a mere handful. I soon realised, as had been suggested to me at my interview, that I had a daunting situation on my hands and that a sizeable building task was needed, this despite Sydney Watson's jocular comments that 'one thing is certain about your going to Ripon—it can't get any worse'.

A further snag was that Ripon Cathedral was very much the poor musical relation to Leeds Parish Church with its considerable musical resources, so it was not only a matter of building up the choir but of boosting morale. Initially my boys may have been few in number, but they sang with the natural, confident, and full-blooded sound for which Yorkshire is rightly renowned. Even so, I had to exert considerable coercion, as when before Evensong one day my best boy was missing and reputed to be swimming in the river. I jumped on my bicycle, found him and persuaded him to forsake the river for Evensong with the promise of fish and chips as a bribe. We both just made it in time. On another occasion this same boy sang his heart out one evening in 'Love one another with a pure heart fervently', the treble solo in S. S. Wesley's *Blessed be the God and Father*, while we all knew that next morning he was to appear before the magistrates for shoplifting.

The men of the choir were fairly elderly and vocally past their best, though with one notable exception. The repertoire had become so run down that we were virtually repeating music every two weeks or so. The overall situation was not helped by the Dean, who had been Chaplain-General to Field Marshal Montgomery during the war and who, instead of backing me up in emphasising chorister attendance, tended to encourage the boys to abscond and follow their own pursuits, such as after Evensong one summer evening when he said to them, 'It's far too nice an evening to have been in church. You would have been better employed enjoying yourselves swimming'.

My initial reconnaissance through the music library revealed a mass of Victoriana which no self-respecting musician would ever inflict on his choir, even in 1954, so I had huge bonfires and more or less started all over again. Unfortunately, I enlisted the help of the choristers who were willing stokers of these conflagrations, but word of this got back to Moody who, I am told, exploded with rage at the impertinence of 'this young whippersnapper'. Admittedly I was only 30 and this was my first cathedral, but he underestimated my determination to make, as

I saw it, a clean sweep and rethink most things. After half a century under one organist some fairly drastic changes were imperative and long overdue.

So much for my early and at times frustrating days at Ripon. All the portents were that this was obviously going to be my first major challenge; nor would it by any means be my last.

Fairly soon after I arrived, two interesting opportunities came my way. After my Eton initiation into choral societies I was eager to have my own such choir, and here was what seemed to be the ideal opening. Ripon Choral Society had been defunct for some years, so I resurrected it. Over 60 singers came to the first rehearsal for which Elisabeth was the accompanist. They not only stayed but the choir grew in size over the coming months. This was my first experience of regularly training a choral society, so I was able to put into practice much of what I had learnt from observing Sydney Watson, especially when I was on the receiving end as one of his chorus members.

For our first concert we gave the Christmas music from Handel's *Messiah*, always a box office draw anywhere and an especial money spinner in Yorkshire, so we were heartened, and certainly encouraged, to find 1200 people in the audience. We were later to perform standard works such as Haydn's *Creation* with Isobel Baillie, which the Princess Royal attended, Handel's *Samson* and the first three parts of *The Christmas Oratorio*. Towards the end of *Samson* the score is peppered with frequent references to a chorus of virgins, and Ena Mitchell, who was the soprano soloist, should at one point have sung 'May every hero fall like thee'. Without realising it she sang 'May every virgin fall like thee'. After the concert, Michael Griffith Jones, the tenor soloist, was quick to suggest to Ena that in the ensuing statement 'and pass through bliss into eternity' she might have substituted 'maternity'.

The Choral Society rehearsals were entered into with much vigour by these good Yorkshire souls some of whom never missed a trick, such as when I was explaining some point and I happened to scratch my bottom inadvertently, one of the tenors remarked 'Ee, lad, hasn't that tooth koom through yet?' After rehearsals some of us would repair to the Black Bull and then go

95

on to the fish and chip shop. If the rehearsal had not gone too well, the favourite taunt would again be to suggest I pay for my own drink.

We got to know some of the Royal Engineers then stationed in Ripon and on my happening to mention to the Commanding Officer that we would soon need a larger and better platform for the chorus and orchestra, he volunteered to get his men to construct one as a training exercise, so the REs would invade the cathedral prior to each concert with Bailey bridge equipment and even a crane. While once erecting this splendidly solid contraption a soldier dropped a crowbar on to his foot and uttered what to him was probably a familiar oath, to which the sergeant major promptly responded 'Watch your language, man, you're in the house of God'.

The second opportunity which came my way was for me the unique one of being invited to become conductor of the Harrogate String Orchestra. This I greatly enjoyed and valued for it gave me my initial encounter with orchestral conducting and proved such good experience in paving the way for Exeter where I would do so much in this sphere. Their season of concerts was very much a part of the Harrogate scene, as witness the impressive list of distinguished patrons whose names were proudly printed in each programme. With this accomplished group of thirty players I learned much of the standard repertoire and worked with such soloists as the pianists Denis Matthews and Nina Milkina, the violinist Frederick Grinke, and the Australian tenor William Herbert whom I recall giving a hauntingly beautiful performance of Finzi's *Dies natalis*. The orchestra also played for me at the choral society concerts in Ripon Cathedral.

The Harrogate orchestra was 'managed' and promoted with much efficiency by Dorothy Yeoman whose husband was a distinguished rheumatologist. 'The Duchess', the name by which she was affectionately known, mothered me in no uncertain way, and it was at their lovely home in Swan Road that Elisabeth and I first met John Barbirolli and where, after every concert, there would be a full scale white tie dinner.

In Ripon we bought our first car, a second-hand Morris Minor, and how proud we were of it, as we were of our first refrigerator. We felt we had now really arrived, especially when we packed so much into it, and on top of it, to venture with the family down the Great North Road and the A6 to Henley on Thames where Elisabeth's father was now Rector. We would leave Ripon at the crack of dawn, sometimes even earlier, and reckon on arriving in Leicester in time for breakfast at the Grand Hotel where its four star rating much impressed our young family. In those days, and with so small a car, this journey was something of a feat, especially in the winter and without any heater, but we thought little of it.

I was now a fully fledged member of the Cathedral Organists' Association and felt rather important when I attended my first conference, which was at Leicester, where I met some of the distinguished names in cathedral music, many of whom I would get to know well in future years. Doc H told me to say nothing nor in any way to express an opinion when business matters were being discussed. 'Leave it to the older and more experienced members' was his firm directive, loud and clear. How totally different from today when it is the younger members who do so much of the talking while the older, or the retired, ones quite rightly do most of the listening. It was I think during my second conference, held at St Paul's Cathedral, that word came through of the birth of Mary, our second daughter. Juliet was also born at Ripon, though she decided to make her début while our doctor was out sailing, so the midwife recruited me to assist her which I did somewhat reluctantly. This was long before the time that fathers became as willingly involved in such matters as they do today.

Probably because I was the new boy and something of a novelty—even perhaps a relief—after 52 years of Charles Moody, I was kept busy giving organ recitals, playing at Huddersfield, Leeds and Bradford Town Halls, as well as in Hull, Otley, Ilkley, and a whole host of churches in the Ripon Diocese. I also gave a number of broadcast recitals on the cathedral organ and never ceased to rejoice in the glorious sounds that magnificent instrument produced. It was, and still is, one of the finest of cathedral organs. Knowing of my Windsor sojourn seemed to make me fair game for giving talks on my life there. As my four years there included three Garter Services, two royal funerals and a Coronation, there was plenty of material to draw on.

In Ripon, no less than at Windsor, a considerable amount of teaching was to be my lot, but as my cathedral salary was by no means lavish, the extra money was a great help. The work proved in the event to be more varied than at Windsor; there was the High School for Girls, St Olave's Prep School, the Teacher Training College, and Grosvenor House, a very friendly prep school in Harrogate, each of which demanded a different and individual approach which I found stimulating, and consequently enjoyable. I also began to collect a number of private pupils.

At Ripon I of course encountered my first experience of working with, and being responsible to, a Dean and Chapter. In this instance, as so often, they were an interesting group, each with his individual, and usually entrenched, viewpoint on most matters. The Dean, Frederick Hughes, was an evangelical with a love for playing his guitar at Sunday evening services, as well as composing ballads which he would sometimes sing and play in place of a speech at official dinners. Canon Wilkinson, known as 'Wilkie', had been a missionary in India and suffered from recurrent malaria which could make him extremely short-tempered, while Canon Bartlett was an old-fashioned Anglo-Catholic who had been responsible for building the magnificent church of St Wilfrid's, Harrogate, the finest example of Temple Moore's work. He and his wife were also devotees of gipsy life on which they were considerable authorities. Finally, there was Harry Graham, the volatile bachelor Archdeacon of Richmond, a lonely soul who as a result drank rather too much and, whether sober or otherwise, was the root and soul of all indiscretion. The Chapter were, I think, so relieved to have a new, young, and co-operative musical broom that they were unfailingly receptive to the ideas and projects I suggested to them for their approval. In any event, there was certainly a pressing need for new thought and new ventures.

On our days off, and before we had a car, we explored on our bicycles the country around Ripon with Rachel in a carrier on the back. When we had acquired our car we were able to venture further afield, and how we enjoyed this, whether it was going westwards to the Dales or east to the Vale of York and the Wolds which I had first encountered during the Army days at York. At Ampleforth we met Walter Shewring, then a master at the college. From time to time he would come over to Ripon to play early music on the cathedral organ, the morning rounded off by his taking me to lunch at The Old Deanery which was renowned for its splendid food and cellar. At that time I was unaware of his long friendship with Eric Gill, simply because Gill's work had not then come into my orbit of interest, something I was to take on board enthusiastically some years later.

On Saturdays I would regularly take the choristers for cycle rides, a favourite trek including the signal box at Thirsk Station where, on the London to Edinburgh route, there was the longest straight stretch of track in the country, and where we would watch the trains roar past at great speed. Expeditions such as this, as well as football, though the boys must have soon realised that I was hopeless at this, did at least help to keep the choir together as a team, and were an invaluable way for us to get to know each other off duty.

As a family, we greatly enjoyed some good holidays during those years. Elisabeth and I elected to plan these so as to revolve round certain parts of the country. In this way we got to know the Worcestershire of Elgar and the Shropshire of A. E. Housman, both of which were virgin territory for us. We visited birth-places—Elgar's at Broadheath and Vaughan Williams' at Down Ampney in Gloucestershire, not far from the source of the Thames at Seven Springs. We climbed Bredon Hill and were thrilled not only by the magnificent views in every direction but also to realise there really were 'the coloured counties around us in the sky' which I had so often visualised with a dreamlike nostalgia when reading *A Shropshire Lad* in distant Egypt. On this holiday we first visited St Michael's College, Tenbury and the Cluns—'Clunton and Clunbury, Clungunford and Clun are the quietest places under the sun'.

In 1956, during the choir holiday after Easter, I was once again in Paris with John Sanderson who by then had begun to disappear suddenly from the scene without a word of warning. He would even more suddenly reappear without volunteering any explanation. He was eventually to be out of circulation for some years, having said he was going to Kenya following an alleged illicit affair with the wife of the Rector of the church in North London where he was then organist. It was not until some years after we had moved to Exeter that he appeared on our doorstep as casually as if he were our next door neighbour passing the time of day. No explanation of what had happened was forthcoming and I knew that any such enquiry from me would be met with a stony silence. He thus became one of those people who, no matter how long it may be since you last met or made contact, you instantly pick up the threads as if there had been no gap. Even so, John's eccentricity, which began as a delightful and amusingly harmless trait in his character, began now to assume something of an embarrassment to his friends. But more of John later.

One of the joys of Ripon was in our being near to York and our seeing quite a lot of Francis Jackson, now married and organist of the Minster. He would give recitals for me, playing with such apparent ease while conjuring from the organ all sorts of sounds and colours none of us had ever thought possible. Healey Willan, the eminent English organist and composer who had carved out for himself such a reputation in Canada where he had lived for many years, was at this time given a Lambeth Doctorate in Music. While in this country to receive it from the Archbishop of Canterbury, he stayed in York with the Jacksons who put on a splendid dinner party to which Elisabeth and I were invited, and after which Healey regaled us men at one end of the drawing room with an endless fund of stories and limericks, most of them fairly dubious in content, for which he was renowned especially when hyped up with liquor. He always delighted in telling people that he was Irish by extraction, English by birth, Canadian by adoption—and Scotch by absorption.

In the early summer of 1956 while staying with Elisabeth's parents at Henley on Thames we explored the Thames Valley and many of its churches, including Fairford with its unique collection of glass. We also visited Bath, Downside, Wells and Montacute, all of which were again memorable first time encounters. Although in later years I would get to know these places well, the initial impressions were unforgettable and yet a further manifestation of things unmistakably English. While we were away we loaned our flat to the Lloyd Webber family, Bill, the father, being a London organist I knew, so our visitor's book has in it the signatures of Julian and Andrew Lloyd Webber, then small boys.

While at Ripon I was approached by Harold Ingham who invited me to be a leader *cum* courier for the then novel tours to the European music festivals which he was successfully promoting. Although in those days travel was by train and fairly basic, with an overnight couchette if you were fortunate, it did provide a particularly valuable first visit with Elisabeth to Salzburg, where on successive nights we heard Richard Strauss's *Der Rosenkavalier* and the Bach *Mass in B minor*, the latter conducted by Herbert von Karajan who, instead of stopping for the customary interval after the Credo, went straight in to the Sanctus. Although tiring for the choir, as I found when I emulated this at Exeter, it did mean that after the exhilaration of the end of the Credo, by which time the chorus would be well and truly limbered up, they sailed on almost compulsively into the majesty of the Sanctus. Seeing *Der Rosenkavalier* for the first time, and in Salzburg of all possible places, was an experience I shall for ever remember, the more so with those lush romantic tunes constantly running through our heads as we roamed the streets of that magical city. It took all of two days, if not more, to come down to earth again.

After Salzburg we went on to Vienna which presented different, though no less exhilarating, experiences, and where in the West Bahnhof we came across fish on the menu translated as 'God baked with potato salad'. The next summer we were at the Aix en Provence Festival.

I was thrilled when in 1955 the Royal Academy of Music made me an Associate—my first honour—and even more so when seven years later I became a Fellow. At Ripon I made my Royal School of Church Music debut, conducting choral festivals in the cathedral and lecturing on the annual course they then held at Grantley Hall.

For some reason, which I find as inexplicable now as then, I began being moody, with fits of depression which would last for days on end and then just as suddenly lift as they would descend on me. These periodic bouts were to dog me through the Exeter years and make me, as I well realised, such a burden and worry to Elisabeth.

In April of 1957 the post of organist at Exeter Cathedral suddenly became vacant. I was called down for interview and appointed. This meant that we were to leave Ripon after less than three years, but I had certainly learned a lot during that time, much of it the hard way. I am sure Ripon was intended as a necessary preparation and discipline for Exeter, though at the time I mercifully had no inkling of the problems which would confront me during my early years there, otherwise I might not have so readily accepted.

Exeter was to prove my longest and biggest cathedral assignment, lasting over fifteen years. The main realisation for me was that I was well and truly launched on my longed for career as a cathedral organist, and I now felt reasonably ready, and confident, to meet the challenge of a major appointment. A jewel such as Exeter was an incentive in itself. I well remember Sydney Watson telling me at the time of the advantage of making one's inevitable fledgling mistakes at a small cathedral rather than in the limelight of a major one. That just about sums up the Ripon sojourn.

CHAPTER TWELVE

Exeter—the early years

The early years—1957-60

As I had anticipated, I was soon to find myself immersed in a much bigger and more widely embracing dimension of activity than ever before. Over the next fifteen years it was to prove increasingly demanding in workload—much of it admittedly self-generated—and in responsibility. It was to be a broadening experience, not least in extending my vision and my outlook, yet it was to be as varied in its challenges, stimulation and rewards as had been each previous chapter in my life. The two new departures here were the scope of musical activity which was possible in a cathedral such as Exeter, and with it the reward of living in so beautiful an environment, not only in The Close and City but also in the rich variety of scenery which is Devon and which I would get to know, and revel in.

All in all, the Devon years were to call for a continuous reassessment of one's life and work, a constant rethinking with forward vision and, not least, learning that greatest essential of all—how to relate to people, and as much to my family as to those whom I worked with.

Throughout my working life we were to live 'over the shop' in a tied cottage which, as the workload increased, would entail my being more and more in my study at all hours, unlike those who travel to their place of work, have fixed office hours and then have evenings and weekends free to be with their families.

As cathedral organist, many of my evenings would be spent in the diocese visiting choirs and clergy, giving talks, organ recitals, or on Saturdays conducting festivals of combined church choirs. This would invariably mean driving considerable distances immediately cathedral Evensong had ended and getting back late at night, with the choristers' rehearsal soon after eight o'clock next morning. As daily Evensong was sung at 5.30 I was, apart from choir holidays, seldom at home when the children were going to bed. At the time this was for all of us, and most of all the children, to be the understood way of life and as such it was accepted without question.

In Exeter, as at Windsor, we were once again lucky enough to live—and not for the last time—in a beautiful house in equally beautiful surroundings, the influence and impact of which were not lost on the children living out their young, formative, and impressionable years in a cathedral close. This is something they have always looked back on with great affection and, as with Elisabeth and me, with considerable nostalgia.

Susceptibility to surroundings has always been an essential stimulus to me, with the drab, the ugly and the colourless acting as depressants. We had now moved from a relatively small north country market town, albeit a very attractive and friendly one, to one of the major cathedral cities. This was something I initially approached with some foreboding and with equal trepidation. Reginald Moore, my predecessor as organist, had left under something of a cloud and initially refused to move out of the flat in Church House which had traditionally been the organist's home, so once again I was to experience a disgruntled predecessor continuing to live on the other side of The Close and who with his wife was regularly seeing the choristers and, so I was told, trying to alienate the boys from me. Some of the senior choristers did in fact give me a rough ride for they liked Moore, despite his temper and the tensions he created. They felt he had been unfairly dismissed and, with an understandable youthful sense of justice and fair play, were firmly loyal in his defence. This was to be the first of many subsequent situations where I had to learn tact, patience and quiet perseverance. Time invariably heals wounds and all my chorister adversaries, without exception, eventually became good friends. It also taught me that children can sometimes be more stubborn than adults.

One good thing to emerge from this was that 11 The Close, which was in the process of being rebuilt after wartime bombing, became the organist's house. It was in every way ideal and was to become a much loved family home with the bow window of its first floor drawing room being for the children a favourite look-out across The Close. Its oak beam pent roof rising to 23ft was fully restored to its former glory, making the room ideal for entertaining, and for music-making. The dining room had a 14ft wide open fireplace of red Devon sandstone, complete with an 11th century squint window.

Felicity, the youngest of our four daughters, was born here, a fifth addition to the family being Dominic, a splendid Dalmatian dog who came to us as a two-week-old puppy and who, during his twelve years, was to become as much loved by the family as we were obviously loved by him. 'Brother Dominic, the Dalmatian dog of Devon', as the children called him, was a familiar and distinctive part of The Close life, even sometimes known to sneak in to the cathedral at Evensong time.

The children duly became King's Messengers and Brownies, while Rachel was Our Lady in the Cathedral Epiphany tableaux, distinguishing herself on one occasion by forgetting to bring the baby Jesus on stage, a deficiency which six-year-old Juliet was quick to perceive and remedy by producing the missing doll with great aplomb. Meanwhile, Felicity's interest in bell ringing was to come to fruition at Addington, though her apprenticeship at Exeter was invaluable when the vergers allowed her to ring the bells before weekday services.

Next door to us at No 10 were Wilfrid and Ruth Westall, he then Archdeacon of Exeter but soon to become Bishop of Crediton. While Ruth was very much a home bird and a willing baby sitter for us, Wilfrid was constantly out and about in the diocese. Around his warm and somewhat eccentric Anglo-Catholic personality many stories were related. He invariably drove to parish engagements wearing not only his purple cassock but purple biretta as well. One dark and stormy night, his car having died on him on Dartmoor, he thumbed a lift into Tavistock from a lorry driver who, looking the bishop up and down, commented 'Lumme, guv'nr, what a night to be going to a fancy dress party'.

Wilfrid was much in demand exorcising ghosts, stories of which he would recount with splendidly elaborated license. He was well known as a broadcaster, frequently being a member of the 'Any Questions' team which at that time was exclusively a BBC West Region programme, with Freddy Grisewood as the question master.

Wilfrid also had an abiding love for railways. Those were still the days of the old GWR steam locomotives, which had to work all out on the steep incline up from Wellington to Blackball Tunnel, half way through which the gradient suddenly changed for the downhill run to Tiverton Junction (not Tiverton Parkway as British Rail have for some reason elected to rename it). That point in the tunnel coincided with the county boundary between Somerset and Devon, which invariably prompted Wilfrid to make the sign of the Cross as the train gathered speed and he was safely back in his beloved Devon. Those were also the days of the slip coaches which thrilled us all when the rear carriage of the Cornish Riviera parted company with the main train and neatly came to a solo halt at Exeter St David's while the main body of the train sped on its way.

It is little wonder that Wilfrid was in constant demand as an after dinner speaker, a role which gave him ample opportunity to recount his seemingly endless fund of stories.

During my years at Exeter I was to work with only two Deans. Ross Wallace was one of a number of headmasters to be made a Dean on retirement, having been at Sherborne and Blundell's. Three years after my arrival he was succeeded by Marcus Knight, a canon of St Paul's who, some years previously, had been a minor canon at Exeter. He was a stickler for doing everything correctly, not least in his communications to me which initially were 'Dear Mr Dakers': then I progressively became 'Dakers', 'Lionel' and finally 'My dear Lionel', though it was not until some time after I had left Exeter that he told me 'I think you may now call me Marcus.' He was unceasing in his quiet observance of all that was going on, not least anything unusual or amusing during services, and which when later recounted at a dinner or a party would equally reveal his quick capacity for wit.

As time went on I tended to be away from the cathedral a great deal, either in the diocese or examining overseas, all of which was fully supported by Marcus, even if it sometimes seemed that I was absent from the cathedral more than I was there. This once prompted him, when introducing me to an audience, to say 'Here is our cathedral organist on one of his rare visits to Exeter.'

In my early days the residentiary canons were equally colourful. Ted Hall, who later retired to Leusdon on Dartmoor, where he served as the faithful parish priest until well into his nineties, had been a boyhood friend of T. E. Lawrence, about whom he would reminisce at some length. Henry Balmforth was a bearded Francophile who after Evensong would invite me in to 6 The Close for red wine and Gaulloises and, as a Latin scholar and pundit, would sometimes call me to account over the choir's pronunciation in a Latin anthem. Previously, he had been Principal of Ely Theological College. His wife was a strange soul who, having taken to her bed one day many years previously, stayed there until her dying day, though the extent of her malaise, if indeed there was one, was in some doubt. Swathed in shawls and silks she would receive her carefully chosen guests with much solemnity at her Walsingham House bedroom, which prompted the students to call her 'Our Lady of Walsingham'.

When Wilfrid Westall became Bishop of Crediton, Dick Babington, who had been vicar of St Mary-le-Tower, Ipswich, was appointed Archdeacon of Exeter; he and his wife Ruth lived next door to us at 12 The Close and became much valued friends over the years.

Prebendary Llewellyn, familiarly known to all as Uncle Reggie, had been Succentor for longer than anyone could remember. Although he could be cantankerous with all and sundry, no one could deny that he knew his job through and through. He would never be caught out on ceremonial or procedure, unlike another Priest Vicar who, slow at giving the intonation for the Gloria one Sunday at the Eucharist, prompted Uncle Reggie in the ensuing silence to shout up to the altar 'Glory be to God, you fool'.

Finally, there was John Dams, currently Succentor, and about whom many colourful anecdotes were in circulation. His sense of pitch when intoning was unerringly correct and a great comfort to the choir, which is more than can be said for some of the others who sang the services.

Invariably, walking home across The Close after Evensong with one or other of the Canons would be followed by sherry, or Dick Babington's beloved Madeira, over which we would work out plans, musical or otherwise, for the future.

The Prebendaries, clergy rewarded with Honorary Canonries for their service to the Diocese, preached in turn at Sunday afternoon Evensong. This gave them an opportunity, as they perceived it, to spread their wings, sometimes at considerable length and with parallel incomprehension. Many of them added to the somewhat eccentric individuality which was so intriguing a part of the Devonian clerical scene, and about whom so many stories, real, exaggerated or apocryphal, were related, such as that of the elderly Prebendary who sat behind our family at the Sunday Eucharist and who on one occasion when the Gospel was announced, greatly amused the children by loudly saying 'This, methinks, should be interesting'. One North Devon Prebendary delighted in fermenting his home made cider in a vast cask to which he added a bottle of gin, while another liberally dispensed bottles of Scotch around The Close at Christmas. When the Greater Chapter (which included the Prebendaries) met *en masse*, we would witness a blatant example of how not to process, with many of them failing to take in their instructions and consequently wandering off in all directions.

Exeter, as with many cathedral communities, was never slow in making sherry the excuse for a party. After morning service on each of the three great festivals there was an open invitation to The Palace where the Bishop's sons delighted in surreptitiously mixing gin with other spirits for a certain Minor Canon who spent most of the party expectantly hovering around the drinks trolley, while Robert Mortimer, the Bishop, once asked what he was giving up for Lent, was reputed to have said 'Drinking before breakfast'.

Although Exeter was in so many ways quite different from Windsor, I soon became aware of the influence of the cathedral's history, with its patina of centuries of worship, witness and music. Exeter shared with St George's Chapel the distinction of being virtually a complete architectural entity of one period. I well remember as a teenager standing by the west door of Exeter and revelling in the vista before me of the longest unbroken Gothic roof in Europe. Its glorious 17th century organ case stood high on the screen, and I thought how wonderful it would be to become organist here. Despite my daydreaming, little did I then suspect that some years later the dream would become a reality. When this came about I was to experience the added bonus of an impeccable conduct of services and distinctive well ordered ceremonial going hand in hand with the music. Not least were the Propers, the Lent Prose, the Advent Prose, and the plain-chant which was then so prominent a feature of the ordination service and the liturgy for Maundy Thursday, the Bishop presiding over splendidly Anglo-Catholic ritual which included his celebrating the Mass wearing cloth of gold gauntlets. Much of this was the development of foundations laid by Dean Matthews when Sir Ernest Bullock and Sir Thomas Armstrong were his organists.

The diocese, as with neighbouring Truro, had a predominant-ly high church tradition, its many elegant churches with their medieval wooden screens, and distinctive towers amid the red soil of Devon, being features I would get to know and revel in.

Presiding over it all, both literally and metaphorically, was Bishop Robert Mortimer, one of the last of the prince bishops of the Church of England, though his predecessor but one, the bearded Lord William Cecil, and often likened in looks to St John the Baptist, was no less a character. When once travelling by train he could not find his ticket and told an enquiring guard at Sidmouth Junction that unless he found his ticket he would have no idea where he was meant to be travelling to. On another occasion, his love of the countryside prompted him to pass the time of day with a shepherd to whom the Bishop confided that he also had a large flock of sheep stretching all the way across Devon, to which the farmer responded in broad Devonian, 'What a time you must have during the lambing season'. It was either Lord William Cecil, or the equally legendary Bishop Montgomery Campbell, who confronted one of his clergy with the enquiry 'Was it you or your brother who was killed in the war?'

Blunt though the Yorkshire people were, and forthcoming in their comments, they were basically as warm-hearted as the Devonians, many of whom I got to know extremely well. Frequent were the occasions when I would return from village churches with a gift of local cider, even though I may have failed to correct the instinctive Devonian singing of 'a loight to loighten the Gentoiles'.

Devon offered so much natural beauty whichever way you went from Exeter. There was East Devon with its gentle and lush contours punctuated by its picturesque rivers, and towns such as Budleigh Salterton, Colyton and Salcombe Regis. The roads northward to Barnstaple and Bideford were punctuated by villages which seemed sleepy and deserted no matter what time of the day or night you drove through them. Westward were wide vistas and equally picturesque villages with the rather different and more rugged spaciousness of Dartmoor as a back-cloth. Urged on initially by Henry Ley who was now living in Ottery St Mary, we were in the coming years to develop a great love for Devon and all it had to offer: its ever twisting narrow lanes, their tall banks a mass of primroses in spring, the village pubs, the smell of a log fire in the bar, and the omnipresent broad Devonian way of speaking. We became well and truly caught up in the magic of the West Country and not least in Exeter itself, its friendliness, its narrow streets, The Close with the Royal Clarence Hotel a constant meeting place, next door to which in those days was Cummins' splendid second-hand bookshop, even though I was seldom able to afford some of the treasures I found there.

At the cathedral, in addition to daily Evensong, there was in my early years choral Mattins on Tuesdays and Fridays, and how we had to work at the psalms set for the mornings, which we sang so infrequently by comparison with the evening ones. Mattins on Fridays was unaccompanied, with the singing of the Litany invariably thrown in for good measure, though weekday Mattins had later to be curtailed when more time was needed for the choristers' mounting academic studies.

When I arrived in Exeter, Mattins reigned supreme on Sunday mornings with a monthly hole-in-the-corner sung

Eucharist preceding it, for which the Voluntary Choir would sometimes provide the music. The growing emphasis on the Eucharist as the central Sunday service was then beginning to make its impact everywhere and by the time I left Exeter it had become the main Sunday service, with the roles of the two services entirely reversed.

As at Ripon, many opportunities were there for the grasping, such as extending the tradition the Exeter choir had for specialising in contemporary music, the enjoyment of which the choir shared with me. The medieval Liturgy of Bishop Grandisson on Christmas Eve, sung in Latin and by candlelight was, and remains, a major attraction in its uniqueness, while during Advent the Great O's were sung before and after the Magnificat during the week preceding Christmas. Ronald Jasper was one of the minor canons and his visionary awareness for matters liturgical, later to be fully realised when, as Chairman of the Liturgical Commission and Dean of York, he would be largely responsible for the Alternative Service Book. His foresight paved the way for the first of the Exeter Advent carol services with their then novel symbolism of the light coming into the world. Four choirs singing antiphonally in different parts of the cathedral gradually converged at the High Altar. For me, one of the features of this service was the great Advent hymn 'Creator of the starry height' sung to the haunting medieval tune *Puer nobis nascitur*. And what a wonderful time Advent is, penitential though it may be, with its strength of words and music, not least those Great O's, pointing the way at every stage towards Christmas.

As the years passed, life in the cathedral was to become as busy as it became varied, with more and more special services, concerts and recitals, though all of them were secondary to the priority of the daily round of the offices—the Opus Dei for which cathedrals primarily exist. In many ways Exeter became a pioneer for many of the musical events which nowadays we tend to take for granted as part of the contemporary scene in many of our cathedrals.

Much of my time was spent as ever before in teaching piano at the cathedral school where life in those earlier days was distinctly Dickensian. When the then headmaster, Howard Treneer, retired, Dean Wallace took it on himself to appoint someone who claimed he could revolutionise the school finances, then sorely in the need of attention. He proved to be a crafty manipulator of funds who thoroughly hoodwinked the Dean and Chapter, lined his own pocket and, when cornered and exposed as a fraud, promptly committed suicide. This resulted in my becoming the stopgap, and certainly unofficial, headmaster for a term before Dick Babington had the brainwave of persuading Tom Evans, a Suffolk priest, to take over. This dedicated bachelor was the epitome of all that is best in a prep school master and who, in his quiet but firm way, moulded his charges for their future life and, by no means least, in preparing them in their spiritual life as Christians. His appointment proved to be an inspired choice, for he put the school on an even keel, increased the numbers, raised the scholarship and consequently set the school on its present highly successful course.

Elisabeth devoted many hours to teaching choristers the piano and was frequently amused by some of their comments, such as the small boy who chanced to have a lesson on the Feast of the Annunciation and then proceeded to explain that it takes nine months to have a baby, adding as a rider to the mother of four children 'but I expect you know all about that'.

Having always admired the Royal School of Church Music's policy of helping choirs, especially small, remote and often struggling groups, I made a point of being out and about in the Diocese as much as possible and in a pastoral way tried to help those concerned with matters musical as did the Bishops in matters spiritual. The annual Diocesan Choral Festival was an ideal basis for this. Each summer I would take up to a couple of dozen preliminary rehearsals in various parts of the diocese as a build-up to the thousand or more singers who took part in the Festival in the cathedral each June. As the interest grew and the numbers increased, I inaugurated a special RSCM Festival each November, specifically for village choirs and with music less demanding than for the June Festival. In both instances, as with other smaller regional gatherings, the object was not only for singers to have the thrill of being part of a large choir but also, and more importantly, to go back to their home churches with new repertoire, new experience, new incentives, encouragement and hopefully, inspiration. This paid handsome dividends and one saw the standard of singing improve each year. The RSCM also asked me to take on quite a lot of work, not only in the Diocese but further afield conducting residential courses.

Even so, despite all one's efforts to help choirs realise their potential, their capabilities—and their limitations—there were always some who had an inflated idea of their abilities and who, having perhaps heard one of the top cathedral choirs sing a most demanding anthem, would proceed to emulate it, however inadequate or incomplete their resources. They would seem quite oblivious to the embarrassment this could cause to those on the receiving end, simply because such choirs had little concept of standards when it came to their own efforts.

One of my greatest rewards was that of conducting Exeter Musical Society and the opportunities to develop their repertoire, spurred on not only by their infectious enthusiasm but also by the support of the public for our concerts, so much so that we were quite depressed on the rare occasions when we performed to a cathedral less than fully sold out. The Society consisted of a chorus of more than 300, and an orchestra which had previously by tradition merely acted as accompanist. We later gave them concerts in their own right, the first of these including Beethoven's 3rd piano concerto with Colin Horsley.

Elisabeth was accompanist for the chorus rehearsals, also playing the harpsichord or chamber organ continuo for works such as the Bach Passions which I was conducting for the first time. Eric Greene was the Evangelist for my first *St Matthew Passion*, sharing with us both his long and wide experience, and not least his visionary approach which was an inspiring eye-opener in itself.

Elisabeth became as much part of the EMS as I was, and in the years to come she was to play an even more prominent role. Early on we thought up the concept of a fairly informal Christmas concert in which audience participation in carols featured prominently. Within a couple of years these were extended to three successive nights each Christmas with the cathedral packed on each occasion. We gave the proceeds to charities and, as the overheads were relatively light, we were able to donate considerable sums each year.

In those days I became subject to something approaching a fiery temper which was easily aroused when things went wrong. This prompted the choristers to tell the headmaster that 'fiery Fred', my second name being Frederick, 'was in a burze at choir practice'. This extended to the Musical Society where whenever I called Elisabeth 'darling' the chorus knew that an explosion was brewing. On another occasion, just as I was about to take a choristers' rehearsal, Elisabeth and I had an argument about something and, as I was about to slam the door of No 11 and go across The Close to the rehearsal room, I shouted out 'I'll have it out on the choir', to which Elisabeth tartly responded 'Good luck, and I hope you have a lousy rehearsal'. As the years passed I became less turbulent and realised in the process that I then got far better results from my forces.

Elisabeth became more and more a part of the wider Exeter musical scene and we worked together on many projects, as well as making music together in so many ways. I continued to value greatly her womanly intuition concerning people she had doubts about, while so often when I and other males had agonised over certain matters, she, usually late at night in the bathroom, would quickly size up the root of the matter which had eluded us. She also possesses, as with many mothers, great staying powers and energy long after we men have wilted. I well remember her playing for the EMS rehearsal one week while heavily pregnant and then playing for the next rehearsal two weeks later, Felicity our fourth daughter having been born in the meantime.

Our concerts and recitals entailed a lot of extra work for the cathedral staff, and when we left Exeter the Head Verger told me, with a twinkle in his eye, that he dare not think of how many thousands of chairs he had moved in the cause of my so-and-so music making. In addition to this there was the erecting and dismantling of the tiered platform in the nave in front of the organ screen, a formidable task as it seated 300 singers. It was bought by the chorus who donated each week at their rehearsal towards the cost of the materials until we had raised the full sum.

It was built by the cathedral workforce and then given to the Dean and Chapter by the Society.

Central to all our musical ventures was Charles Goddard, manager of the local music shop. He was a great enthusiast, never ceasing in his labours in dealing with the mechanics of the concerts such as box office, ticketing and publicity. He also sang in the chorus which he entered into with equal enthusiasm. How bereft Exeter was when he died.

During the early Exeter years I conducted the Bournemouth Symphony Orchestra for the first time in a performance, sponsored by the National Federation of Music Societies, of Brahms' *Requiem*, in which a number of West Country choral societies took part. The response and precision of a large professional orchestra was a great, and novel, thrill for me, my being so accustomed to the somewhat less disciplined approach of the local and mainly amateur orchestra. This, however, provided rich rewards in enthusiasm and determination, with up to a dozen rehearsals for each concert providing me with invaluable orchestral experience which I gained the hard way.

Another interesting concert was Haydn's *Creation* as part of the Devon Festival, and in which thirteen choral societies joined forces.

During this period I was invited to be the guest conductor for some of the smaller local groups and for a short time was responsible for Torquay Philharmonic Society which proved to be a somewhat frustrating and unrewarding experience. Most of the choir were rather old and suffered from illusions of grandeur. Ena Mitchell sang for me in the Bach *Magnificat* and, writing to me after the performance, said 'It's a difficult work full of pitfalls, but the choir only fell into one, though I admit it was a sizeable crater'.

After a while I formed Exeter Chamber Orchestra, a group of around twenty of the best local string players, led by the Dartington String Quartet who regularly took sectional rehearsals, the 'cellos in our kitchen, the violas in the drawing room and the violins next door in the Bishop of Crediton's house. Altogether we gave fourteen concerts, which widened my knowledge of string music, not least of the 20th century, and gave me the opportunity, and invaluable experience, of working with soloists such as Isobel Baillie, Osian Ellis, Leon Goossens, Cyril Smith and Phyllis Sellick.

For these and the Musical Society concerts the soloists stayed with us and the supper parties Elisabeth put on at 11 The Close after each concert were such fun and very relaxing after the rigours of a concert preceded by two or three hours' full rehearsal. In this way we got to know many people, including Janet Baker and John Shirley Quirk, when they were commencing their careers and were virtually unknown. We later learned that we had established quite a reputation in the profession for our hospitality.

There were also other concerts in the cathedral, the most memorable being the annual visit by the Hallé orchestra with Sir John Barbirolli. He would come to the house for post-concert parties and we got to know him well, as did the children to whom he always gave much affectionate attention, even sometimes having Felicity, then rising seven years old, on the rostrum with him at rehearsals. I always cherish the memory of his playing Vaughan Williams' *Tallis Fantasia* and commenting afterwards in his husky Cockney voice that 'it's music such as this which grows out of the stones of a great medieval cathedral and then, when it's finished, it goes back again into the stones'. In those days we always sang a hymn instead of having an interval, with JB's conducting of the audience invariably an unforgettable experience, not least the *pianissimo* he would extract from 2000 people.

Sir Charles Groves was at that time conductor of the Bournemouth Symphony Orchestra which spent much of its working life on tour in the West Country and which used to give two concerts on a Sunday in the now demolished Exeter Theatre Royal. Later, when the University Great Hall was built, they gave monthly Friday evening concerts which were invariably a sell-out. By this time I was reviewing concerts for *The Express and Echo*, the Exeter evening paper for which I also wrote a monthly chit-chat column, as I did for the University's Northcott Theatre magazine. This was a further challenge for me in that it gave me the opportunity and invaluable experience of writing

With my parents, 1928

'The bus conductor'
and my father's car

At Rochester
Cathedral
Choir School
1931

The schoolboy organist

*All Saints'
Cathedral,
Cairo
1946*

St Mary's, Slough, 21 April 1951

The family at Exeter, 1971
(back row left to right) Juliet, Mary, Rachel
(front row) Felicity and Dominic

Four organists of Christ Church, Oxford
(left to right) Dr Sydney Watson, Dr Henry Ley, Sir Thomas Armstrong
Sir William Harris

Addington Palace

With the
Housekeeper
in my
office at
Addington
Palace

Relaxing at the Taj Mahal, India

With Dr Robert Runcie, then Archbishop of Canterbury (now Lord Runcie), at our farewell party, Addington Palace, January 1989

In my Stall as a Lay Canon of Salisbury Cathedral

on all sorts of subjects and topics far removed from the church music scene. These sometimes included profiles, one of the subjects being Paul Patterson who, as a local schoolboy, played the trombone in the Musical Society orchestra. He was then beginning to compose, and some of his earlier avant-garde works were written in our drawing room.

These years also saw me embarking more on writing, having been invited to contribute regular church and organ music reviews for *The Musical Times*. I even wrote to *The Times* deploring the singing of carols two or three weeks before Christmas. This not only provoked a lively correspondence but even resulted in a third leader.

Despite a fairly full diary we nevertheless found time to lead an enjoyable social life mostly confined to smallish dinner parties which were then very much in vogue, and much more rewarding in getting to know people than the mammoth and noisy sherry parties which nowadays have become the easy way of entertaining considerable numbers of people *en masse*.

We explored Devon fairly thoroughly, though as much for work as for pleasure. During the post-Easter break we would sometimes spend a week on a farm in North Devon near North Molton, which the children much enjoyed, not least because of the animals. For summer holidays we would often go to Cornwall, staying with friends at what then was a quiet and sparsely populated Rock, where the children could paddle out a long way in relative safety. By this time Elisabeth's father had become Rector of Henley on Thames which we would regularly visit, staying in the handsome Georgian Rectory on the banks of the Thames. From there day visits to London by train were so easy, allowing me to indulge in visiting second-hand bookshops. In those days it was a long drive from Exeter to Henley on the A303, with few by-passes, no dual carriageways, and no car heater. We would leave at 6 am and then stop at the Dolphin Hotel in Wincanton for breakfast which was always a much anticipated event for the family.

On occasion we would travel abroad and, among other places, visited Oberammergau again, though this time with the four children who had arrived since our previous visit to the

Passion Play twenty years before. One summer we towed a caravan to the Dordogne. Wherever we ventured on holiday *en famille* there was always the pleasurable anticipation heightened by loading up the car with clothes, food, children, and often Dominic, the Dalmatian. As these expeditions usually came at the end of a long summer term, there was on arrival at our destination the chance to relax and for me to settle down to catching up on reading, though the urge to be back at work again would soon emerge, for I have never found it easy to unwind and fully relax, the more so over the years and with them increasing demands and pressures. Even so, we had some memorable family holidays as the many photos and slides remind us.

John Sanderson was by this time married and living near Lyons. On a number of occasions Elisabeth allowed me to spend New Year there, which was an enjoyable time, for the Sandersons lived well, while France at that time of the year was always an attractive lure.

CHAPTER THIRTEEN

Exeter – a continuing saga

The Middle Years (1961-66)

Many of the projects I initiated during my first four years at
Exeter were now to be extended and consolidated, though the
daily round of cathedral services rightly continued to be the basic
raison d'être of my work. Domestic problems in the cathedral
school having now been resolved we settled down to a more
peaceful, happy, and consequently productive, period. This was
to be despite warning signs from the Dean and Chapter over the
cost of the musical foundation, though the launching of the
Cathedral Campaign, to include generous provision for safe-
guarding the music, proved fruitful and saved the day. The
cathedral choir gave a number of recitals in the Diocese and, by
dint of sheer hard work, including a cathedral *Son et Lumiére* and
a flower festival, the necessary money was raised, much of it
through willing effort and support in the Diocese and county.

Highlights of 1962 included the BBC televising 'live' our
Christmas Eve midnight mass, a radio programme on the
cathedral featuring John Betjeman and the cathedral choir, and
myself becoming for a while the introducer, or presenter, of the
BBC Songs of Praise programme on television.

The cathedral organ was by now due for an extensive
overhaul and rebuild, but not before HMV had asked me to
contribute to their 'Great Cathedral Organs' series of LP
records. During the months when the organ was silent, Elisabeth
or my assistant joined me on two pianos for the services and
voluntaries, or sometimes to accompany Second Evensong on
Sunday evenings, a long-standing popular Nave service at which
the Voluntary Choir sang. The rebuild of the organ completed,
the opening recital was given by Fernando Germani, the distinguished recitalist who was then organist of St Peter's in Rome.

119

Until the advent of Tom Evans as headmaster there had never been an Old Choristers' Association at Exeter. When he set about forming one and suggested Easter Monday for the annual reunion, most of us felt this would be a disastrous day for such an occasion but we were proved wrong and Easter Monday it has always subsequently been, with 70 or 80 old choristers of all generations not only foregathering for a reunion and dinner, but also singing Evensong with the cathedral choir. This always was, and still is, an inspiring occasion, not least in the hymn 'Ye choirs of new Jerusalem' with its great onsurge of unison sound in the verse 'Triumphant in his glory now, His sceptre ruleth all'.

Notes in my office diary at this time reminded me in hindsight to tell the choir what to do, or not to do, when a certain occasion next came round, such as at Epiphany when we sang Crotch's *Lo, star-led chiefs*. In 1966 the diary said 'The Larghetto section must be softer than last year, with boys being particularly careful to tune their C naturals and C sharps'.

The work of the RSCM continued to grow, fuelled, I venture to suggest, by the results of successive events. I much enjoyed overseeing these occasions, especially directing the rewarding choral festivals in North Devon and not least the journey there and back, especially on summer evenings. The Diocesan Choral Festival grew to such an extent that we eventually had to turn choirs away, there being no more space available for them in the cathedral. By inaugurating a separate festival for the Plymouth area in St Andrew's Church, we were able to cater for the west of the Diocese, which also saved choirs having to travel long distances to Exeter.

On the secular choral front I formed the Festival Chorus in 1961. This was a choir of getting on for 600 singers comprising the Musical Society augmented by the University of Exeter Choral Society with contingents from St Luke's College and Dartington Hall. Our objective was from time to time to perform works needing large choral and orchestral forces. The first such venture was Elgar's *The Dream of Gerontius*, followed by the Verdi *Requiem* and then in 1964 Vaughan Williams' *A Sea Symphony*. In all instances we used the Bournemouth Symphony Orchestra.

In order to provide opportunities for performing small scale choral works, with or without orchestra, I formed the St Peter's Singers, who developed into an efficient group giving recitals in various parts of Devon. Vaughan Williams' *An Oxford Elegy* and *The Pilgrim Pavement* were among the works included in the early concerts, while later we gave a number of Britten cantatas including *St Nicolas* and *Noye's Fludd*.

By this time I had got to know Sir Adrian Boult, this through my father-in-law who was his contemporary at Christ Church, Oxford. He was most helpful to me in my coming to terms not only with conducting some of the more complicated scores but also in giving me invaluable tips on working with highly professional players such as the Bournemouth Symphony Orchestra.

1966 was a particularly busy year, with the Musical Society, together with the cathedral choristers, giving one of four West Country cathedral performances of the then new Britten *War Requiem* with the BSO conducted by Charles Groves. This was an especially tough and demanding assignment for the choir but, as with Vaughan Williams' *A Sea Symphony* and the Verdi *Requiem*, it gave the chorus the opportunity of coming to grips with varying styles, idioms and, not least, challenges, which through dint of sheer hard work in preparation they took in their stride. The more works we learned, the more experienced and versatile they became.

Each summer, after the run-up to the Diocesan Choral Festival, followed closely by the cathedral patronal festival on St Peter's Day when we really 'went to town', I always looked forward to what was then a quiet few weeks with the cathedral choir on holiday. The main events at that time of the year were the six summer organ recitals in the cathedral, which invariably drew large audiences especially among holidaymakers in Devon.

These led on to the much anticipated family summer holidays with Cornwall continuing to be a firm favourite, though one year we went to St David's in Pembrokeshire where I had been invited to give an organ recital in the cathedral and for which the then handsome fee of £15 paid for a week's rent for the house we had in The Close.

121

By this time, we had taken on a succession of *au pair* girls from the continent who helped Elisabeth with the family, and in 1966 we towed a caravan *en famille* through Holland, Germany and Denmark visiting their homes and staying with their families.

My interest in collecting modern first editions and private press books was now growing apace, though dictated by what I could reasonably afford, for we had considerable school fees to meet for our children. It was at this time that Harry, son of the author Henry Williamson, came for a voice trial for the cathedral choir. It was a great relief to find how musical he was, so we readily accepted him as a chorister. I consequently got to know Henry, whose writings I had admired and collected since the wartime days in York when I was introduced to *Tarka the Otter* and *Salar the Salmon*. Henry frequently visited us when he came to see Harry, while he and I would meet at his home in Georgeham when I was visiting choirs and clergy in North Devon. On one occasion I stayed in the hut he had built at Ox's Cross high above Braunton Sands and the glorious coastline. I even slept in the bed T. E. Lawrence had slept in, which for me was such an occasion for hero worship that I was awake for much of the night.

On the cathedral scene, apart from lonely spinsters with a religious mania who habitually seem to haunt cathedrals, two of whom were a continual nuisance to me and the family, Exeter was no exception in attracting religious eccentrics such as the heavily bearded gentleman known as 'Whiskers'. He lived in a tent in a field at Dunsford where he kept a miniature ark ready at hand for the end of the world which he believed would be at any time and in the form of a great flood. He would sit immediately behind the choir and contribute a loud, and hopelessly inaccurate, tenor line in the hymns, even when the choir were singing in unison.

There were other characters one remembers so well, not least Michael Dykes Bower, an eminent eye surgeon. His three bachelor brothers included John, the organist of St Paul's Cathedral. Michael lived in a lovely Regency house in Southernhay where he was looked after by his manservant Ridgeway, who, whenever you telephoned, would inform you that he would summon 'the master'. Michael would also sit immediately behind the choir at cathedral services and would loudly sigh if anything went amiss in the singing. In the early days we did experience certain choir problems, and Michael sighed rather a lot. In those days the back row of the stalls in the Quire was strictly men only and the entire congregation stood for the anthem.

Every year the four Dykes Bower brothers would meet for Christmas dinner. They would drink to another year of bachelorhood followed, so it is said, by Michael sighing heavily and commenting 'England has never been the same since women were given the vote'.

In 1965 I paid my first visit to the United States, directing the RSCM's summer school at Wa-Li-Ro, an insect ridden summer camp on the shores of Lake Erie where I was initiated into the mysteries of volleyball. Leo Sowerby, the American composer, who visited the course annually, later lent me his house in Washington DC where I gave an organ recital in the National Cathedral and savoured for the first—and only—time an adjustable pedal board which, instead of the more familiar adjustable stool, you could raise or lower as you wished.

The previous year had seen my first overseas tour as an examiner for the Associated Board of the Royal Schools of Music. This lasted for all of three months with Elisabeth being with me for the first part. I began by examining in Switzerland at the English Schools at Montreux where John Sanderson and his wife joined us. From Venice, of which we saw all too little, we took a Greek boat to Egypt, travelling via Athens, the Corinth Canal and Rhodes. We spent a week in Cairo, my first visit there since the war. We stayed at the Semiramis Hotel now restored to its former glory and looking splendid with its lush Victorian decor, not least there being a metal hook in the bathroom on which was embossed 'For razor strop'. It was so good to visit All Saints' Cathedral again after a gap of nearly twenty years, and even more to find Aziz, the faithful and efficient verger, now ordained and a priest on the staff. This being Elisabeth's first visit to Egypt, we did all the expected things such as exploring Old Cairo, the Mouski and the Tutankhamun treasures in the

Egyptian Museum. Having taken Elisabeth to see the Pyramids we returned there one evening for Son et Lumière which began as the sun was setting in the desert in a characteristic blaze of incandescent red; it proved to be a memorably moving production.

Flying on to Addis Ababa and then to Nairobi we experienced for the first time the sight of an African dawn breaking as we flew low over the game park coming in to land, and with it our first sight and the never to be forgotten sounds of Africa, to be repeated and to rejoice in on countless future occasions. After another all too short stop-over we found ourselves on what transpired to be BOAC's first commercial flight by VC10 to Salisbury in Southern Rhodesia. Here we stayed with Alan and Rosemary Milton, Alan having been Professor of Education at Exeter University and a keen violinist in my orchestras. He was now vice-principal of the University in Salisbury. In between examining and a fairly hectic social round we visited the Wankie and Inyanga game reserves, we saw the Victoria Falls and sailed up part of the Zambesi river, saw Fort Victoria and the ancient ruins of Zimbabwe before moving on to Umtali where we stayed at the cosy old Cecil Hotel, visiting the Vumba, the Eastern Highlands, and the Mirfield Fathers at Penhalongha. In Bulawayo we spent a day driving and walking in the Matopos where we saw Rhodes' grave high in the hills before I went on to South Africa, leaving Elisabeth to return to England.

Of all the many parts of the world I have since visited, it is always the anticipation—and the reality—of Africa which never fails to thrill me, whether it be the smiling Africans singing their hymns and songs, or the ubiquitous richness of blue skies and the wonderfully brilliant cloud formations as seen nowhere else in quite the same way. Add to this the vividness of everything when you are 6000 feet above sea level, and you have something which always fills me with pangs of nostalgia as does little else. Perhaps it all springs in some measure from East and South Africa being the first places I was to visit outside Europe other than my brief visit to the United States.

The Royal School of Church Music asked me to make contacts while in Johannesburg and I did this to such an extent that it took up a great deal of what little spare time I had, but it gave me a useful insight into the church and its music in the Southern Hemisphere, even though so much of it was almost more English than in England. This was never more so than among the Africans themselves who, as I was to see again and again over the years, felt that God was not being properly worshipped unless it was with *Hymns Ancient and Modern* and a pipe organ, the latter even in churches in the bush. Even so, I was able to visit a number of the more truly African churches and rejoiced in hearing all sorts of instruments as well as, to English ears, their slightly unusual though intriguing approach to singing in parts. Hugh Tracey was one of the great scholars of indigenous African music and he revealed to me many insights of a rich tradition which is much better known today than then through recordings, radio and television.

St Mary's, the Anglican cathedral in Johannesburg, was in those apartheid days unique in having a mixed congregation of Africans and Europeans. I was there on most Sundays and got to know the organist Roger O'Hogan and his family who were exceedingly kind and hospitable to me. I enjoyed helping Roger by taking choir rehearsals and sometimes by playing on Sundays. One of my examining visits was to Machadadorp to which I travelled by train. This was near the Kruger National Park where I was taken for a day visit. Although we set off at 4 am and arrived back late at night, on that occasion we saw relatively little wild life.

My work in South Africa ended, I went on to Mauritius for a further three weeks of examining. In those days it took over six hours flying time from Johannesburg, virtually all of it over the Indian Ocean. When I got there I found in this smallish island in the middle of an endless expanse of sea something quite different from what I had either anticipated or previously experienced. Looking now at my letters home, I am amused at how explicit and observant they were, and almost extravagantly flavoured with the excitement of novelty at every turn, this time with a strongly Indian element which accounted for the Creole emphasis. The south-east trade winds produced a vast amount of rain on the eastern side of an island little more than thirty miles wide and given over in the main to growing sugar. Those winds blew themselves out midway, an extraordinary sight to witness, for the western side of the island was as dry and sunny as the east was wet. In most parts there was high humidity, especially in the capital, Port Louis, a delightful city with its French influence matched by an equally English atmosphere with the statue in the square of Queen Victoria benevolently surveying the scene.

I stayed at the delightfully old fashioned, now demolished, Park Hotel in Curepipe and this was to be the first of many occasions when the British Council, who were responsible for the Associated Board's work in Mauritius, would be so helpful, and not least here through their representative, Guy Sells, and his charming French wife.

Mauritius was a thoroughly delightful island to explore, especially in the late afternoon when I had finished examining and would go for walks through fields of sugar cane and up on to the hills. On one such walk along a country road I came across a manhole cover on which was embossed 'J. Brown, Maker, Deptford, London. S.E.'—this a real reminder of the days of Empire.

I never tired of the glorious sky, as blue as an air mail sticker, nor of the vivid red sunsets night after night, and of going out in a flat-bottomed glass boat to look at the incredible beauty of the coral reef. On the lighter side was my chancing to see an Indian correspondence school which proudly sported that it was called Knowledge College, while the sleek teenage lady candidates intrigued me with their split skirts which revealed so much, and no more. This was something which would become an everyday occurrence when I was later to examine in the Far East.

While I found much to write home about, I was saddened at hearing so infrequently from my parents. In a letter to Elisabeth I commented 'When they do write, it's only to tell me that either the garden at Uplands needs rain or else that the wind had played havoc with the plants and shrubs'.

I was still in Mauritius when the Musical Society chorus rehearsals began after the summer recess. On this occasion, as on many more in the future, Elisabeth was to take the rehearsals in my absence. This was a contrast which the chorus much enjoyed and, as one of the tenors later confided to me, 'when it's your wife conducting we all watch the beat much more'.

CHAPTER FOURTEEN

Farewell West Country

The Latter Years, 1967-1972

The final years in Exeter were rewardingly happy ones with a further awareness of what I had either set in motion, or had tried to further during the earlier years, now seeming in many ways to be coming to fruition. Even so I was more than ever aware of the projects which somehow had seemed to hang fire or were less well fulfilled, this the more so as with increasing hindsight I realised that much of any failure or fault in this respect lay with me. As I grew older and as my responsibilities, as much for Elisabeth and the family as with my work, increased and widened, so I believe I became more mature, less volatile, and more understanding, rather than dismissive, of the feelings and needs of others. How invaluable Elisabeth was to this process and in helping me to see—often the fairly hard way—the error of my ways. She was a truly stabilising influence. Our now working together on so many musical projects also helped me to forge and maintain a greater rationality in our way of life.

With all that was now happening, the demands on my time increased more and more, but, because these were so wide-ranging they were the more rewarding. Life had now settled down to a pattern, though never a dull routine, at the core of which was the cathedral and my work there. The problems of the earlier years had now, thank God, fully resolved themselves and I was able to build up the cathedral choir on to a surer, and certainly steadier, foundation. BBC work and recordings were an added incentive and stimulus for the choir, although the daily round of rehearsals and services was the ongoing priority for us all. The cathedral was now being used more and more by the diocese who increasingly came in to their mother church for all sorts of events and in doing so I believe became more aware of what it stood for, not least in its unique beauty and musical resources. This process, and my visits into the diocese, helped to cement what each of us in our various ways were doing.

There were also many casual one-off deflections, most of them extremely enjoyable, such as talks for Rotary and Women's Institutes. I was now on the auditioning panel for the BBC in Bristol and found this also served to widen my interests and my critical faculties. As time went on I became caught up with more and more committees and I confess to enjoying much of this work, especially when it took me to London with increasing frequency. I went willingly, for my love of London born in the 1930s and 40s had never diminished.

On the home and diocesan front I was subject to increasing contact with the clergy, and they with me. More often than not, whether individually or in discussion groups, we were meeting on more or less equal terms and with equal purposes in our respective sights—the enrichment of worship through music. We realised the power of music, be it in cathedral or in village church, to enrich worship, or, if ill-prepared and ill-presented, to impoverish or in dire circumstances even destroy it. And all of this was in the wake of the *Honest to God* syndrome of the immediately preceding years, the radical thinking which John Robinson's book engendered, and not least the problematic influences which resulted.

The Diocesan Choral Festival each year was now one of the major features in the life of countless church choirs up and down the county, while the November festival for village and small town choirs was no less popular. On both occasions we now had to enlist the help of the police in marshalling the many coach-loads of choirs and their parish supporters which descended on the restricted spaces of the cathedral close.

I for my part much valued and enjoyed my visits into the diocese and my contacts, especially with the many small though dedicated choirs, those who trained them and those who played for them. All this was of course before the Royal School of Church Music's 'Reluctant Organist' project was launched, a training scheme which converts pianists to enable those with basic skills to play the organ for services in churches where no one else is available. The needs at that time in Devon were urgent and there was for me the realisation, as I suspect there was for those on the receiving end, that I genuinely enjoyed trying to help them in their efforts, to which they responded in full measure and, in doing so, often attained heights they—and I—would never have felt possible. This is something I now realise was impelling me on as a rather special part of my Exeter work. Although I did not realise it at the time, it was valuable preparatory work for the tasks which would be very much mine in my RSCM years. God moves in a mysterious way . . . .

Meanwhile the annual menu of RSCM events in the Exeter Diocese proceeded apace. Each year these were now in excess of twenty, not put on to impress through numbers, but because there was clearly a necessity to cater for many diverse needs. For example, rural North Devon was a very different proposition from Torbay, and even more so from the Plymouth area. We therefore planned a broad-ranging programme intended to help all, whatever their resources or expertise, and it was reassuring to see the mounting enthusiastic support and, more importantly, choirs and organists themselves realising what they could do and what they could achieve through hard work backed up by perseverance—and by encouragement.

In 1967, together with the Bishop of Exeter and Gerald Knight, Director of the RSCM, I arranged four festivals for congregations, although these were equally to help the clergy, choirs and organists. We had already promoted study groups and hymn-singing festivals through which I was able to emphasise the importance not only of congregational participation in those areas where it was needed, but also to show how well they could take part to advantage. It was the giving of guidance, and an awareness of how important congregational input could be to the musical completeness of worship, and at a time when there were many more choirs than today. In other words, they were not merely hangers-on in the body of the church, but integral to what was happening in chancel and sanctuary.

During these years Exeter Musical Society continued to give its annual quota of concerts in the cathedral with, in the summer of 1967, our playing Mendlessohn's *Reformation Symphony*, the

Schumann piano concerto with Denis Matthews, and a performance of Paul Patterson's *Symphony Study 1966*. It was at this
concert that the Dean and Chapter allowed applause for the first
time. Although nowadays virtually never called into question in
churches and cathedrals, it was then quite unique and prompted
a man to shout out as he made a dramatic exit, 'This is a
cathedral, not a concert hall'.

In 1967 I also became a member of the Council of the
Royal College of Organists while, on the proposition of Henry
Williamson, I was elected to membership of the Savage Club.

Looking through our visitors' book for these years, it seems
remarkable how Elisabeth, with four young children, not only
coped with so much piano teaching and other commitments, but
managed to have so many people to stay, or for dinner parties. It
certainly makes for interesting reading now, and, as with the
scrap books, concert programmes and press cuttings, brings back
a whole host of memories, and of otherwise forgotten events and
people.

During 1967 I went to the Far East for five months examining for the Associated Board, my long suffering Dean having
given me permission for an even longer absence than before. He
would always cite three things—earning extra money would help
me pay the children's school fees, that all would be well if I made
provision for all my responsibilities to be covered during my
absence, which meant a lot of extra work for Elisabeth and for
my loyal and gifted assistant, Paul Morgan, while thirdly the
Dean felt it was good for the name of Exeter Cathedral to be
made known through me in distant countries.

For the first two months I was in Singapore staying at the
Cockpit Hotel, one of the older hotels, with a lovely garden, in
Orchard Rise. Here on Sundays was as excellent a lunch, a
Malaysian Rijsttafel, as was the curry and beer on offer at the
Tanglin Club. The examining may have become as tedious and
repetitive as the heat and humidity, but the vitality of the city
never failed to appeal to me, despite the volume of traffic being
as enormous as it was predictable. The *Singapore Times* just
about summed it up by reporting one day that 'there were only
forty accidents in the city yesterday: one of the lowest figures

this year!' Even so, Singapore in 1967 was still a fairly gentle and smallish city while much of Orchard Road contained green open spaces, with C. K. Tang's Emporium and the downtown Robinson's store focal points swamped today by vast building projects. Even so, the relative quiet surrounding the Anglican cathedral and the cricket ground on the padang still retained a certain aura of Singapore's imperial past.

John Rigg, the company secretary of Jardine Mattheson, happened to be an old St Paul's Cathedral chorister. He frequently entertained us examiners, who included among our number Douglas Hopkins, one-time sub-organist of St Paul's. On one occasion we were part of a dinner party in the garden of the Riggs' lovely home near the Botanical Gardens where we were given English fish and chips in newspaper. Together, we also spent a memorable weekend in the ancient city of Malacca where St Francis Xavier is buried.

After Singapore there were two months in Hong Kong where we examiners stayed in the recently opened Mandarin Hotel, which was with justification hailed then, as now, as one of the five great hotels in the world. As elsewhere, I was drawn into church music life at St John's Anglican Cathedral where I frequently played on Sundays and took choir rehearsals. The crowded vitality and effervescence of life in the colony was quickly apparent and we soon became caught up in its impelling and infectious atmosphere, not least the restaurants such as Jimmy's Kitchen, and Le Trou Normand just behind the Peninsula Hotel where, when funds allowed, we would have pepper steaks in the dining room, which in those days afforded a view across the harbour to the Peak, a panorama now obscured by the seemingly never ending onsurge of new skyscrapers, hotels and office blocks.

When we were short of money we would eat in the roof garden restaurant of the YMCA opposite the Star Ferry and the railway station which was the terminus of the line which once went from London's Victoria Station through Europe, Russia and China, and where the original timetables were still on display in the booking hall.

The day's examining ended, Douglas Hopkins and I would regularly take the Peak tram and walk in relatively peaceful seclusion around the Peak with its breathtaking views of the southern side of the island and the South China Sea. When we got back to the tram the sun would be setting as it sets only in that part of the world and then, as the thousands of lights came on in Kowloon, we would ride down into the city for dinner.

On Saturday afternoons Douglas and I would invariably take a ferry to one of the many outer islands of the colony, often in company with the Hakka women in their distinctive headwear making their way to the villages of the New Territories. We would also visit the now demolished Repulse Bay Hotel and revel in its gardens and food. This was the time of the Hong Kong riots when bombs were deposited in various places. On one occasion Douglas inadvertently left his carrier bag containing his swimming costume on a seat in the hotel garden. When he returned to Hong Kong and he realised what had happened, he telephoned the hotel who told him that the servants had found a 'suspect' package on a seat and had called in the military to blow it up. 'Your swimming costume is, alas, no more, sir'.

We also visited Macao, then similarly in a state of tension and with anti-imperialist slogans daubed on the walls of the British Consul's residence.

Hong Kong was in every way such an exhilarating city to live in. The lobby of the Peninsula was a frequent meeting place, whether for gin and tonic, chicken and pineapple salad at lunch-time, or merely for watching the world go by, as it did in no small way there.

Later visits to Hong Kong have disenchanted me, with vast hotels and office blocks mushrooming on every available piece of ground, while the harbour is progressively being reclaimed on the Kowloon side to allow even more building. No—Hong Kong will never be quite the same again for me as it was in the 1960s, any more than it probably was then for those who knew it in earlier years.

Work in Hong Kong ended, there remained five final weeks in India. Calcutta seemed such a contrast, and a depressing one, my first impression being of the road into the city from Dum Dum airport, full of potholes, with people everywhere and paramount to it all the sacred cow to which all traffic gave way.

I stayed at the Oberoi Grand which faces the Maidan. A Sunday afternoon spent at the Tolleygunge Club showed that the Raj way of life was by no means defunct. Tennis in a setting so reminiscent of England was followed by bearers bringing cucumber sandwiches and tea in silver teapots.

From Calcutta, which I was not sorry to leave, I flew up to Bagdogra and then on by car and train to Darjeeling. On the way up we stopped for refreshments at a railway station and were guided to a room with, over the door, a faded notice which proudly proclaimed 'For upper class European Gentlemen only'. I stayed at the Windermere Hotel where, because of the altitude, I was glad of thick blankets on the bed, plus a hot water bottle. Apart from the Alps, I had never before seen really high mountains, so the view from Darjeeling along hundreds of miles of the highest mountain range in the world, crystal clear in the early morning sunlight, and crowned by Kanchenjungha, all of 28,000 ft high, was in itself unforgettable. The sight was surpassed only by my going to Tiger Hill the next morning to witness that great expanse of snow-capped mountains turning pink for all too brief a moment as the sun rose on the full length of the Himalaya, as far as the eye could see, with Everest clearly visible over a hundred miles distant.

Later that day I was examining at a convent in Darjeeling and recounted to one of the old nuns what I had seen. 'Yes, my friend,' she said, 'you have seen the sun rise on the highest spot in God's creation. When you see such beauty the words of the *Benedicite* become very real'.

The bustling vitality of Madras was in marked contrast to the relative spaciousness and quiet of Darjeeling. It was here that I first experienced the Liturgy of the Church of South India which would later ring familiar bells when the highly derivative Series 3 Holy Communion was launched in the Church of England.

I travelled on the fascinating narrow gauge railway up the Nilgiri Hills to Ootacamund, passing through Wellington and Coonor with their array of army barracks built by the British and looking so reminiscent of Sandhurst. It was a long and steep haul up to Ooty, as it is familiarly called, and which with proud justification proclaimed itself 'Queen of the Hill Stations'. Here I stayed in the Kiplingesque atmosphere of the Savoy Hotel with its lawns and English flower beds. After dinner a log fire would be lit in your bedroom, for at that height it could be very cold at nights. 'Snooty Ooty' retained many vestiges of British India, such as hunting, racing, polo, golf and tennis. The countryside was in many respects reminiscent of Devonshire, the Scottish Highlands and Sussex all rolled into one, with houses which could have been transplanted straight out of a rural Surrey village. There were quaint cottages with equally English names, gardens and ubiquitous roses. With its rolling countryside, mountain streams and closely cropped green open spaces it was in such marked contrast to the noise and the dry barren plains far below. There were then a number of English schools in and around Ooty where I examined for some days. I was later to pass through Madurai, with its magnificent temples, on my way to another hill station, Kodaikanal, or 'Kody' as it was familiarly called. Later I would travel from Bombay's impressive Victorian railway station on the Deccan Express to Poona where I stayed, as I recall, at the Royal West Indian Turf Club, a hark back at every turn to imperial splendour, where in the mahogany-panelled dining room there was still a portrait of Queen Victoria. In those days the Wantage Sisters had a school in Poona where I examined, as also at another English school in Panchgani. The tour ended with a week or so working in Bombay. Here I stayed in even greater splendour at the red-domed Taj Mahal Hotel where I had a bedroom overlooking the Apollo Bunder and the Gateway of India.

Back in England, 1968 proved by marked contrast to be a relatively quiet year, and probably needed to be. This was particularly so as regards special events and gave some breathing space to prepare for the following year. Exeter was by this time twinned with Bad Homburg in Germany. Their church choir, when they gave a recital in Exeter Cathedral, showed just how proficient and disciplined a choral group they were. Seeds sown at this time matured over the years with visits by all and sundry in either direction. Later on I visited Bad Homburg to give an organ recital.

In November I was invited by the RSCM to play the organ for the British Legion Festival of Remembrance in the Royal Albert Hall. This was a new experience and an occasion I found most moving, not least in playing that magnificent organ, and doing so with the massed military bands, while being part of a highly organised exercise which is always mounted with such precision and professionalism.

As anticipated, 1969 proved to be one of the busiest of the Exeter years. The cathedral duly celebrated the 600th anniversary of the death of Bishop Grandisson, who completed the cathedral in virtually the same form as it stands today. As the centrepiece of the celebrations, the Queen Mother and the Archbishop of Canterbury attended a great service for which Paul Patterson wrote brass fanfares. A full programme, in which musical events featured prominently, was spread over the year. These included a BBC Songs of Praise with Exeter Musical Society, and a splendid BBC Music Programme weekend divided between the cathedral and the University Great Hall.

A Worship and Arts Exhibition took place in the Chapter House, while Son et Lumière ran nightly in the cathedral for three months during the summer. Donald Swann, together with his musicians and actors, presented 'Soundings with Swann' and in doing so started a long association with Elisabeth and me which extended well into our Addington days. The Musical Society orchestra performed Tchaikovsky's B flat minor piano concerto with Enloc Wu, a young pianist from Hong Kong, while the Festival Chorus and the Bournemouth Symphony Orchestra once again gave Verdi's *Requiem*. To crown it all, the cathedral was the scene for a wonderful flower festival in which the county was heavily involved.

That year Erik Routley, who was one of the greatest authorities on hymnody in our time, paid his first visit to us. This led to a firm friendship which lasted until his sudden death some years later. As a member of the RSCM Council he greatly influenced my subsequent thinking and work. I owe much to him. But more of this later.

Erik's razor-sharp mind was quick to size up any situation, and always with such reliable credibility of judgement. Late one evening I gave him two sizeable books to review. At breakfast next morning he had not only read both books but written a full length piece on each. This Congregational minister, who so enjoyed his food and his drink, was best summed up by my Dean who once claimed that Erik, a distinguished minister in the United Reformed Church, knew more about the Church of England and its Liturgy than many Anglican experts.

The Routleys had a holiday cottage at Halton Lea Gate midway between Newcastle and Carlisle, and here we spent one of our summer holidays exploring the Northumberland country-side with the family and Dominic, our Dalmatian, who, although only a few months old and very active, had already become so much a part of the family and would remain so throughout his life.

Looking back in retrospect I realise the number of hours I must have spent in those days learning scores, most of which were new to me, if not as music, certainly in terms of training a chorus and of knowing what it was all about. When I used the Bournemouth Symphony Orchestra we had at the most one prior rehearsal with them without the chorus. With the Musical Society orchestra there would be ten or more weekly rehearsals before a concert and so to an extent I learned my scores with the orchestra.

The reviewing of concerts and recitals for the local evening paper took more and more time as the number of events con-tinued to increase. The work taught me how to conclude quickly what to write, to write it with brevity, and then to get my piece to the paper's office before midnight. Not only did I learn a lot in terms of reporting but I equally widened the range of my musical interests to include a whole host of orchestral works new to me, as well as the opera productions at the University's Northcott Theatre.

On the home front, family life went on in much the usual way, with the children seeming to weather without undue problems my being away from home so much. Elisabeth was adept at moulding the family life in a sensible and rational way, with the seeds she then sowed coming to fruition now with our grandchildren, our delightful sons-in-law and the tightly knit family unity which, I venture to suggest, is almost uniquely ours, and for which we are constantly grateful. On 16 July 1969 I see that Rachel wrote in my desk diary 'Daddy and Mummy at St Monica's. Rachel's last day at school ever'. St Monica's School was at Warminster where Mary, our second daughter, had joined her. Rachel went on to Florence for a year, living with the Camelloni family at Fiesole and helping to look after their musically gifted daughter. Later, Rachel did a secretarial course in London before becoming secretary to Sir Keith Falkner and then Sir David Willcocks, successive Directors of the Royal College of Music. She was also a competent pianist and a flautist.

David Calcutt, who had been a chorister at Christ Church, Oxford, with Elisabeth's brother Patrick, was by this time a successful barrister working on the Western circuit. He was frequently in Exeter for cases and would often stay with us. When he was married at Edington Priory he enlisted no less than six cathedral organists to play in turn before the service, each of us being allocated one of the Bach Orgelbuchlein preludes. David, now knighted, was until recently Master of Magdalene College, Cambridge, and has become a successful QC holding a number of tribunal appointments arbitrating commercial and professional disputes, by dint of which he is much in the limelight.

The next three years which, in the event, were to be our final ones in Exeter, were years of mounting busyness which I much enjoyed and revelled in. I seem to thrive best when under pressure, working at all hours and using every minute to advantage. Waiting for trains and planes and then working in them, as in hotels, are always valuable opportunities for uninterrupted writing or reading, while to spread out your papers in a train usually frightens off would-be companions. I have always seemed to be at my best when I have my back to the wall and problems with people or situations to be worked out.

My first book, *Church Music at the Crossroads*, which Sir John Dykes Bower as adviser to Marshall, Morgan and Scott, asked me to write, was published in 1970. The writing of this infused me with the urge to put pen to paper and to write a number of books which I did on various occasions during my Addington years.

1970 saw the cathedral choir giving a recital at Buckfast Abbey, with the Roman Catholic Abbot and the Anglican Bishop of Exeter not only sharing the honours but each pronouncing their respective Blessing, something hardly ever encountered, if at all, in those days. In the cathedral we recorded for BBC Television two not very successful Complines for Holy Week, one traditional and the other Taizé. That year Covent Garden promoted the English Opera Group in a West Country tour with Exeter Cathedral providing the ready-made backcloth for Britten's *Curlew River*. The Vienna Boys' Choir sang in the cathedral and when they came to the house for refreshments after the concert the family were amused to see thirty sailor caps neatly stacked by size on the hall table. The Musical Society gave Tippett's *A Child of our Time* which I found a most moving work to conduct, and which the choir particularly revelled in.

After Easter I went to Malta for three weeks for the Associated Board. Though Malta was now independent, life there was still empire-orientated in its atmosphere. It was also quiet, which it certainly was not when I again examined there twenty-one years later and found the island all but completely given over to tourism. I stayed at the Xara Palace Hotel in Mdina, the fascinating medieval walled city high on its hill in the centre of the island, and so full of atmosphere and history. The hotel was the permanent home of a number of eccentrics voluntarily left behind when the British Navy departed. Retired bachelor naval officers revelled in exploring the island, much of it on foot, and would recount the day's exploits over dinner, to which a deaf old widow, aided by her enormous ear trumpet, would add pungent and noisy comments. To this Somerset Maugham type of gathering was added Mabel Strickland whose name, together with that of her father, Lord Strickland, just about summed up the old Malta.

My examining ended, Elisabeth flew out to join me for a short holiday during which we explored and revelled in the beauty of the island with the spring flowers then at their best and in such abundance. There were few tourist attractions in those days and virtually none of the plethora of building now to be encountered at almost every turn.

After Malta we went to Sicily, where we found so much of historic interest, though in Syracuse we were stranded for some days by a rail strike—a *sciopero*, as we were so frequently and frustratingly reminded—before visiting Palermo and Rome.

In the summer we were in Europe as a family, hauling a caravan for some hundreds of miles. On this occasion the children were responsible for the first of the family holiday scrapbooks in which each day was written up in turn. The title page of the book tells us that it was 'published by Juliet'. Getting up after our first night in Belgium, the diary relates that 'the balloon went up. Daddy couldn't find his clothes anywhere and he made a great scene until we discovered that they had fallen out of the caravan window'. We stayed with friends in Bad Homburg and then visited Ulm before going on to Oberammergau to see the Passion Play. Later we stayed near Salzburg where the children were intrigued by my liking for Paprika Käse at breakfast, this being a type of cheese uncommon, and probably unobtainable, in those days in England. We also visited Herrenchiemsee to see the castle of the mad Ludwig II, before driving up the Zillertal to show the children Mayrhofen where we became engaged in 1950. On the way home we spent a couple of days in Luxembourg. The scrapbook-cum-diary ends by saying 'we drove 2968 miles in three weeks and one day, and it was an admirable introduction to Europe for the children'.

That Christmas the Exeter Musical Society carol concerts were announced as 'Conducted by Lionel and Elisabeth Dakers', a duality which would continue until we left Exeter.

I have constantly been intrigued by meeting people with whom, as so often happens, you discover the sharing of interests, and frequently of friends in common. For a few years I was a Rotarian but it was that lack of common ground and interests which I found so inhibiting to the conversation which is so integral a part of their weekly lunches. Not being greatly informed, or particularly interested, in the worlds of business, golf, or of meeting colleagues for a drink in 'the local', immediately put me out of court, while I was incensed by those who obviously knew nothing about the work of being a cathedral organist and would ask me if I would be going away on holiday over Christmas or Easter. But, by the reverse token, I never know how to get on to the wavelength of those whose life was so differently played from mine. I usually fail dismally, and invariably utter a disastrous *faux pas*. But what fun it is when you find places and friends shared in common and from which springs a fruitful and often informative discussion.

The bearing, and conduct in public places, of one's fellow creatures, male and female alike, is for me a fascinating, though at times depressing, matter. As life has moved on and I have inevitably come into contact with more and more people, I find so much to admire in many of my fellow creatures. I recall the quiet and dignified bearing of Sir Owen Morshead, the librarian at Windsor Castle. He was a true courtier in every sense of that often misunderstood label, as were others of the Royal Household I would later come into contact with in the RSCM days. His use of his hands was another marked characteristic and as idiosyncratic as Edward Roberts, then Bishop of Ely, who would constantly play with his episcopal ring when thinking out some plan of action at an RSCM Council meeting he was chairing. Into a similar category came Robert Mortimer, my Bishop at Exeter, whose presence could be awesome, but always episcopal.

Today we seem to be so obsessed with being casual in dress, such as men who appear at smart restaurants in faded jeans and open neck shirts while invariably the lady with them will be much more smartly turned out, as will be the restaurant staff. It is encouraging to know that some, albeit too few, restaurants now demand ties and jackets, something which African countries have insisted on for many years after sundown.

Another aspect I always find intriguing is seeing people in their homes, how they furnish their rooms and, if they possess books, what their tastes and interests are. I invariably find that browsing along bookshelves provides a revealing character guide to a person.

Summing up these various observations brings to mind two specific people from the Exeter days, both of whom seemed to me to meet many, if not all, of the qualities one respected. Sir Leonard Daldry had been the head of Barclay's Bank in Nigeria and consequently, under British rule, a member of the government. He and his wife retired to Budleigh Salterton, and when Sir Leonard became chairman of the Exeter Cathedral Campaign we got to know them well. They would invite us to lunch from time to time, after which we took the dogs for a walk before tea. Having changed into black tie for dinner we would drink champagne before and with our meal, as we previously had at lunch. After dinner there would be a game of billiards, which Leonard always won, and then we would stay overnight. Breakfast was as elegant as the house and our previous meals, with scrambled eggs, mushrooms and bacon in heated silver dishes on the sideboard. Our visits to the Daldrys were excursions into a way of life all but new to us then, but for them no doubt a continuation of what they had been accustomed to in Nigeria. When they visited London they would always have a suite at the Ritz.

Sir Godwin Michelmore was a solicitor who, as a retired Major General became the Diocesan Registrar of whom most of us were somewhat in awe, or even frightened by. This always immaculately dressed person became a widower and then married Winsome Holderness, herself a widow. Both were well into their seventies and both became almost childlike and proclaimed that they were 'deliriously happy'. Winsome's brother was Field Marshal Lord Montgomery who gave her away at the small family wedding in St Leonard's Church, Exeter, for which I played the organ. At the reception the photographer said to the Bishop of Crediton, who had married them, 'Will you move a little to the left, my Lord', to which Monty tartly retorted 'There's only one "my Lord" here'.

Another delightful eccentric was Mary Heath, one of those religious, tweedy spinsters who habituate cathedrals, are full of good works, and have boundless energy. She supervised our children when they were Brownies and King's Messengers and also walked them to school each morning. When Wilfrid Westall, the Bishop of Crediton, was in the Royal Devon and Exeter Hospital for an operation, she would make the children genuflect as they passed the hospital.

Our final Festival Chorus Concert, as it transpired, took place in the summer of 1971. Verdi's *Te Deum* and more especially Walton's *Belshazzar's Feast* are demanding works, needing for

141

our resources concentrated and lengthy preparation. This was a tough assignment as much for me as for the three choral societies involved. I had to work extremely hard on learning the Walton score but in the end more or less knew it from memory, which I think helped relay confidence to the chorus when it came to the performance. Whenever I subsequently hear the work I wonder how we coped with the sheer technical demands of the music, and then with the massive orchestral sound which had such an impact on the chorus, who for some weeks previously merely had the piano at rehearsals. This always applied with any heavily orchestrated works, for it was not only the sheer volume of sound in the louder sections but the accumulated instrumentation and the additional rhythmic points which are either lost or not heard on the piano.

We also included the *Kindertotenlieder* of Mahler. John Shirley Quirk had never performed the work before—nor had I—and, as he was due to sing it in Germany the following week, asked if he could come in on any preliminary rehearsal I might be having with the Bournemouth Symphony Orchestra. I much welcomed this and I know that the resulting performance of the Mahler benefited greatly as a result.

In looking back to our final years with Exeter Musical Society there was for both Elisabeth and me a certain sense of pride and achievement, for in 1967 I had inherited a small and not very efficient chorus with whom we both worked hard, as they did too. By the time we left there were 300 singers. The orchestral side was perhaps the hardest of all, for one was so reliant on good local talent and, with only one or two players to a part in the wind and brass sections, any uncertain sounds were obvious to all, whereas in the chorus the sheer numbers helped to cover up any less efficient singers for, as Sydney Watson claimed, an amateur choral society is where two and two make five.

One of the most rewarding aspects was the friendships which emerged, some of them, as with the retired Brigadier flautist and 'the honorary unpaid second bassoon' as the eminent Exeter gynaecologist termed himself. Then there was the obvious stimulus of the successful concerts and the resolution by the performers to do so much better next time if they knew they had failed to fully deliver the expected, and anticipated, performance. All concerned were certainly determined to rise to the challenge of every occasion and never more so than in our latter concerts with the orchestra giving my beloved fifth symphony of Vaughan Williams and Beethoven's *Consecration of the House* overture, while Phyllis Sellick played Beethoven's fourth piano concerto. Our final concert, the Bach *B minor Mass*, somehow seemed to sum it all up with the majestic sound of the *Dona nobis pacem* being the finale of a particularly happy and, I believe, fruitful part of our Exeter sojourn, for it really did give so many people the opportunity to come to terms with, and perform in public, works they would have never even dreamed of knowing other than by hearing others perform them. Success breeds success, and how they responded in no small measure, rising to occasion after occasion, and time and again when I felt I might have embarked on a work which was taxing them to the utmost. And, additionally, how rewarding it was that we should be making music in the beauty and ambience of so wonderful a cathedral.

Reflecting back, I cannot help but feel that we must have got away with a lot which would not pass muster today when standards in amateur music making and expectations are so high. Of one thing you were always certain, that on the night of the performance, however rocky some of the previous rehearsals may have been, the choir and orchestra would give you 110% in concentration, determination and enthusiasm—sterling qualities in any situation.

John Norman, the organ builder, had earlier taken us for our first visit to Glyndebourne where we rejoiced in Cavalli's *La Calista* with Janet Baker singing opposite James Bowman, the counter-tenor. I was also asked to become a member of the Organs Advisory Committee of the Council for the Care of Churches, of which I was to become chairman when Sir John Dykes Bower resigned four years later. 1971 also saw me as President-Elect of the Incorporated Association of Organists, visiting Cambridge for their Congress that summer and being given VIP treatment which, I have to confess, I enjoyed. I see that I gave the Royal College of Organists lecture at the Congress on the subject of 'The Organist in the Permissive Society', though I have no recollection now of what I said about so thought-provoking a matter as it obviously was in the early 1970s.

That summer we hauled a caravan to France for a holiday in the Dordogne. This time the scrapbook related that it was 'stuck together by Felicity'. We visited Bayeux and its tapestry and what was left of the Mulberry Harbour from the D-day landings in 1944, before eventually putting our roots down on a very pleasant camping site near Sarlat, where we would buy wine each morning and cool it in the nearby river. One night there was a frightening thunderstorm with eight-year-old Mary telling us she was so scared that she kept on repeating the 'Our Father' as fast as she could. Next morning there were, according to the diary, 'hailstones the size of Maltesers still on the ground six hours after the storm'.

As the family, unlike me, wanted to sunbathe and swim, I went off on various solo expeditions exploring Souillac, Rocamadour, Perigeux, and other parts of this fascinating quarter of France. Henry Balmforth, the francophile Canon of Exeter, had lent me Philip Oyler's book *The Generous Earth*, and armed with this I visited a number of the places he had colourfully written about, not least Queyssac-les-Vignes where they produce the yellow *vin paillé* made from grapes allowed to ferment on straw.

Immediately the Christmas Services at the Cathedral were over that year I willingly forsook damp, cold and dark Devon for South Africa, something I would do on future occasions to direct one or other of the RSCM summer schools in the Southern Hemisphere. Less than a day later I was revelling in high summer in Cape Town. I stayed with John and Barbara Badminton, he an old chorister of Christ Church, Oxford, whom we had met some years previously in Bulawayo. He was now director of music at Bishop's, the public school in Rondebosch. My visit included a splendid dinner, the first of many, at the Mount Nelson Hotel, and taking the cable-car up Table Mountain before breakfast on an unforgettably beautiful New Year's Day. A couple of days later we drove a thousand miles through the scorching hot Great Karroo Desert to Johannesburg for the course at St John's,

144

Houghton, another fine boys' school. Here I worked with a choir of 130 which included four lady tenors. Some of the participants had travelled considerable distances, including a group of boys from Rhodesia, over a thousand miles to the north. Our services took place in the splendid school chapel designed, as was the school, by Sir Herbert Baker who was responsible for so much of the architecture in South Africa.

The Sunday services ended, I travelled on the overnight BOAC plane to London and was correcting ARCO examination scripts at the Royal College of Organists at Kensington Grove at 10 o'clock the following morning. I was by now accustomed whenever I returned from South Africa to being subjected to jibes. On this occasion a priest in Exeter confronted me with 'How can you be a Christian and go to that country?' The very reason for my going there was of course to help the Church through its music.

When 1972 began I did not entirely foresee it as being our last year in Exeter. I knew that Gerald Knight was due to retire as Director of the RSCM. Rumours, unofficial soundings-out and the like tended to suggest that the directorship might perhaps come my way, but I took nothing for granted and was certainly not going to count any chickens before hatchment. I had seen too many people hurt and disappointed by setting their heart on something which in the event failed to materialise.

I felt I had said and done all I could in Exeter and for some time I had anyhow been increasingly drawn towards the administrative area of music. I felt ready for a move and for the challenges I knew this would involve, but equally I knew it would be the end of cathedral life for me and that in any event, unless I was very lucky, I was unlikely to move to one of the five or six top posts in the cathedral hierarchy.

In April I was interviewed by the Council of the RSCM in the Jerusalem Chamber of Westminster Abbey. While the Council deliberated, I waited in the Nave and could not help but think of similar occasions during the war years when I said my prayers in that very place, and now, thirty years later, those prayers were again answered for I was given the job and was to move on to new pastures.

I realised this would be the time to test my powers and judgement to the full and to do so in other directions than before, not least in a worldwide dimension. But, as I was so enamoured of travel, the globe-trotting my new job would entail appealed to me the more. I firmly believe that all that had gone before—York, Cairo, Windsor, Ripon, and now Exeter—had provided me with a broadly based training ground which had not been solely confined to church music. I sensed by what I had been told and what I had observed that the RSCM had tended to become static, inward-looking and, as a consequence, was only more or less ticking over, with so many possibilities waiting to be explored. In other words, the time for RSCM change was as ripe and as ready as change was for me.

But, for the immediate, I was due to go to East and South Africa for the Associated Board for all of five months, a tour for which I had been signed up nearly two years previously. While the RSCM wanted me to commence duties in September they appreciated the situation and the problems the Board would face in finding someone to replace me at such short notice and for so extended a tour. I consequently left for Africa with mixed feelings, not least for Elisabeth who would be left to deal with so much in my absence, for Exeter provided no secretarial help.

My final Musical Society orchestral concert had anyhow taken place in May and when I returned in November I was to find that Elisabeth had very thoroughly done all the preparation with the chorus for the Bach *B minor Mass* and the carol concerts.

During my absence Elisabeth also had to deal with all the business of where we should live at Addington Palace, the headquarters of the RSCM high on the Surrey hills south of Croydon. It was eventually agreed to be Golf Cottage, an 18th century house which, with its walled garden, had been the laundry of the original Palace. This was an attractive proposition and we renamed it Nicholson House as a reminder of the RSCM's founder. Dame Betty Ridley, whose husband was Rector of Finchley when I was organist at St Mary's in the late 1940s, was now a member of the RSCM Council and was of immense help to Elisabeth, as was Vincent Waterhouse, the RSCM's secretary. Between them they worked out redecorations, with Elisabeth sending me samples of wallpaper the size of a postage stamp and asking whether I would like to wake up each morning to see this or that design on the bedroom wall. Elisabeth also proved to be a most efficient secretary and general factotum in my absence, as the desk diary bore witness.

Arriving in Uganda, I once again experienced the rapid transition by jet from Europe to Africa, this time flying overnight to Entebbe and then on to Kampala, which I found very tense. Idi Amin's reign of terror was gathering momentum and one regularly heard gunfire at nights. It transpired that I would be the last Associated Board examiner to visit Uganda. My work there concluded, and with a visit to the source of the Nile included for good measure, I crossed into Kenya to examine at Kisumu on the shores of Lake Victoria, where I also adjudicated at the West Kenya Music Festival. I then moved on to Eldoret where, outside the delightfully old-fashioned hotel, was one of those blue enamelled tin signs so reminiscent of the England of my youth which said 'You may telephone from here'. Nakuru, Naivasha, and Equator railway station were all taken in, as were the stupendous scenic views at that altitude, much of it so like Scotland, before I arrived in Nairobi to stay once again in the Norfolk Hotel, a real survival of the early settlers' days, though now resplendently modernised without losing its character. I much enjoyed the famous terrace where most of Nairobi, together with planters and farmers on leave, are likely at one time or another to foregather.

Examining in Nairobi included the schools for which it was renowned in Colonial days, many now renamed, such as the Duke of York's which had become the Lenana. Limuru High School for Girls was set in scenery so reminiscent of rural Surrey or Devon: it was here that I first met Brian and Mary Russell, he the RSCM's representative for Kenya. They lived in a delightful house on her father's tea estate high among the hills and from where you looked down to the city and across to the distant mountains. Brian was organist of the attractive little stone church in the village. While in Nairobi I also adjudicated at the Kenya Music Festival.

I also examined briefly in Mombasa with wonderful vistas of Kilimanjaro on my way down to the coast, then on to Dar es

Salaam before spending a week in Malawi, the old Nyasaland, staying at Ryall's Hotel in Blantyre. On then to Rhodesia to Marandellas to examine at the schools there which included Ruzawi and Peterhouse before moving on to Bulawayo where a letter awaited me with the news of Lucian Nethsingha's appointment as my successor at Exeter. By a strange turn of coincidence, Lucian, who came from Ceylon, had some years earlier stayed at the Rectory in Slough on his arrival to study at King's College, Cambridge. He subsequently became organist of St Michael's College, Tenbury.

Arriving once again in South Africa cemented more than ever my love for this fascinating country, its scenery, people, climate and its then more stable and still peaceful way of life. How well I recall, as on later visits, being moved by the beautiful and vivid cloud formations so unique to Africa, the red soil, the dry bush and grass of summer and the sunsets which night after night gave way to the myriads of stars such as you see only in the southern hemisphere. The distinctive smell of wood fires at the roadside, with the equally distinctive and omnipresent rondavels in which so many Africans live, are for me such a nostalgic part of the scene.

I visited Johannesburg, Port Elizabeth, East London and Pietermaritzburg, and was intrigued by Grahamstown in the Eastern Cape where life, particularly on a Sunday, was reminiscent of the quietness of the England I knew as a boy in the 1930s, while in Bloemfontein and Kimberley you would hear in the small hours of the night the high-pitched whistle of steam locomotives as they shunted their loads in the goods yards.

I was in Cape Town for two months staying either in the delightfully quiet atmosphere of the City Club or with Barry Smith, the organist of the Anglican Cathedral. He and his mother lived in Oranjezicht where in the evening we would as a nightly ritual sit on the balcony, read the evening paper and revel in the view over the harbour as we drank our gin and tonic before dinner. There were periodic visits to the Mount Nelson where in those days a sumptuous six course dinner at this five star hotel cost all of 45p. Although my diary reminds me that while in Cape Town I was at dinner parties on seventeen successive nights, I much enjoyed Sunday visits to Bonteheuval on the Cape Flats where the Anglican Church drew a vast congregation and where George Schwartz, later to become Bishop of Kimberley, was the parish priest, and where Henry King presided over a large, enthusiastic and most efficient choir. I was also in Stellenbosch and stayed for the first of many times in the lovely Lanzerac Hotel which nestles among mountains so reminiscent of Austria in that beautiful wine producing part of Cape Province.

Urged on by Gerald Knight to whom I had perhaps rashly said 'use me', I found myself much in demand as Director-elect. People seemed anxious to meet the 'new boy' who was obviously something of a novelty after the many years of Gerald Knight whom they had become accustomed to. For me it was a useful bonus experience and an equally useful fact-finding mission; when not examining I made contact with bishops, clergy, choir directors and choir members, all of whom seemed anxious to tell me what they expected both of the RSCM and especially of its new management. This in its turn gave me an invaluable insight into how the RSCM operated in a vast continent where the East African countries were thwarted by currency controls and were so different from South Africa, yet shared the same basic problems and ambitions, all of which—and more—I would be confronted with in the years which lay ahead.

Returning to England I found a busy two months ahead of me, with farewells and presentations from the various organisations Elisabeth and I were involved with.

Immediately the Christmas services were over and the choristers had gone on holiday we moved out of 11 The Close. There were many wrenches in leaving a home, cathedral, city and county which had come to mean so much to us as a family during fifteen years. While I was looking forward to the new work and life, for Elisabeth it meant the end of her teaching, her involvement with the Musical Society and with the life of the cathedral. Never again would we live in the community of a cathedral Close—and Exeter was such an exceptionally happy one—nor would I be involved again in the musical life of such a virile Diocese as Exeter, and never again would I have the joy of playing for the daily round of the psalms, surely one of the most rewarding of tasks facing a cathedral organist. Even so, the RSCM was the job I had hankered after for so long and the reality of the anticipation would, I knew, stimulate me as much as the realisation of all I equally knew there was to be done.

The early years at Exeter with their various traumas now seemed so distant and well and truly exchanged for a settled life in which we had been able to build so much. I always reverted to the cathedral, its services and its influence which, after all, were the prime reasons for my being there, enticing though the liberal icing on the cake was—and how lucky I had been in having so many extra interests and concerns over those years instead of being merely cathedral organist and little else. In this, all of us involved owed so much to Tom Evans, the faithful and much loved headmaster of the Cathedral School who not only sorted out the many problems he inherited but quickly put the school on an even and successful scholastic keel. As far as my side of the work was concerned he was such an ally, probably because we each knew that our respective tasks could not be fully realised without the support of the other. I realised that if the choir was sub-standard, parents would not enter their children for voice trials, while Tom appreciated that if the academic side was not up to the mark we would not attract choristers. The fact that we both depended on each other resulted in a mutual understanding and, not least, a warm regard for each other in the process.

Tom was helpful in implementing aspects of the choristers' lives which I held to be essential—neat processing, the spoken parts of the services, kneeling properly, and an embargo on chatter in the vestry before and after services. These matters, together with an understanding of precisely what we were in the cathedral for day after day, were disciplines we jointly insisted on as part of the process of training for life and, not least, through the Christian faith. Nor did it, as far as I was concerned, stop with the choristers, for the attitude and bearing of the Lay Vicars was of equal importance, and I rejoiced at their ready willingness to go along with this.

For my part, I know that my personal religious life was deepening, and growing into an Anglo-Catholic leaning, much of this the influence of Elisabeth, and she through her father. I more and more moved into this ambience with my serving at the seven o'clock Mass each Friday morning becoming a much valued part of the process.

At this time I read, and was fascinated by, *The Later Cecils*. In it, one of the Cecils, though I cannot recall which, wrote 'As I grew up, doubts began to press on me. Nothing profound, just the general sensation that I lived in a world in which I could see and hear and touch, and that religion—belief in God and Christianity—was beyond the reach of ordinary senses. Could it be true? . . . But I will not claim that I am even now one of those fortunate people who never feel a qualm of doubt. "Lord, I believe: help Thou mine unbelief".' This seemed to mirror for me some of the reasoning which had from time to time surfaced and worried me during the Exeter years, as it continues to do.

Looking back to Exeter I realise just how hard I had to work, and willingly so, impelled on by the awareness of what needed to be done, and with new insights constantly being revealed to me. And how lucky I had been with my Deans and Chapters over those years, with whom I always sought to work happily, as they did with me. Always at hand was for me that splendid little prayer 'Lord, though we may disagree, help us not to be disagreeable'. I wonder who wrote it.

Not least in all this was our family life, even though I did not see as much of Elisabeth and children as compared with some fathers. Exeter gave the Dakers family so much, a wonderful house in a glorious Close with Devon all around us, and surrounded by so many friends. Our new life at the RSCM would never be quite the same, but we all knew this and accepted it, though Exeter was the mould which formulated so much for all of us and to which we constantly look back with affection and regard. They were certainly memorable years.

CHAPTER FIFTEEN

A totally different existence

The first eight years—1973-80. The work at Addington Palace and in the United Kingdom

On arrival at Addington Palace my immediate and salutary realisation was how different my new life was from that of living and working in a cathedral close. I swiftly found myself immersed in an entirely different way of life, thrown in at the deep end of a job which placed me at the centre of a large 18th century house which was once the home of the Archbishops of Canterbury, with some thirty or more administrative and office staff. Unlike my previous existence where I was but part of an overall team, I was now all but King of the Castle, daily surveying the scene and cogitating on all I perceived from the holy of holies—the directorial chair at the head of the lunch table. I must confess that from the outset I rather enjoyed it all.

I knew, both from what was intimated when I was interviewed by the Council, and from subsequent discussions, what was expected of me and where my priorities lay. At this initial stage and for some months to come, Addington Palace took precedence over all else, this because the College of St Nicolas, the small residential arm of the organisation, was under threat both financially and from the shortage of suitable students coming forward to take up places. So—I observed and listened. In the process I was offered plenty of advice, much of it unrealistic, however well intentioned, which was directed towards me from all and sundry. Many were intent only on preserving the *status quo* at all costs, while looking nostalgically backwards with a blinkered refusal to accept the realities of the present day. As a result, I was not always popular as I tried honestly and impartially to see some positive and productive way forward.

It soon became abundantly clear to me that much of the RSCM, and not merely the college, was insular and inward-looking, with a smugness almost amounting to self satisfaction and which was seemingly oblivious to the overall spectrum of church music. Over the years, seeking to widen the horizons and the contacts proved to be a slowish haul. But in the end it paid off, and by involving a wide cross-section of respected names in the musical world as lecturers and tutors, we gained greater credibility and certainly more recognition from individuals and bodies alike, which in the process ultimately gained us more respect in the wider echelons of music.

For the present I was faced with a college which aped Oxbridge in its wearing of academic gowns, and the holding of candlelit dinners on any pretext, while ostentatious summer garden parties, often drawing in all the wrong sort of people, seemed to me to be irrelevant superficialities, taking precedence over what the RSCM should be all about. Worse than these displays of outward show was the confirming of my suspicions that much was in fact lacking in the way of a sound academic basis. It soon transpired that a lot of the syllabus and the teaching were less than satisfactory, while at virtually every turn so much smacked again and again of living—certainly in more recent years—in a none too glorious past. All in all it was a classic head-in-the-sand situation.

Was the college sufficient to meet the challenges of educational processes then current? It was certainly far too small to be academically viable and, more to the point, it was unsound financially. This last was the crux of the matter and proved to be the ultimate determining factor.

While changes were certainly expected of me by some, these were not always relished when they happened. I therefore came in for considerable flak, much of it from people I felt should have known better.

I soon realised that the entire concept and image needed rethinking, and fairly drastically at that. Little by little I began planning to this end, though initially much proved to be a sort of patching-up process of expediency. A joint course with the London music colleges had been proposed and was partly operative before my arrival, though much of this in practice revolved around those who happened to lodge at Addington while being full-time students in London. They owed little allegiance to Addington, which was in many respects understandable. One of the most futile features of this scheme was the Mass sung with a full complement of music at 7.30 each Friday morning. Because it was so early, absenteeism, legitimate or otherwise, was rife, while the service, because it was resented, was seldom what it ideally should have been.

The future of the college was pertinent and it was crucial that changes be made, and quickly. The considerable resources of the house were grossly under-used, it having a strangely empty feel about it, and it is no understatement to say that whatever may have been achieved in the past—and in the early days the achievements had been considerable—the college now made little impact, nor did it command much respect or regard in the musical world.

In some respects my task was easier than it might otherwise have been, if only because for some time previously I had these misgivings reinforced by subsequent observations. I had dreamed dreams, as had Elisabeth, of what we felt we could do with this glorious house which had been beautifully restored and extended by Norman Shaw at the turn of the century. Within six months or so of my arrival, and having seen what I believed to be the chinks in the armour, I felt fairly confident about making recommendations to the Council. Addington Palace was not then a happy place for either students or staff, and this was an added concern for me.

While it was relatively easy to sum up the various faults and one's reasons for proposing the abandonment of the *status quo*, it was a rather different matter to come up with a viable alternative. I had long felt that the resources of Addington were ideal for short courses, both residential and non-residential, and I had a vision of creating an ecumenical education centre for church music, the more so as matters interdenominational were then very much in vogue, even if not fully realised in the event. I therefore recommended to the Council a far wider and more all-embracing range of instruction which would use the house and its facilities more effectively and usefully—and, I hoped, provide more revenue in the process.

But first there was Gerald Knight, my predecessor as Director, to contend with. I suspected it would be difficult to convince him, for much of the inception of the college and its subsequent history was his and he would therefore be likely to defend it to the full. How well I remember, while driving with him to a meeting in Brighton, unfolding with not a little trepidation, my thinking and thoughts for the future. Gerald had the reputation for being a touchy and difficult bachelor and it was much to my surprise that he not only took on board all I propounded but supported me fully in my subsequent proposals. I suspect he was in fact more fully aware of the situation and its implications than we gave him credit for.

A much more broadly based and widely respected teaching staff was needed, for few of the big names in church music would have anything to do with what they saw as the constricted, yet self-sufficient, attitudes and approach of the college and the RSCM as a whole, as they then were. Being the new boy gave me a certain initial credibility, though I had no illusions about the need for me to prove myself in the immediate rather than in the distant future. Time was only to a limited extent on my side. My other main consideration was that the college should not cater solely, as in the past, for the top end of the profession. So much of church music was now increasingly amateur, though this was by no means necessarily detrimental, nor as denigrating as some would believe.

I outlined to the Council a broadly based scheme for 'The Church and its music today', with the emphasis on the needs of today, though in 1973 this was a far less turbulent situation than twenty years later would prove to be. Newly found liturgical processes were rubbing shoulders with the rebels for or against traditional considerations, with the promotion of 'happy-clappy', DIY spontaneous music deliberately calculated in many instances to even undermine, or at best negate, any concept of a need for standards or quality.

The resulting plan was for all aspects, all needs, and all levels of ability to be catered for, amateur and, to a degree professional, alike. Liturgy, choir training, organ accompaniment, improvisation, religious drama, composing, religion and music in schools, and choral workshops, were all to be taken on board as part of the initial course structure though, as time went on, the less popular—which were presumably the less needed—aspects were abandoned for what seemed to be more relevant projects. Never failing in popularity, year in and year out, were Sir David Willcocks' annual choral workshops, my own pre-Christmas Carol Days and the yearly workshops on the Bach Passions.

I presented the new scheme to the Council early in 1974, the revamped course structure became operative in the autumn of that year, though not before we had adapted the house to the resultant changing needs. Three or four students had previously shared the larger bedrooms which we partitioned and furnished as single unit entities complete with all the necessary amenities.

In all my thinking and planning I never failed then, as throughout my years at Addington, to be grateful for the wisdom of Vincent Waterhouse, the RSCM's Secretary and Chief Administrative Officer. We worked very much as a duo, while his being an organist meant we both spoke the same language. Even so, there were inevitable occasions when he told me quite firmly that the funding I wanted in order to promote a project was not possible, but his advice and his encouragement overall were a great source of support to me over the years in the various projects I set my hand to, as was his friendship.

Elisabeth had by this time become Housekeeper, so we were now again working in tandem, though in a somewhat different way from Exeter. She was full of ideas and rearing to go, for she was now very much under-employed and had been marking time since we left Exeter. For a start she organised ecclesiastical embroidery and, to a lesser degree, flower-arranging courses, with the former developing into regular weekend residential events which over the years would result in new altar frontals, vestments and kneelers to beautify the chapel at Addington and elsewhere.

From the outset, in order to use the plant to the full, we encouraged what we termed 'outside bookings' in the shape of bodies connected either with the Church or education, to use

Addington for their residential conferences. Over the years this was to develop significantly with many of the Church of England's General Synod committees coming to us on what transpired to be a long-term continuous basis. Our own courses also attracted considerable laudatory press coverage, which helped the cause. This was especially true of the bigger one-off events such as the Flower Festival Elisabeth organised as part of the RSCM Golden Jubilee celebrations in 1977, when she spent well over a day at London's Heathrow Airport collecting the many exotic blooms which had been sent to us by members from all over the world.

As many of the students under the old dispensation came from overseas I saw the need to make provision for, and even widen, opportunities in this particular area. So, in the first year of the new scheme we included a nine-week summer course exclusively for overseas students. This provided for a three-week gap in the middle for visits to music festivals or for the students to get to know England or Europe. The course subsequently became a six-week 'crash' event which proved very popular and was invariably over-subscribed. Part of the programming was for well known visiting tutors to work and live with the students for a week at a time. This gave those attending the course the opportunity to get to know such people, as did our guest nights each week, with a speaker informally talking in the Common Room after dinner to those present. Many of these speakers, such as the Archbishop of Canterbury, the Speaker of the House of Commons, and Richard Baker, the television personality, were not necessarily musicians, though a regular visitor for many years was Herbert Howells who never failed to delight the Americans with his reminiscences of Three Choirs Festivals, Elgar and Vaughan Williams.

'Come and Meet' days were similar favourites, with Sir David Willcocks, Sir Charles Groves and John Rutter among those directing choral classes and introducing the students and others to major choral works. These summer courses included visiting the Southern Cathedrals Festival (Chichester, Winchester and Salisbury annually in turn) and staying in the host city for the entire event; also a weekly outing to cathedral cities such as

Oxford, Cambridge, Canterbury and Guildford. Whenever we visited Cambridge I rejoiced in hearing the comments of those entering King's College Chapel for the first time. It was almost as if they had arrived at Valhalla.

By this time we had seven organs at Addington, these being additional practice incentives to organ students. The small and extremely versatile mobile instrument I had asked Peter Collins to build became a never-failing favourite for recitals in the Great Hall by players such as Gillian Weir, Francis Jackson and Peter Hurford.

The short courses generally caught on and in doing so proved the need for the kind of help they offered. In the early stages we learned much by trial and frequently by error as to what was needed and what was merely peripheral, though perhaps desirable. I was especially encouraged by the involvement of those who had previously had little or nothing to do with the RSCM and who would now come to lecture when invited.

Careers were an important factor so we put on events to help those preparing for the Associateship and Fellowship diplomas of the Royal College of Organists, also those intending to apply for choral and organ scholarships at universities. David Willcocks was a regular part of these occasions and was extremely adept at helping these young people with guidance on interview techniques. We also engaged well-known singing teachers such as Marjorie Thomas and John Carol Case to help singers.

The needs of country organists and choir directors were also specially catered for, with one-day events ranging from psalmody and hymnody to ordinands and plainchant. Everything we did was intended not only to provide for all needs but also to emphasise the rightful place of music in worship. Furthermore, we dealt with the worsening relationships emerging between the clergy and their musicians, the courses having something of a psychological basis in underlining the human weaknesses and failings in all of us, with suggestions as to how these might be overcome.

Weekends for bell-ringers were also popular, though nothing caught on so much and so consistently as Janette Cooper's genius for converting pianists into organists. Her encouragement and patience resulted in many people feeling able to play in country churches and so provide music when otherwise there might not be any. Later, when Janette became Warden of Addington and responsible for the administration of the courses there, she was able to extend this work. As I went round the country I would frequently meet people who would proudly tell me 'I'm one of your "reluctant" organists'.

With my interest in design and typography, I much enjoyed devising course brochures and seeing them through the press. We issued four course brochures each year, containing information on around seventy events. An attractive house design was essential and I experimented with different colours, though on one occasion the orange ink I chose proved in the event to be well nigh illegible and resulted in a small response of takers, so here I really did learn by trial and error.

At the same time, although so much emphasis needed to be laid on the work at Addington, I was fully aware of the need for rethinking and revitalising the work in the country as a whole, much of which was either tired or moving along in a half-hearted way. We relied very heavily on people at local level initiating and administering our affairs in these areas. Some of the regional committees were effective, others less so, while in some instances virtually nothing happened. The membership had every right to expect a measure of specifically local return for their subscription, such as choral festivals, workshops and other events relevant to local needs. I therefore embarked on a nationwide reorganisation process, aimed at getting the right people as chairman and secretary to head an area committee. As each area was usually synonymous with an Anglican Diocese, our work had in many instances been overseen by the cathedral organist, with varying degrees of success or otherwise, this for a variety of reasons.

I saw reorganisation firstly as an opportunity for getting rid of dead wood and bringing in as chairmen those with business skills who had a real interest in and concern for the Church and its music. All sorts of people emerged, from solicitors, dentists, deans and bishops, to chartered accountants and the recently retired Secretary of the British Council. Not all were Anglicans, and this was no bad thing when, in an ecumenical age, so many still believed the RSCM to be an exclusively Church of England organisation, which it had ceased to be in 1945. One prospective chairman in inviting me to his London club, wrote 'Please arrive at 12.45 when I shall detain you for lunch', a quaint and certainly original turn of phrase which I felt could augur well for the future—which it did.

As a general help towards the additional need for binding together neighbouring areas, I arranged and conducted two series of regional choral festivals, the first taking place between 1974 and 1976 at Bath Abbey, York Minster, and Liverpool, Guildford, Coventry and Ely Cathedrals. The second group took place four years later in the cathedrals at Durham, Bristol, Manchester, Southwark, Peterborough and Worcester. These were sandwiched between the Golden and Diamond Jubilees of the RSCM, which in their turn were highlighted by festivals in London's Royal Albert Hall. Both sold out well in advance which meant over six thousand people attended in addition to the choirs taking part. For the 1977 Festival people even placed requests for tickets in the Personal Column of *The Times*, side by side with similar needs for Wimbledon. For this festival we invited 750 singers to take part, and I travelled around the country taking seventeen sectional rehearsals in the month before the event. Canon Joseph Poole, the liturgical expert and Precentor of Coventry Cathedral, devised a splendidly grand service in which we used the first orchestra from the Royal College of Music.

I commissioned works from Peter Aston and Arthur Wills, who set T. S. Eliot's moving text *O light invisible* with its lovely phrase, 'our gaze is submarine'. The Archbishop of Westminster and the Moderator of the Free Church Council both took part in the service, thus emphasising the growing ecumenical stance of the RSCM. The occasion was tele-recorded by the BBC for Songs of Praise, while Abbey Records brought out a long-playing disc of the musical highlights. Queen Elizabeth, the Queen Mother, was present as our Patron and afterwards wrote to say this was something she 'will always remember with feelings of gratitude and happiness'.

John Barrow, the assistant secretary of the RSCM, was painstaking in being responsible for the organisation of these big festivals. He planned the regional rehearsals down to the last detail, as he did the arrangements on the day itself when, with his posse of helpers, he assembled and marshalled the hordes of singers in the bowels of a building hardly equipped to deal with so many performers.

In marked contrast, I conducted, also in 1977, a small scale festival of village choirs at Childe Okeford, a church in rural Dorset which in 1927 was the first ever to be affiliated to the then School of English Church Music. As we solemnly processed through the village from the school hall to the church, a local farmer was driving his cows past us in the opposite direction. He greeted us in a delightfully broad Dorset way, a rural touch which forcibly served to remind me of the RSCM's humble beginnings and how it had developed over the years, though always with much emphasis on the village church and its musicians.

There was also a garden party at Addington that summer. Two dinners were held, one in York for the North of England, while the Southern one was held in London at the Connaught Rooms, the Archbishops of Canterbury and York being the main speakers. The year also saw many locally arranged events up and down the country. The BBC made a documentary radio programme about the RSCM, while Elisabeth and I were invited to dinner at Lambeth Palace. The year ended with a special Evensong in Westminster Abbey. This took place on 6 December, the day on which the RSCM had been founded fifty years previously in Jerusalem Chamber.

1977 also saw the launching of the pointed, or singing, version of the Alternative Service Book Psalter which Cyril Taylor, Roy Massey and I had been responsible for. Collins, who published this, sent me round the country to promote the new book. That autumn I recorded for the BBC World Service nine *Reflections*, each lasting five minutes and based on music which had some special significance for me. As the spoken part of each broadcast was limited to one minute, I learned the virtues of getting my message across with brevity, in which I was greatly helped by a first-rate producer. There was also an exciting festival in Arundel Cathedral for Roman Catholic choirs; here I first experienced the Roman Catholic *animateur*, a *basso profundo* whose improvised singing at crucial points in the Ordinary of the Mass was taken up and copied by the choirs and congregation.

During these early years at the RSCM many matters were to claim my attention both at Addington Palace and in the field, as we termed the nationwide work. The publishing operation had always been an important feature, uniquely catering for the specialised needs of the average, or less than average, choir, as well as for the equally relevant needs of the choir with depleted forces, which comprised one of the main areas of membership. These publications were a useful teaching aid in their own right in that they provided material with a degree of difficulty by no means demanding yet challenging, and rewarding in its musical interest. So great was the need for this that it became one of the largest single aspects of the RSCM's work and generated a sizeable income, the profits from which were ploughed back into providing the best possible service for our members. Even so, it was quite obvious that the catalogue was too narrow in concept, too monochrome, and unashamedly Anglican; nor did it reflect the needs generated by changing worship patterns and the resulting demand for material consequently needed in each and every situation.

I came up against quite a lot of resistance to change from within, the apparent security, even satisfaction, with the known seeming to me to be strangely unambitious, the more so as much of the RSCM publications catalogue contained such dull and pedestrian works. But gradually during those early years I managed to widen the scope of our publishing ventures, though some items inevitably sold less well than others. Once again we learned by trial and error. The service we provided included stocking many of the works from other publishing houses for resale to our members. This was all but entirely mail order, and through it we built up a reputation, especially among our overseas members, for a speedy despatch service.

As time went on, I recruited a number of composers who had the knack of writing simple music which was full of interest, which was what so many choirs needed, and which helped them to widen their expertise as well as their repertoire. Peter Aston, Martin How, Richard Shephard and Harrison Oxley were but four of those who became something akin to house composers and whose work continues to enhance and widen the range of the catalogue.

Church Music Quarterly, the house magazine published specifically for RSCM members was, and is, in many respects the RSCM's ongoing link with its world-wide membership. This, by its very nature, tried to be all things to all people and as such did not always fully succeed. Director's notes, articles, teaching hints, promoting publications, salaries, working conditions and clergy/organist relationships were all pertinent matters regularly and rigorously claiming our attention. I edited an annual collection of essays called *The World of Church Music*, a rather more scholarly publication which aimed to take into critical account a wide range of subject matter either directly or indirectly connected with church music. For this we enlisted specialist scholars and writers as contributors for each topic.

As time went on I was out and about a great deal: the membership needed contact with the centre and I strongly felt the need to meet as many people as possible. Although the demands on my time grew more considerable I somehow managed to slot in most things such as, for example, being in Scotland one Saturday evening to conduct a choirs festival in Perth, then travelling overnight on the train to London so as to be at Bishops Stortford to preach at a service in the parish church on the Sunday morning.

Although much of the work was inevitably routine, it was never dull and was from time to time relieved by one-off events, many of them proving to be memorable, such as the first of a number of choir festivals I was to direct in King's College Chapel, Cambridge. I found this a wonderfully inspiring building to work in, as it surely was for the choirs taking part, many of which came from village churches in the Ely Diocese. There were also the initial festivals, and very memorable ones too, in St Paul's Cathedral and Westminster Cathedral, and I took great pleasure too in going back after many years to Rochester

Cathedral and St George's Chapel, Windsor Castle, to conduct massed church choirs. No less rewarding were Saturdays, virtually every one of which, apart from the holiday periods, became more and more earmarked for the conducting of Diocesan Choral Festivals. By the time I retired I had directed such events in nearly every cathedral and major parish church in the land, and sometimes on more than one occasion.

I quickly learned not only how to adapt to the individual acoustical and other problems which most cathedrals present but, more importantly, how to encourage choirs, many of them small, often incomplete, and perhaps from a small country church, to give of their best as part of a larger group performing in a very different and invariably inspiring environment. Time and again they would rise to the challenge in quickly adapting to unfamiliar surroundings and produce exciting and frequently memorable sounds as a result.

'Meet, Eat and Sing' evenings emerged during these years as popular occasions for meeting choirs informally over a buffet meal and then leading them through the singing of some new or recently published RSCM works. Elisabeth often accompanied the choirs and sold publications, and with encouragingly lucrative results. Martin How, who was seldom lost for a word, christened these events 'Slurp, burp and chirp'.

We also forged links with the Army, with some of their highly disciplined and gifted musicians coming regularly to us from Kneller Hall, the Army's School of Music at Twickenham. We put on special courses for them, from which we on the staff also learned much.

Each summer we promoted Cathedral Courses in which forty or more boys and young men would sing the services for two weeks at a cathedral, in place of the regular choir. When Rediffusion, and then BET, sponsored the Choirboy of the Year competition, we would take their directors to the cathedrals concerned for them to hear these course choirs which they supported financially. One such course took place each summer at Canterbury, where Canon Derek Ingram Hill would take us into the cathedral to experience the extraordinary ambience and beauty thrown up by the flood-lighting in an otherwise darkened and empty building. These were always memorable evenings for all concerned, not least when we were told to lie down on the steps under the great Bell Harry tower and look up at the unforgettable sight of the vaulting high above us, and floodlit from the outside.

My predecessor, Gerald Knight, died in September 1979 only a year after retirement. He expressed a wish to be buried at St Michael's College, Tenbury, and the night before his funeral I was staying at The Athenaeum. As I had been delegated to convey his ashes to Tenbury, his remains rather aptly spent their last night above earth in my bedroom, in a building he so loved and habitually inhabited.

There were increasing comings and goings at Addington, not only of individuals but of organisations such as the American Association of Anglican Musicians whose members, roughly akin to the English Cathedral Organists' Association, spent a week with us during the summer of 1978, with their annual conference including visits to a number of cathedrals. Later on I much enjoyed similarly planning a study programme for Westminster Choir College in Princeton, New Jersey, which in many respects is the American counterpart of the RSCM. BBC Television came to us for the New Year's Eve Watchnight Service in the Great Hall, with Donald Coggan, then Archbishop of Canterbury, giving the address. The BBC also used the Great Hall for 'Seeing and Believing', at that time a popular weekly religious documentary. Erik Routley, Cyril Taylor and I took part in one of these when music in worship was the focus, a subject at that time grossly overworked by the media. Like so many such discussion programmes this proved to be as unsatisfactory and inconclusive for those of us involved as it probably was for viewers.

A number of services were broadcast from the Chapel at Addington, while for some years I presented a Christmas Sunday Half Hour on the BBC, using material I had found on my overseas visits. Africa and the Southern Pacific were especially fruitful in this respect, with one year an intriguing carol from the Solomon Islands which included the jaunty refrain 'Black man, white man, he love God' sung in delightful pidgin English.

There were also the inevitable radio interviews, nationally and locally, on various topical issues as and when they arose. On my overseas visits, these would come up without fail, with local radio stations in countries such as New Zealand using farmers or businessmen who had a refreshingly natural and easy approach which, as with all good interviewers, drew out the best from the person being interviewed.

While at Exeter I had greatly enjoyed being part of television services and programmes but later felt much less at home in this medium than in sound broadcasting, something I am sure producers realised, for the television invitations latterly became fewer. In the Exeter days television was not the sophisticated, high-powered and searchingly demanding force it was later to become and which in its turn was to make me feel less than relaxed when on the receiving end of the cameras.

More and more I seemed to be asked to do an ever widening range and variety of things, whether directly or indirectly concerned with the RSCM. These I much valued for they helped to broaden my overall perspective—and my knowledge—especially the regular visits to clergy and to most of the theological colleges, to which I gave a high priority. The influence of Bishop John Robinson's *Honest to God*, a book which in the 1960s put the cat well and truly among the pigeons, seemed especially to influence the rationale of many of the colleges and, in terms of church music, to downgrade it as peripheral and therefore of no great import. Also, as our new liturgies emerged, with a rightful prominence given to congregational participation, many clergy and ordinands concluded that there was now no place for traditional music and that a robed choir was *per se* élitist, and consequently ripe for redundancy. Choruses and guitar groups took off in a big way and were imposed willy nilly on many a congregation.

In my dealings with all concerned I sought to stress that music is an inescapable and integral part of most worship, and that although ordinands were not expected to be musicians, nevertheless the role and expectation generated by music was part of their ministry and responsibility; that it could enrich worship just as much in its own right as badly prepared and badly presented music detracts from worship, and in the ultimate can even destroy it. Such is its power. This was particularly true of some of the new look approaches in church music where unrehearsed and casual attitudes were, and still are, in many instances, promoted as the order of the day.

Consequently, during much of my time at the RSCM, I was continually at pains to 'preach' that while church music may now have many faces, what works in one situation might well be entirely out of place in another. This was not always easy to get across, for inflexibility was then as rigid a part of many a church scene as now, though within a few years the tables had in many instances turned in no small way, with unstructured free-for-all services frequently resulting in disastrous consequences. The visits to the theological colleges were therefore doubly important, especially in meeting and talking with angry young men (and some not so young) who vowed when ordained to revolutionise any parish they were sent to serve. The sad part was that such people concluded that the RSCM—and I—were stuffy, outdated, and conservative *in excelsis*. While none of this was necessarily true, some absented themselves from my lectures and so denied themselves, and me, what could have been a lively exchange of views.

Other interesting departures, some of which were to become annual events, included my taking part in the 'Come and Sing' series in Westminster Abbey, which dealt with various aspects of hymnody, another rapidly changing scene. In 1975, Rediffusion, as I mentioned earlier, launched 'The Choirboy of the Year' competition, to which they gave much prominence through extensive media coverage. As it was directed to the parish and not the cathedral scene, it did much at a particularly vulnerable time to encourage the boy, and later the girl, chorister movement. This annual competition went on for some years in conjunction with the RSCM. Sir David Willcocks and I were the two permanent adjudicators and we were joined each year by someone not directly associated with church music, such as Sir Charles Groves, Richard Baker, Evelyn Barbirolli, Donald Swann or Ian Wallace.

While I was at Exeter I succeeded Gerald Knight as Secretary of the Cathedral Organists' Association and was responsible for arranging two conferences each year. The work at one period entailed taking part in discussions with the Labour Party over the future of the choir schools, which they at that time proposed to penalise and eventually destroy together with the rest of the independent sector when they came to power. The happier situation now prevailing is due in some measure to those discussions, difficult and frustrating though they were. Even so, I would not by any means suggest that we are completely out of that particular wood. Because these matters greatly affected Deans and Chapters, a permanent working party was set up, consisting of Deans, Provosts and Cathedral Organists. This has resulted in a better understanding and liaison between bodies previously inclined to work in isolation, though not always intentionally. The situation has been further improved through the Choir Schools' Association now having a permanent seat on this committee.

For three years I was President of the Incorporated Association of Organists. My first annual conference had been planned to take place in Exeter before I knew we should be moving, so we went back in the summer of 1973 for the usual round of conference fare, which for this occasion included John Rutter writing for me his lively anthem *O clap your hands*. A sizeable part of the IAO commitment entailed my visiting organists up and down the country for talks and dinners, something which has gone on even into retirement, and with mixed fortunes, for some were less organised and certainly less interesting occasions than others.

Soon after I arrived at Addington I was invited to become one of the five-man Board of Directors of *Hymns Ancient and Modern*. This meant that I became one of the editors of *More Hymns for Today* and more recently of our latest supplement, *Worship Songs Ancient and Modern*. The A and M commitment has been a widening one in extending my interests towards hymnody.

For some time I was a member of the Council of the Musicians' Benevolent Fund, an important part of their work highlighted each November in the St Cecilia Festival and the Royal Concert. When Sir Edward Heath opened the Ivor Newton House in Bromley, one of the Fund's homes for retired musicians, we were given a delightful mini-recital by a trio of octogenarians—a performance of Bach's *My heart ever faithful* by Isobel Baillie, Leon Goossens and Ivor Newton.

While at Exeter I was elected to the Council of the Royal College of Organists and in 1976 became President for two years, another role I much enjoyed. These various offices resulted in some attractive invitations to such events as Livery Dinners of the Musicians' Company, the Goldsmiths' Company, the Parish Clerks' Company, and on a number of occasions to the Madrigal Club where, after a splendid dinner in the Tallow Chandlers' Hall, madrigals were sung while the port was passed round as a suitable lubricant—and an invaluable aid to finding one's notes. For Elisabeth, the sad thing about so many of these occasions was that they were for men only. My regaling her with what we had eaten and drunk on these occasions would be countered by a terse comment such as 'and all I had was scrambled egg on my own in the kitchen'.

CHAPTER SIXTEEN

The joys of globe-trotting

My Initial Visits

During the first three or four years visits abroad were occasional, certainly as compared with later on. I needed, as I hinted earlier, to concentrate firstly on the work at Addington and in Britain generally. These were immediate priorities. In any event, my predecessor, Gerald Knight, was now Overseas Commissioner for the RSCM and would be a member of my staff for five years. He lived very much out of his suitcase and became an almost perpetual Thomas Cook peripatetic.

Even so, not a few opportunities for travel came my way, and for various reasons, not the least being that people overseas seemed to want to make contact with the new Director. I soon found that an initial invitation would become the starting point for a longer tour and trigger off my planning all sorts of things around it. In my enthusiasm to take in as many ports of call and contacts as possible, I found I would tend to fill up every moment of virtually every day and leave no spaces to relax or to do at least some sightseeing. As time went on, and when I knew I would be taking in some especially interesting places, I learned to keep more free time available and, in the process, recharge my batteries, a *modus vivendi* which paid dividends. I am lucky in that I find air travel relaxing and am not usually much affected by jet lag.

The first tour of this nature was the forerunner of a number I would make to the British Army of the Rhine where I met both chaplains and choirs. During my first year at Addington I directed the annual United States Summer Course which on that occasion took place at Lawrenceville near Princeton in New Jersey. The weather was typical of the eastern seaboard in its steamy midsummer humidity which, for the boy choristers taking part, was more conducive to sport and swimming than singing. Elisabeth joined me for this, after which we visited New York as guests of Lee Hastings Bristol, a wealthy devotee of the RSCM who arranged a number of delights for us which included seats for *A Little Night Music*, the then current Broadway spectacular.

At the end of the following year I ventured on my first round the world tour, planning out for myself as comprehensive a programme as possible. I began in East Africa taking in Nairobi, Blantyre, and Salisbury as it then was. Much of this retraced the Associated Board tour of 1972. I also saw the Victoria Falls once again, this never failing to be an awesome spectacle in its sheer immensity and in its thunderous noise. The breakfast flight from Salisbury by Viscount, one of those sturdy pre-jet aircraft, was followed by a drive through the bush and then a cruise on the Zambesi. I was intrigued to see the still extant, though long since disused, Imperial Airways jetty where the flying boats would tie up overnight on their way from London to Cape Town so that passengers could see the Falls and spend the night at the Victoria Falls Hotel.

I was in Bulawayo at the turn of the year staying with Allan Shaw, the Dean of the Anglican Cathedral. His elegantly furnished home was so unexpectedly English in so strangely unreal a setting and his hospitality was sumptuous. I recall the dinner on New Year's Eve and our seeing in the New Year to the accompaniment of steam locomotive whistles, a nostalgic harking back to boyhood days.

I moved on to Johannesburg and then to Sydney and Melbourne before going to Tasmania for the RSCM Australian Summer School, taking place that year in Launceston. This was the initial reason for this extended tour, which on the way home took in Hong Kong, where in the New Territories I visited the Gurkhas at the request of the Army Chaplains' Department. This concluded a tour of 34,000 miles in just under a month, something which gave me a useful insight into church music in widely contrasted situations. It also whetted my appetite for even more travel which over the next few years would be fulfilled in a variety of ways.

Soon after this I was in the Netherlands for the first of a number of choir weekends at the English and American Church in The Hague, later visiting SHAPE, the headquarters of the European Forces near Mons. I was also in Berlin, again for the Army, travelling from Hanover on the splendidly appointed military train where I ranked as an officer and was wined and dined in considerable style. Less alluring was the entry into the Russian sector with the train and its occupants ruthlessly examined by the Russian military complete with guard dogs. That year also saw the first of a number of visits to conduct the combined choirs of the chaplaincies of the English Churches in North Europe, this particular festival taking place in the pro-cathedral in Brussels.

In the summer of that year, 1976, I was in Washington to attend the conference of the Association of Anglican Musicians. As with so many things American, this was organised on lavish lines and included visiting the White House, with dinner at the British Embassy, the splendid Lutyens house in Massachusetts Avenue. I went on to preach at the Cathedral of St John the Divine, New York, on the occasion of the 50th anniversary of the inception of their musical foundation, before going down to the deep south for a couple of days work in Nashville, Tennessee.

Two months later I again crossed the Atlantic, this time to oversee the Toronto Diocesan Choir School at Port Hope, after which I was in Ottawa as the guest of Sir William McKie, my organ tutor at the Royal Academy of Music. He had by then retired as organist of Westminster Abbey and was living in a beautiful apartment in the city, this previously staunch bachelor having surprised us all by recently acquiring a wife. I was also with church choirs in Montreal and was driven on to Quebec where I spent a night in the legendary Chateau Frontenac Hotel.

At the end of 1976 Elisabeth joined me for a lengthy visit to South Africa, triggered off by my being asked to direct the summer school taking place that year in Grahamstown, the attractive old world university city in the Eastern Cape. After a start which included three frustrated attempts by our aircraft to leave Heathrow, (though on the second try we did at least get as far as Zurich where snow further delayed us), we eventually arrived in Johannesburg twenty-six hours late. But, as always, it was such a joy to be transported in the matter of hours from a dark and damp December England to the brilliance and warmth of a South African summer, a carrot I invariably dangled in front of prospective takers when inviting them to be in charge of this particular course, which was hosted in turn by each of the five RSCM Branch committees in South Africa.

The course ended after our duly celebrating the Epiphany, and not least in music. We hired a Volkswagen Beetle from the delightfully named Tom Tit's Travel Agency and drove down the Natal coast to Wilderness, then up to Oudtshorn before negotiating the Swartberg Pass, much of which was then unmade road. Coming down the other side of the mountains was, if any-thing, more hair-raising than the ascent, but we were rewarded with magnificent views such as South Africa so uniquely offers. Driving on through the Great Karroo we stayed at the Lord Milner Hotel in Matjiesfontein, the entire 19th century village being the latest acquisition of the Rawdon brothers, and which they had restored as tastefully and elegantly as they had the Lanzerac at Stellenbosch, the attractive 17th century Dutch farmstead nestling beneath the mountains near Cape Town.

In Cape Town I shared with Elisabeth pleasures I knew of old, such as visiting the church at Bonteheuval on the Cape Flats, the Cape of Good Hope, Clarke's bookshop in Long Street and the delights of dining at the Mount Nelson Hotel. Our many friends in and around Cape Town were as generous as always in their hospitality before we set out on the Blue Train to Johannesburg, a journey which proved a remarkable combination of gracious living with endlessly wonderful scenery to con-template as we climbed through the Hext River Valley and into the Great Karroo.

The following March I was particularly sorry not to be in London for the Benjamin Britten memorial service in Westminster Abbey, but this coincided with the first of several visits I was to make to Redlands, a Methodist University some ninety miles inland from Los Angeles. The sizeable and certainly high-powered church music department was under the efficient directorship of Jeff Rickard, a discerning choral director. Apart from music making with an enviably high standard of expertise and performance, this visit was memorable for me in two respects, my initial experience of a doggy bag, and being taken by the students for breakfast high up in the snow capped mountains of Southern California. After an early morning drive in what were distinctly fresh conditions, a large and hot American-style breakfast went down very well.

I then flew up the west coast to San Francisco and Vancouver before travelling on the Canadian Pacific train which then went through the Rockies and alternated magnificent scenic views with tunnels of amazing engineering complexity.

For the remainder of 1977 I was preoccupied with arrangements for the celebrations being planned to celebrate the RSCM's Golden Jubilee, and I would not be able to be abroad again for any length of time until the summer of the following year when I would once more be in Toronto for the church music conference arranged by the local RSCM branch, at which Francis Jackson, Erik Routley and Martin How joined me. Immediately this had ended I was on my way to Africa once again but, because there was no route other than via London, I travelled the best part of 10,000 miles in thirty-six hours. On this occasion I was to be in South Africa for five weeks consolidating and seeing forward work and projects initiated on previous visits, for I had soon discovered how essential it was to do just this in all the overseas work, while additionally encouraging other projects and initiatives at local level had of necessity to be done by our local representatives.

On this tour I made a point of including as many centres as possible, such as Pretoria, Kimberley, Bloemfontein, Durban and Cape Town, even to the extent of flying in a four-seater aircraft to Newcastle where there was a keen, if smallish and flourishing, cell of activity. I also took in Port Elizabeth and East London, the east coast always being an attractive proposition in itself. This I did in company with Kenneth Oram, the Bishop of Grahamstown, who was the hard-working and supportive Chairman of the RSCM Eastern Cape Branch. It was on this occasion that I was castigated by a group of charismatic clergy who without compunction told me that if I had not been renewed in the Holy Spirit then I was a second-class Christian. I was so incensed by this arrogant attitude, typical of many 'born again Christians', that I commented on this in the RSCM magazine. This led to my being denounced by Bill Burnett, the charismatic Archbishop of Cape Town, as being unsympathetic to renewal movements within the Church. While this was not in any way true, I did—and still do—find the hardline intolerance of some clergy and laity the world over hard to accept, not least their automatic 'we are right and you are wrong' approach.

I also took the opportunity to include Salisbury and Nairobi in my itinerary once again. The trip ended with a short visit to the British Army of the Rhine at Rheindahlen thrown in for good measure on my way home. While there I visited, and observed with some envy, the West German conservatoire of church music at Herford, one of five such establishments funded by the state government, with resources which made the mind boggle when compared with what the RSCM had at its disposal.

Early in 1979 I was once again in the United States, going first to the elegant city of Charleston in South Carolina with its wealth of beautiful houses—and bookshops. In the summer I represented both the Royal College of Organists and the RSCM at the Royal Canadian College of Organists' Convention in Edmonton, a thoroughly enjoyable occasion which included a trip to Banff and the Rockies. November saw me in Washington DC, together with Allan Wicks and Alec Wyton, for 'Church music Yesterday, Today—and—Tomorrow?' a conference held at the College of Preachers. That month I was again in the BAOR, centred on Frankfurt, with the Chaplains' Annual Dinner an occasion not to be missed.

In June 1980, Vincent Waterhouse, the RSCM's Chief Administrative Officer, joined me in the USA for discussions pertinent to the setting up of an American office and base. This included our being in South Carolina where, at Raleigh Durham, Donald Hinshaw's sizeable publishing company was situated. He was later to enter into a publishing and retailing partnership with the RSCM. On this occasion we also visited Princeton, New Jersey, another RSCM stronghold.

175

I was now beginning to be away from Addington, either in Britain or overseas, almost as much as I was at home. Hardly back from the United States, I embarked on another round-the-world tour, not in 80 days but near enough to it in 63 days. This worked out as a fairly balanced combination of work and pleasure, the latter made the more enjoyable as Elisabeth came with me. We flew direct to Hong Kong where the small RSCM membership was anxious to keep in contact and gain help. We were also lavishly entertained by Rediffusion whose tentacles extended worldwide and in a way far removed from the original 'Choirboy of the Year' contacts created in London. We went on to Penang, mainly for a holiday, and stayed there at the E and O, the Eastern and Oriental Hotel beloved by Somerset Maugham, where our bathroom was considerably larger than the sizeable bedroom. The hotel still breathed the aura of empire, with its gracious, if now slightly faded decor. There followed a short stay in Singapore, where the demolition of attractive Malay buildings and the erection of huge skyscraper blocks was rapidly depriving the city of its character and making it a carbon copy of any modern city anywhere.

In Western Australia I directed the RSCM National School in Perth, a most happy and musically productive week centred on Guildford Grammar School with its elegant and spacious chapel. The course, then far less sophisticated or up-market—and less anti-English orientated than some of the later occasions in the east of Australia—was one of the best and most rewarding ever, made so by the keen and efficient musicians I worked with. In Sydney we stayed with Elisabeth's brother before going on to New Zealand where, in the company of Nigel Werry, the RSCM's resident secretary, we spent a week or so touring much of the South Island. Here, at virtually every turn, we revelled in the ever-changing and varying scenery for which New Zealand is justly renowned. This included a hair-raising drive through Skipper's Canyon, which in retrospect seemed far less frightening than the reality of narrow and precipitous tracks high above valleys some thousands of feet below, and made less than reassuring by the speed at which our driver negotiated some of the narrow bends perched above yawning chasms. Dunedin, where for some days we were marooned in the vicarage at Mosgiel by sudden floods, gave way to Christchurch, and then Auckland, with yet another summer school to be responsible for.

We later spent some days' holiday in Fiji before a stop-over in San Francisco on our way home. The *Church Times* wrote up this tour under what I felt was a none too complimentary headline, calling me 'Church music's Dr Kissinger'.

In August I was in the Southern United States for the Mississippi Diocesan Conference on church music and liturgy. By flying me out first class the organisers were perhaps sugaring the pill as a preparation for the appalling humidity which particularly afflicts that part of the States in summer. In the event it proved to be a rewarding occasion, particularly as I was working with James Litton, one of the best—and nicest—of all church musicians I know. He and I, together with David Hurd, seemed to make a good trio, with our teamwork hopefully reflecting on those attending the course.

I then went on to Dallas, San Francisco, Vancouver, and Victoria, flying over that particularly spectacular part of the United States which includes the Grand Canyon, the Colorado river and the Hoover Dam, all of which we saw to advantage 35,000 feet below. On that flight I asked the stewardess, in my best American, for a tom-ay-to juice, to which she responded 'You mean tom-ar-to juice. I'm also English'.

In the autumn, Vincent Waterhouse, Monty Durston, the vice-chairman of the RSCM, and I were in Washington tying up loose ends from previous administrative visits, although the American lawyers conjured up all sorts of snags and demands before finalising the not-for-profit corporation status of the RSCM in America, which would lead on to our opening an American office and appointing an American co-ordinator. At the end of a hectic two days of meetings we must have looked tired as we checked in at Kennedy Airport, for we were immediately upgraded to first class and revived ourselves on the splendid dinner and all that went with it. Unfortunately, Laker, on whose airline we were flying, went into liquidation a few weeks later, though we hoped his generosity to us was not the cause of this.

In so many of the countries I visited there were such spectacular mountain backcloths—the Canadian and American Rockies, the South Island of New Zealand and the magical, almost mysterious, ranges of East Africa. Every time I saw Kilimanjaro it seemed more beautiful, though nothing could ever rival for me the grandeur and sheer immensity of the Himalayan panorama. Then there were the islands of the Southern Pacific, their unique brilliance, dazzling silver sand, the extraordinary clearness of the amazingly blue sea, the reef with the life and colour it revealed. There was always the wonder of sunrise, with never the same cloud formations two days running, especially when you are flying more than six miles above the earth, or the vivid red of sunset which is so much a feature of India. These, and many other memories of such beauty will for ever linger on in the mind, and were as rich in their anticipation as they were in their actuality. All I can say is that I have been fortunate in being able to witness such things and to become more and more increasingly aware of so much beauty in a world which humanity in its headlong urge for progress and, not least in its greed for gain, is doing its best to retard or even destroy, and not always unwittingly.

CHAPTER SEVENTEEN

Gaining momentum

1981-1989

This was to be a period of forwarding and expanding projects I had initiated in the earlier years and which had taken root. Mercifully, the last years never degenerated into a running-down process, certainly not in my own attitudes or in the workload which, if anything, became more and more demanding right through to the end. Living 'over the shop', as I had previously done as a cathedral organist, meant that I was in and out of the office at all hours, frequently starting the day at 7.30 and getting a lot of work done before the mail arrived and the phone began ringing. The same obtained at the end of the day and I often worked on undisturbed until well past midnight. But I thrived on being occupied, and even felt I was at my best when under pressure. Elisabeth was equally busy with her many house-keeping tasks, not least in acquiring skills in managing the bar, while often being responsible for the not inconsiderable task in so large a house of locking up the Palace and turning out lights late at night. Above all there was for both of us the involvement with people, and our interest in them as such.

Saturdays, when the offices were closed, were invariably taken up with travelling, often considerable distances, to conduct choir festivals. Whenever I could I tried to get home the same night, for Sunday travel by British Rail could become something of a mystery tour when engineering works resulted in diversions, sometimes involving having to travel by bus for part of the journey.

When we first arrived at Addington I found Sundays very strange, these having been for almost as long as I could remember the busiest day of the week. Elisabeth and I loved the garden at Nicholson House, but although we would make our Communion at 8 am in the village church, it took a long time for me to feel less than uncomfortable, and certainly less than guilty, at spending much of Sunday in the garden. Whatever the time of the year there were always jobs to be done. I particularly enjoyed the destructive tasks, such as pruning trees, mowing thick grass, and sweeping and burning the mountains of leaves in the autumn, many of which had blown down the hill from the golf course. After a Sunday in the garden, and probably smelling earthy or of bonfire, I would enjoy a hot bath, followed by the Sunday papers and what was always the best gin and tonic of the week. These were relaxing days and very necessary recharging for the week ahead.

For the rest, I worked hard in trains, planes and hotels, where I could be anonymous and uninterrupted. Latterly, I became almost afraid of wasting time, using every minute to the full, even the quarter of an hour train journey from East Croydon to London proving most valuable, probably because I did this journey so often. Now, in retirement, although I have new pursuits and interests, I still cannot cope with not being fully occupied. Elisabeth is the same, with her embroidery always at hand. Busy though we may be as a consequence, there is more time than before to genuinely relax, with life shorn of many of its previous responsibilities.

Overall, the omens were good because they showed growth. I had a succession of hard-working Wardens whose task it was to arrange and oversee the mechanics of the Addington Palace courses, which continued to number between sixty and seventy each year, though by the time of my retirement the course structure involving the use of Addington and its facilities was all of fifteen years old and beginning to show signs of being a little tired and probably in need of new vision.

The course for overseas students was a major feature each summer, attracting people of all ages from many parts of the world. Although something of a marathon which gave little respite for any of us during its six weeks, it was always a worthwhile event. Here, as in the other courses, we increasingly used the chapel which over the years Elisabeth and I had completely refurbished and reordered. Substituting free-standing chairs for fixed pews gave much needed flexibility for the many different types of services we now had, while Elisabeth and her accomplished band of embroiderers continued to make beautifully designed vestments, altar frontals and kneelers. Being the conservatory of the original house, there was a lot of light, which made early morning services in the summer a particular joy. Looking through the windows behind the altar to the ancient beech and cedar trees, some of them up to 200 years old, helped to produce a particular atmosphere which made the chapel conducive to saying one's prayers. Sadly, many of the trees became victims of the two hurricanes in the 1980s.

In my personal work I was helped by some very good secretaries, especially latterly when Marian Hughes became such an efficient and willing PA and on whom fell a considerably enhanced workload. She was always one step ahead of me in booking travel tickets, sensing how I would deal with correspondence and with visitors only too ready to take up too much of one's time with trivia. She took a huge load off my shoulders and in the process became a valued and always cheerful friend to the entire Dakers family.

Early on I had established annual workshops on the Bach Passions, St Matthew and St John in alternate years. Until the last minute we never knew how many were coming to sing or what the balance of voice parts would be, but in the event it usually worked out and after three or four hours' rehearsal we would perform among ourselves a truncated version of the Passion music with soloists to complete the narrative. Elisabeth, with Martin How or the Warden, would provide the accompaniment on two pianos, to which we sometimes added the organ.

At this time the *Alternative Service Book* was launched, with clergy and musicians wanting help and clarification on how to cope with new-style musical demands. These we tried to meet through workshops. I also contributed a small guide book on possible ways of singing the psalms to advantage. It was inevitable that in all these matters some clergy and musicians would go their own way, though in shunning advice and help they invariably got it all wrong in the process.

From time to time I returned to Exeter, on two occasions conducting the festival for village choirs which I had initiated early on in our years there. In my last year at the RSCM I was even asked to give the address at the Diocesan Festival and found I was the first layman to do so.

Each November at Addington there was a Fair, and what a marathon this was in its organisation, which for some years was to be my lot. At it we sold everything from cakes, sweets, provisions and books, to full scale Christmas lunches. At the end of the day we would have made at least £5,000 which would go towards enhancing the house in various ways. It also made possible our buying the small purpose-built Peter Collins organ. Elisabeth organised two Arts and Crafts weekends, each of which attracted some thousands of visitors, occasions on which I found myself recruited as a car parking attendant endeavouring to persuade drivers to park 'prettily'.

When the 'Choirboy of the Year' awards were ten years old, the organisers, then BET, not only invited back all the previous adjudicators for a dinner but spent a lot of money and effort at further promoting these events which were doing so much to highlight the boy, and later the girl, chorister movement which at that time, as now, needed all the encouragement and publicity possible.

1987 was a particularly busy year when we fully celebrated the Diamond Jubilee of the founding of the RSCM in 1927. We held a dinner in Leeds with Archbishop Coggan as the chief speaker and in London at the Middle Temple Hall with Sir Edward Heath. I found myself invited to conduct a whole host of choral festivals in the provinces, though the centrepoint of the year was 'Let All the World', a great festival in London's Royal Albert Hall with 850 singers in the choir, more than 150 of them coming on this occasion from overseas. As the service was being televised by the BBC and recorded by Decca, we could take no chances, and every singer had to guarantee to be note perfect well before the sectional rehearsals—23 of them in all throughout the country—which I conducted during the weeks leading up to the Festival. Being note perfect applied in particular to the overseas contingents whom I only met as a body the day before the service and who, having learned their notes in twos and threes in scattered parts of the world came together that day in such a way as to provide one of the most thrilling aspects of the whole operation.

We chose music ranging across the entire spectrum of the repertoire, with specially commissioned works by Richard Shephard, Paul Patterson and William Mathias, whose setting of part of the *Venite* ended with the audience joining the choirs in the hymn 'Let all the world in every corner sing'. Sir David Willcocks orchestrated the hymns, making full use of the Michael Laird Brass Ensemble and percussion players. The hymns were for me the most thrilling part of the service, when I found myself conducting 7000 people. It was the sort of thing which really did send shivers down one's spine, and most of all in the final verse of *The day thou gavest*, a never to be forgotten highlight of the entire festival. Her Majesty The Queen, as the RSCM's patron, attended the festival together with the Duke of Edinburgh, while the Archbishop of Canterbury and Cardinal Hume were among those taking part in an event which did much to highlight the standards of performance church choirs can achieve. At a time when we are constantly being told that young people do not join traditional church choirs any more, it was revealing to see that boys and girls, not adult singers, comprised by far the soprano line. In the final analysis, if asked to single out the most memorable occasion in my career, 25 June 1987 would rate very high, if not at the top. The year also included recitals in the Great Hall of Addington Palace by John Shirley Quirk and the King's Singers, while the festivities concluded with Evensong in Westminster Abbey on 6 December, the day on which, sixty years previously, the RSCM was founded in Jerusalem Chamber.

1987 also saw a number of one-off events. The American Association of Anglican Musicians once again held their annual conference in England, centred as before on Addington, while the International Congress of Organists took place that summer in Cambridge, attracting more than a thousand delegates from many parts of the world. For this I was a member of the organising committee. Because of the RSCM's celebratory year

I was invited to preach at the Southern Cathedrals Festival in Winchester Cathedral and to lecture at the Worcester Three Choirs Festival.

From time to time I gave the address which formed part of the Bach Vespers sung regularly in the Lutheran Church in the City of London. I was intrigued by the shape and content of the service which was basically the same as in Bach's time and was reflected in hymns, readings, cantata, and sermon revolving round the theme for that particular Sunday in the Lutheran Church. A workshop performance of Stainer's *Crucifixion* held in Guildford Cathedral with some 400 RSCM singers taking part, alerted me to how splendidly dramatic a conception this is—apart from the words of the hymns. I also much enjoyed directing for two successive years the RSCM summer school at Salisbury, which provided the choral services for a week at a time in the Cathedral.

Not least in importance to me were the steadily continuing links with the Roman Catholic and Free Churches whose music conferences I frequently attended as a visiting lecturer. In the process of doing so, I realised more and more the extent to which music speaks a common, uniting language which, in our universal quest for ecumenism and togetherness, plays a more crucial role than we sometimes give it credit for.

In the summer of 1982, Queen Elizabeth the Queen Mother, who was our Patron, as was the Queen, spent an afternoon with the Overseas Course, a delightfully relaxed occasion which brought as much pleasure to the staff and students as it gave to the Dakers family who had gathered *en masse*. It was during rehearsals at Exeter Cathedral for a Christmas *Songs of Praise* I was conducting for BBC Television that I learned I was to become a Commander of the Order of the British Empire (CBE), in the New Year Honours List. When it was duly announced I was amazed to receive more than 300 letters and messages, many from people I had not seen, or heard from, for many years. The pleasure these brought were capped when I found it was to be the Queen Mother who would invest me at Buckingham Palace.

It was around this time that I discovered a loophole in the Church of England legislation which in so many words permitted the clergy to dismiss their organist without the person concerned having any recourse to legal appeal. We set up a small group chaired by Dame Betty Ridley who successfully steered suggested amendments through the General Synod. It was a lengthy process to amend the offending statute but I hope it curbed the excesses which some of the clergy had previously resorted to without any compunction. As there was a happy outcome, it was well worth the time and energy spent.

Although European Music Year, designated to celebrate the tercentenary of the birth of Bach, Handel and Domenico Scarlatti would be in 1985, the committee formed to plan this was drawn together in 1983, for there was much to be done in this country as well as on the continent. As a member of this body I valued the meetings, working under the chairmanship of the Duke of Kent, with people who had little or nothing to do with church music, which I was there to represent. This in itself helped to widen my perimeters and horizons and was something I much appreciated, for too much of my life seemed to centre round the confines of English church music—and by definition that meant a sizeable diet of the Anglican chant. When it came to 1985, European Music Year was launched with a high-powered concert in Westminster Abbey followed by a reception in the Banqueting Hall in Whitehall. Although the programme for the year was well planned, varied in content and well supported, we were hampered, as compared with most other European countries, through lack of central government funds and business sponsorship.

One of the enviable features of being Director of the RSCM was the variety and interest generated by enticing extras. Some of these, especially latterly, were ongoing tasks, such as the Archbishops' Commission in Church Music which was formed in 1988 under the chairmanship of the Bishop of Portsmouth. The last such commission had sat more than forty years previously and I felt, as did others, that the time was more than ripe for a thorough survey and assessment of the current situation which in so many respects had changed out of all recognition during the intervening years. On a personal level I also saw this as a means of drawing together the various strands of the RSCM's greatly extended work over the same period and I felt it would for me be a useful and tidy finale before my retirement, though in the event our work as a commission went on well after the time of my giving up the reins. The Commission aimed to incorporate every possible element within the Church and its music today, from villages, the BBC, the Salvation Army and the Church overseas, to charismatic music, musical input in the theological colleges, music in the monastic traditions, and the composing and publishing of church music today. The changed situation had been further emphasised, and broadened, by the inclusion of Roman Catholic and Free Church members among the fifteen of us who comprised the Commission. We completed our report in 1992 and included in it a wide range of recommendations in addition to our observations.

Other ongoing tasks include the Conservative Party Advisory Committee on the Arts and Heritage, an interesting group whose responsibilities included museums, the theatre, opera, ballet, art galleries, architecture and music generally. Being Chairman of the Friends of the Musicians' Chapel, which is centred on St Sepulchre's, Holborn, and where we hold the annual service, is a further interest.

Each summer, during the Overseas Course at Addington, the BBC would record a service involving the course as a choir. This was then broadcast on the World Service. It was always enjoyable moulding the students into a choir, coming as they did from many parts of the world and from a wide range of denominational backgrounds. Under the guidance of good producers, we were able to give the service a different format each time. On one occasion this even extended to my being asked to give the address, which was something I valued since it gave me the opportunity—at least in theory—to speak again to many of those I had met on my overseas visits.

Through Michael Leighton, the cultural attaché at the South African Embassy in London, I got to know Denis Worrall, the then Ambassador. Between them they promoted a series of concerts in the elegant theatre of the Embassy which was designed, as was so much South African architecture, by Sir Herbert Baker. They also gathered round them a group of people who were anxious to maintain cultural links with South Africa, a need I was particularly sensitive to and felt should not be jeopardised by political considerations or pressures. I was therefore glad to be able to play some part in this with especial regard to the music of the Church.

At the Organs Advisory Committee of the Council for the Care of Churches, much of our time and deliberations were taken up over a considerable period with the continuing, and seemingly never fully resolved, saga concerning the pros and cons of the pipe organ as opposed to the electronic instrument. All parties concerned certainly took up entrenched positions and invariably held forth with prolonged eloquence, while I as Chairman sought to achieve a rational, balanced, and impartial assessment. This was not an easy task.

One-off events were always welcome, and invariably enjoyable extras, especially if they were only marginally connected with my work. It was one thing to be invited to the Archbishop of York's enthronement in York Minster, and the Royal College of Music's centenary service in Westminster Abbey, with Sir David Willcocks excelling himself as always in his conducting of so many different contributions, but it was rather different to be invited as the principal guest to the dinner in Blackpool of the Rating and Valuing Association. The President of the Valuers on this occasion happened to be an amateur organist, which is probably why I was asked, though much of what I had to say, and my stories, were, I suspect not very much on the wavelength of those attending. I felt much more at home each summer when Robert Ponsonby, the BBC's Controller of Music, and his successor, John Drummond, would invite us to a couple of the Prom concerts where it was good to meet so many interesting people among the wide circle of guests in the BBC's box.

CHAPTER EIGHTEEN

Keeping the airlines busy

For a number of reasons I had for some time begun to really emphasise the work overseas where, since Gerald Knight's retirement as Overseas Commissioner, there was no longer the permanency of ongoing links with Addington. By contrast, in the relatively small confines of Britain there were three full-time people working in the field. If you add to this the remoteness of many church choirs in the vast spaces of Africa, Australasia and North America, and the need for the maximum possible help, then personal contact—and the encouragement of feeling you belong—must surely be high priorities.

Unlike Gerald Knight, whom we teased for planning his overseas tours to coincide with the best of the weather, so that he could indulge to the full in his beloved swimming, I went as and when I was needed, and frequently encountered some very cold weather as a consequence, for Africa and Australasia can be particularly unpleasant in their winter season, the more so as they have so few facilities for heating houses since so much of the year is comfortably, or even uncomfortably, warm.

I never ceased to marvel at the ease of air travel which on the whole I used to find relaxing though, as we all know only too well, when delays occur they are usually sizeable inconveniences.

A particularly happy work *cum* holiday tour in the summer of 1982 began in Canada where, with Elisabeth, and in company with Allan and Elizabeth Wicks, Allan having just retired from being organist of Canterbury Cathedral, we spent a glorious few days relaxing in the Rockies at Waterton Lakes, a quiet area south of Calgary, prior to a conference in Toronto where Allan and I were to lecture. Here, amid those wonderfully unique wide Canadian skies we did a lot of walking and enjoyed the string quartet which played each tea time in the hotel lounge, a survival of the teashop music I remembered so well from the 1930s. We would buy steaks and cook them on log fires we made beside mountain streams in which we cooled our wine. In our wanderings we seemed blissfully unconcerned by the warnings which were regularly posted in the village about the proximity of bears. We were told that if you rattled pebbles in an empty Coca Cola tin any bears would take fright and move on. I suggested much to Allan's amusement that if we sang them an Anglican chant they would even more readily take to their heels.

I then flew on to Australia and New Zealand for some weeks and was back in England for only three days before going to New York for forty-eight hours for an RSCM Board meeting. This added up to being my longest single tour so far.

In Australia I visited all six branches into which the RSCM is divided in that vast country, the sheer size of which you realise if you superimpose a map of the British Isles on to a map of Australia, where it sits like a forlorn postage stamp. In Queensland I called on choirs and clergy in some very remote areas which included flying up the coast from Brisbane to Townsville. When I enquired of my ex-mining engineer host how long the flight would take, he said in his broad Australian accent 'As long as it takes to drink four cans of beer or, if there's a head wind, six cans'. Because I wanted to get the best possible view of the Great Barrier Reef, though little realising just how far out to sea it was, I asked when I checked in at the airport for a window seat, only to be told they were all window seats—four on each side—for it was a small eight-seater plane.

Sydney, and some of the many RSCM churches there, led on to Canberra. While in Melbourne I went up to Geelong and its renowned grammar school. In Western Australia I spent some time in Perth, while in Tasmania I relished the extraordinary beauty of that island while working in Launceston and Hobart. Back on the mainland, one of the most memorable drives by car was all of 600 miles from Brisbane to Sydney, going well inland to Grafton and Armidale. Although much of the countryside was in the grip of an extended drought, the sheer beauty and immensity of it all was indeed impressive.

I then went on to New Zealand, making contact with our committees in the main cities, while the familiar cycle of conducting festivals, giving talks, meeting the clergy, press interviews and broadcasts, all emerged with unfailing regularity.

In the spring of 1984 I was in Nairobi with a one day visit to Uganda included. Edward Nsubaga was a wealthy businessman working in London. He had arranged for me to fly in his private two-seater plane to Entebbe, a journey which gave a succession of amazing vistas over the Rift Valley and then across the northern part of Lake Victoria. In Kampala I found some hundreds of singers assembled in the Anglican Cathedral at Namirembe, and could hardly believe the expertise of the singing of these local church choirs whose tone, artistry and style were such as to make it hard to believe I was in Uganda and not in an English cathedral. This was in many respects the more remarkable as the country was barely beginning to recover from the excesses and cruelty of Idi Amin, who had all but raped Uganda bare. There was certainly no lack of food and liquor over lunch at the Nsubaga house, after which I spoke to some of the clergy, all of them Ugandan, who reiterated what I had often heard before in Africa, that worship was not complete without the old standard edition of *Hymns Ancient and Modern* together with a pipe organ, for, as one of them said, 'God cannot be properly worshipped without an organ', such was the teaching and influence of the missionaries who no doubt went out to Africa armed to the teeth with *A & M.*

After Uganda I was once again in South Africa with engagements in most of the main centres, which this time included the Dutch Reformed Church at Potchefstroom not far from Johannesburg. This was very much a novel departure into a denomination which had always been a closed door to the RSCM, and certainly to me. Not for the first time was I much encouraged to see white, black and coloured singers joining together for special occasions, something which at that time was anything but the norm, even if many had recourse only to tonic solfa instead of the normal staff system of notation.

My work in South Africa finished, I flew non-stop—and first class, which was always a rare and much enjoyed experience—

from Johannesburg to New York, once again for a brief Board meeting before returning to London.

By this time Canada was a familiar port of call, with the Toronto Summer School regularly coming up. In January of 1981 Ned Hanson had arranged a 'Lionel Dakers Weekend' at his Toronto church, St Simon's, Bloor Street, after which I visited Montreal and Ottawa, the latter providing the coldest weather I have ever experienced anywhere, though this was soon forgotten with the hospitality and kindness of John and Jean Churchill, he then being Professor of Music at Carleton University, having many years previously been a fellow student with Elisabeth at the Royal College of Music. I stayed at Niagara-on-the-Lake with John Sanderson whose lovely house on the Parkway overlooked the Niagara river with the United States on the other side. Not the least attraction was John's library, for he had now come into money and had amassed a wonderful collection of modern first editions and private press books, with pride of place given to his Norman Douglas collection, now the finest and most complete anywhere in private hands. His wife Marjorie was Canadian and looked after him with great care and affection, for he was by no means in good health and could easily lapse into moodiness and become irritable, though he always contrived to cheer up when I appeared and we relived old memories of the immediate post-war years and our student days centring on the Royal Academy of Music.

In 1983 I adjudicated at the Kiwanis Music Festival in Toronto and again in 1990 when, in two weeks of judging choral classes, I heard no less than 31,000 singers, the bulk of them school children, such is this particular aspect of musical life, vitality and expertise in Toronto.

Visits to the United States came up with unfailing regularity, thirty-three of them in all during my sixteen years as Director. Much of this was within the period when we were setting up a not-for-profit corporation, the American counterpart of charitable status here in Britain, though a much more complicated and lengthy process to conclude. Having achieved this we then became 'The RSCM in America', with me assuming the somewhat grandiose title of Vice President, and Erik Routley as

President. The setting up of the Board of Management with the required proportions of English and American members was time-consuming and at times frustrating. This frequently entailed being in New York or Washington for perhaps only a couple of days at a time which for economic reasons I would try whenever possible to fit into a longer visit to North America.

While some of these tours were inevitably routine and fairly predictable, others stood out because they were the very reverse, such as my being a lecturer at the Chicago Diocesan Conference, where the clergy lived in considerable style in a country club which rejoiced in the name of Nippersink. Another occasion was at the University of Wisconsin where they operated a trans-Atlantic telephone programme link which I had previously taken part in, and where, in the comfort of my office at Addington, I gave a series of talks on certain aspects of church music followed by listeners from all over the States telephoning questions to me live.

On two occasions I lectured in the music department at the University of Huntsville in Alabama and also visited the nearby NASA research centre, saw examples of space rockets from the pioneer days onwards, clambered into the original capsule which landed on the moon, also the skylab, and had the added experience of being made weightless. On one occasion, after work in St Petersburg, Florida, and having then spent some hours working with my secretary in the Business Class Lounge at Gatwick, I flew on the same day to South Africa. Because I was by now a fairly frequent traveller, British Caledonian gave me this valuable facility which was both useful and relaxing, and which I much appreciated.

On another occasion I combined work and pleasure when I was in Albuquerque in New Mexico and then in Santa Fé with its unique combination of Spanish and Mexican-style architecture, spectacular countryside and a snowcapped mountain backcloth. I was only sad that time did not allow me to drive on to Taos where D. H. Lawrence lived latterly and is buried. On this visit I also took in the Grand Canyon, flying there from Las Vegas in a small aircraft which provided some magnificent vistas, not least of the Colorado River. It was the sheer immensity of the Canyon carved out by the river over the centuries to a depth of nearly a mile, which impressed me almost as much as the incredible shadows and the variety of colours which changed the contours by the hour. What a uniquely spectacular quirk of nature this surely is.

When visiting Dallas I was entertained by Rediffusion, the sponsors of the 'Choirboy of the Year' competition, at their research centre where airline pilots are trained. Here I sat in a simulator and helped bring a 747 Jumbo Jet into Minneapolis, an all too realistic situation which even extended to a sizeable bump as we hit the runway.

On two occasions when in Denver, Colorado, I flew on over the Rockies to Laramie, a ranchers' town in Wyoming where, although life was far less sophisticated as compared with many an American city, they nevertheless took their church music seriously and to good effect. Steaks in Laramie, as later in Des Moines, Iowa, were 'out of this world' in both size and tenderness. While in Des Moines I bought a dozen steaks which, frozen solid and sealed in plastic bags, I strategically placed in my suitcase, sandwiched between pyjamas and underwear. How good they were when back in England we had them for my birthday party dinner.

Over the years I was to pay three visits to Redlands University in Southern California, all of them equally rewarding because of the high standard of the music. The West Coast of Canada and the United States has always attracted me because it is so different, scenically, architecturally, and in its people, from much of the rest of North America. In America religion was also rather different, with a full quota of revivalist, way out, or other less than predictable denominations. I suppose the most ostentatious, flamboyant—and sizeable—of all these churches is the Crystal Cathedral at Garden City, near Los Angeles, which attracts some thousands every Sunday. Its almost bizarre trappings extend to coloured fountains in the aisles which play at strategic highlights in the services. It is the blatant opulence and the subtle manipulation in extracting large sums of money from the gullible, which has always seemed to me to be so alien and so far removed from many a humble church where the Gospel is projected in a much simpler way, with more reliance on eternal truths, rather than gimmicks.

Some of the preaching I have heard over the years on this nationwide Sunday television slot reflects a theology which would seem to be distinctly shaky, frequently questionable and consequently suspect. The music is another matter, for this involves some hundreds of singers and instrumentalists each week and is presented with integrity, even though the choice of music is sometimes questionable. Although I personally find much of the eastern seaboard less attractive than California, I am especially drawn to the Carolinas where Gordon and Dorothy Lyall, long-standing, generous hosts who have the interests of the RSCM very much at heart, live near Chapel Hill. Add to this the charms of Charleston and Savannah and you have a thoroughly delightful prospect, with Bermuda not all that far distant. An island with a speed limit of 20 mph everywhere and with only one car allowed per family, its peaceful lanes look so English. The only snag is the excessively high cost of living.

North of New York I delighted, as does everyone, in the multifarious rich colours of the Fall in New England. In Boston at the seminary attached to the University, I came across an amply proportioned lady student wearing a tight fitting tee shirt across which was proudly proclaimed 'When God created man she was only joking'.

Wherever my travels took me, whether in North America or elsewhere, I sought out bookshops and, over the years, discovered some very good additions for my library, not least editions of T. E. Lawrence, especially when the rate of exchange was so much more in our favour than later.

At the end of 1981 Elisabeth joined me for a fairly extended African tour which began in Johannesburg, where, after leaving behind a cold, dismal and dark Boxing Day, we were the next day relaxing in deck chairs sunning ourselves in the garden of Bishopscourt, with Tim Bavin our host. Tim had been a chorister at St George's Chapel, Windsor Castle, and was now Bishop of Johannesburg, so the links were long-standing and would become stronger in the years ahead. One of the joys there was his chapel which I knew of old, with the quiet early morning Mass each day, which always included the simple but hauntingly moving prayer,

> God bless Africa,
> guard her children,
> guide her leaders,
> and give her peace;
> for Jesus Christ's sake.

We drove on to Cathedral Peak in the Drakensburg Mountains high above Pietermaritzburg and on the border with Lesotho. Here we spent our time walking, reading or just relaxing in scenery reminiscent of Austria yet with that clarity in the atmosphere which is unique to Africa, and particularly so in the mountains. Just north of Durban at Umhlanga Rocks we visited John and Maureen Ferguson, as staunch in their support for the RSCM in South Africa as were the Lyalls in the United States, and both the husbands were priests. Maureen, who virtually never stopped smoking, also sang a very reliable and acceptable tenor line. In Cape Town I was one of the adjudicators at the Organ Festival.

The tour ended in Zimbabwe, centred on what was then Salisbury, now Harare, where we stayed with Jim and Carice Peto, he the RSCM's indefatigable representative who had arranged seventeen engagements for me in seven days. This included a work *cum* pleasure visit to Peterhouse School in Marandellas and a return visit yet again to the Victoria Falls, an experience which never fails to impress me. It seems quite uncanny how awesome, and majestic, water on this scale can be, quite apart from the noise which sounds like six express trains at high speed. I have only once seen the Niagara Falls which, by marked contrast, are so disappointing, though I suppose less so if you have never seen the Victoria Falls.

The work in Europe necessitated much shorter and generally more fragmented visits, though the lion's share went to the British Army of the Rhine which I now regularly visited for the Army Chaplains' Department and where, over the years, I met most of the chaplains *in situ*. To those of us who had experienced Army religion during the war, with compulsory church parades, military bands and rigorous military attitudes, the 1980s revealed a very different approach. The all but uni-style centre of the road churchmanship was now widened out of all belief and surely to advantage. Choirs and organists were now a much more dedicated and committed cross-section of all ranks with, in Germany, a high proportion of civilian input both British and local. I always greatly enjoyed these contacts which often led to people coming on courses at Addington. The chaplains and their wives were also extremely hospitable. Moreover, being wined and dined by high-ranking officers was such a different proposition from my wartime army life as a sergeant when commissioned and non-commissioned ranks were fairly strictly segregated, though Cairo at the Cathedral and Music for All were something of an exception.

I remember in particular one Irish chaplain who, within minutes of arrival suggested as the first priority my buying my duty-free liquor to take back to England 'before', as he put it, 'we got down to the business of religion and church music'.

Most years there were visits to the Diocese of Europe, frequently to conduct the choirs festival which was held in rotation in The Netherlands, Belgium and Luxembourg. I similarly visited the two English churches and the American Cathedral in Paris, also Zurich and Gibraltar, the latter in conjunction with examining for the Associated Board. In 1985 I worked my way through the English chaplaincies in Scandinavia, and twice visited Logumkloster in Jutland, the Danish counterpart of the RSCM.

Round-the-world tours continued to take place from time to time, though these necessarily demanded a lot of planning both at Addington and locally. There were always so many cogs in this particular wheel. In the early part of 1985 I was in Australia for the summer school in Melbourne where we had three chaplains, an Anglican, a Roman Catholic and a Uniting Church Minister. The object of this was my wish to highlight the ecumenical nature of music in worship and how music induces few tensions across the denominations. If anything it does the reverse, for music is the unifying force which this particular project fully revealed, notably at the final service in Melbourne Cathedral—an Anglican Eucharist with all three chaplains taking part and celebrating together. Although this would not have been possible, even allowed, in many other parts of the world, this was very much the order of the day in Australia.

I then went to New Zealand to direct the RSCM Summer School in Hamilton, but not before the timetable allowed me a restful few days at the rather nice and peaceful Sheraton Hotel just outside Rotorua.

It was in the main Post Office in Hong Kong that I chanced to see a tablet on the wall which quoted from the Book of Proverbs what I took to be a rather apt statement, 'As cold waters to a thirsty land, so is good news from a far country'. I also paid my first visit for some years to Singapore where, in its continuing spate of affluence and prosperity, so much of the old was systematically still being demolished with the city losing more and more of its previously delightful Malay character. It was on this tour that I visited Japan for the first time and where, in Tokyo, I found a small Christian community making itself felt, not least in its music. It was a fascinating experience to witness the many faceted culture of a huge city teeming with people, where traffic jams, the extent of which I had never before seen, were the unfailing order of each day. This crowded, bustling, metropolis was quite unlike any other city I knew.

On the way home I was joined by Elisabeth who had flown out to meet me in Bombay where we unashamedly stayed at the Taj Mahal, one of the great hotels of the world. Here we had a magnificent view from our bedroom of the Gateway of India and the harbour. We then flew south and spent some happy days at Ootacamund high in the Nilgiris, which I had visited some years previously when examining for the Associated Board. We did a lot of walking over the Downs with their attractive streams and copses, and stayed once again at the Savoy Hotel. After some days in Madras we moved on to Delhi and stayed there in the Taj Mahal which was as modern as its Bombay counterpart was through and through 'Raj'. Elisabeth rejoiced in the hotel's many artistic displays of exotic flowers. One of the main reasons for our going to Delhi was to see Lutyens' great masterpiece, Viceroy's House. I was by then becoming very interested in Lutyens' work, of which there is probably more in Delhi than in

197

the rest of the world put together. The Moghul Gardens were looking their best in February—and so English—with the lawns immaculately mown, while the herbaceous borders, as I so well recall, were full of enormous sweet pea plants all of six feet high. As in the days of the Raj, small boys were employed to chase away the birds. Our one regret was in not being able to visit inside the palace, though we did drive to Agra to see the Taj Mahal which was even more magnificent than we had anticipated. In Agra we bought a small Indian carpet which now hangs on our dining room wall beside another I later bought when in Sharjah in the Persian Gulf. India concluded, we stopped off for some days in Bahrain to stay with John and Joan Parkinson whom we knew from the Exeter days when he was Vicar of Kenton. He was now Dean of the pro-cathedral and here I worked with his choir and others who came in from the nearby Gulf States for a 'weekend' workshop, which in those parts of the world meant a Thursday and Friday.

Other overseas tours during these final RSCM years included Fiji where for the British Council I adjudicated Methodist Church Choirs. In the 19th century race for Empire, it was the Franciscans who arrived first in the neighbouring British Solomon Islands while the Methodists captured Fiji. The oft quoted statement that Methodism was born in song had a very real meaning in Fiji where in excess of 20,000 singers and supporters came to Suva from well over 300 Polynesian islands for this annual marathon. Many had travelled in longboats while singing their hymns, a wonderful sound and sight. On the first day I adjudicated from after lunch until well into the early hours of the next day. I was told there would be a break for a sandwich supper, with the added enjoiner that I must not stop for more than thirty minutes. After the festival I stayed on to take workshops for choir directors. These were partially productive, although the use of tonic solfa and the unaccompanied singing because they had no instruments, did provide problems over intonation and pitch generally. While I was intrigued by the national greeting 'Bula', which in the United States would have been 'Have a good day!', I did find it hard to come to terms with some of the local Fijian food.

1988, my final full year as Director, resulted in farewells to all and sundry, not least overseas. I made my last official visit to South Africa, and because Barry Smith was abroad, I stayed in Cape Town at the Mount Nelson, a hotel which encapsulates all the good things of this life in both comfort and food, and yet contrives to do so in a gracious and gentle way, which is more than half the enjoyment of it, as are its elegant and spacious gardens nestling under the shadow of Table Mountain. I then went on to Zimbabwe and Kenya where, as in South Africa, I was given farewell dinners and gifts, and how nice it was when I was asked what Elisabeth and I would like; memorabilia of our choice now adorn our home and bring back memories of the visits over the years.

I also went to the United States for the last time, taking Elisabeth with me. While in Chicago Elisabeth had her initial experience of the Eucharist with a lady priest celebrating. This proved no great problem other than her finding the Peace somewhat disconcerting when the lady in question introduced this particular juncture of the service with 'Now folks, up and at 'em', which they responded to in full measure, so much so that at the end she elected to blow a whistle to restore order and say 'That's enough of that, folks, let's get on with the Offertory hymn'.

Neither of us had ever been to New Orleans which we found attractive and surprisingly un-American. What an unexpectedly beautiful city it is with its profoundly French history and atmosphere. Here we were booked in at the Pontchartrain Hotel which was an experience in itself, though less for opulence than for atmosphere and good husbandry. We then went on to North Carolina to stay with the Lyalls. Here I conducted workshops and a choirs festival in Chapel Hill. We also stayed in Charleston and visited a delightful widow who had been on an Addington course for overseas students and who rejoiced in the name of Loving Philips. Visits to Charlotte and Atlanta completed this final tour.

So ended my long round of worldwide RSCM visits extending over sixteen years. On reflection, many churches, their clergy and the musicians I visited in those years included just about every possible facet from Cathedrals to tiny communities in the Australian outback.

I seemed to be frequently asked to preach, though I preferred to call it giving an address. The same sermon often had to suffice in different parts of the world, although as with the clergy in their ministry there was the constant need to reiterate certain things again and again, even if you said this in different ways to avoid what so easily could become the monotony, as much for me as for those listening, of the 'vain repetition' which the Prayer Book mentions. Even so, I kept a careful check so as not to say too many of the same things when I revisited a church.

There were the inevitable contacts with the clergy, either individually or in group sessions, and radio interviews *ad nauseam*, with most of the interviewers asking the same sort of question, whether I was in New York, New Zealand or Hong Kong. Not least in all this globe-trotting was the hospitality and kindness of so many people and, in the even broader context, the contacts these created for discussion and dialogue on a wide range of topics and interests which are surely more of the essence today than ever before. The more we can pursue these essentials in a rational way, the more likely we are, I believe, to come nearer to solving some of the many contemporary problems which face the Church, by no means least in matters musical.

CHAPTER NINETEEN

Overseas Postscript

By the time I retired I had become a fairly experienced and hardened jet-setter. You certainly had to be the latter when you invariably travelled long distances in economy class as I did. The more I found myself south of the Equator, the more I revelled in the warmth of the all but predictable sun, especially now as I grow older I increasingly feel the cold. I love the richness of the blue skies and the brilliant whiteness of the southern hemisphere clouds with everything highlighted by the radiantly clear atmosphere and vast open spaces denied to Europe.

Looking at a map of the world gives little real indication of distances, such as New Zealand being almost as far south of the Equator as England is north. Similarly, the west coast of the United States being six thousand miles from New Zealand, which means twelve hours flying time, and all of it over the sea.

Equally attractive to me, and thoroughly characteristic, are the houses and cottages, many of them single storey, their brilliant white, pink or cream walls as familiar in Africa and Australia as they are in the Mediterranean. And then there are the trees and flowers, many of them so distinctive, the abundance of eucalyptus, or gumtree, poinsettia and protea, while lemons and oranges grow in profusion in gardens as do apples, pears and plums in Europe.

At the end of these varied and colourful years—and how privileged I was to visit so much of the world in the pursuit of church music—it is always to Africa, my first love, that I revert. This is where deep-seated nostalgia is so inexplicably alluring, which I know stems from my first visit many years ago. How vividly I recall the night flight from Europe, and one's first reactions, and thrill, at seeing the extraordinary pink in the sky which prefaced dawn as the sun rose and I saw Africa below me.

I had, after all, never seen anything quite like it before. As ever, it is the first impressions which are the most indelibly memorable, and they have remained with me as such over the intervening years. Today it still thrills me as much as ever when I arrive in Africa, though never with quite the same uniqueness and novelty as on that first occasion. The Great Rift Valley was pointed out to us by the pilot as we flew in low over the Nairobi Game Park to land at the old airport, which was much smaller and more alive with local flavour than the vast new airport which could be a modern international terminal anywhere in the world.

We were greeted by the brilliance of the early morning African sun and the mainly African ground staff in shorts and bush shirts quietly swarming around the plane even before it had come to a stop. Servicing ended, we set off for Johannesburg, flying over the then Rhodesia with its great meandering rivers all but empty in the dry season. Below us all was sunbaked, parched and brown, but always around and above us those alluring African clouds, the 'imperial clouds' as Jill Furze called them in one of her poems.

There and then, though I did not anticipate it at the time, was born my abiding love of Africa. It may have been the novelty then but it has persisted and matured over the years, the more so as we have witnessed the sadness of the African continent struggling in its new-found independence to find its identity and its way forward, dogged continually by tribal factions and with tribal warfare engendering a ferocity and hatred which we in the West find it hard to comprehend. So much has happened, and happened so relatively quickly.

Over the years I have so often observed Southern Africa, its peoples, its way of life and its incredible natural beauty, much of which is somehow particularly encapsulated and epitomised for me every time I drive from East London to Grahamstown. Here you experience something of the vastness—and the character—of South Africa, the tribal villages and the farmsteads, the rondavels, the menfolk in their khaki greatcoats and bonnets and carrying tall staves. As you drive past there is the distinctive whiff of the log fire and the 'Jambo' greeting of smiling children who always seem to be at the roadside, for the awful 'Have a good day'

Americanism had not in those days penetrated the High Veld. When you pass a car, which is not that often for the roads are so empty, the chances are that it will be erratically driven by an African and will be crammed full of Africans and luggage, though perhaps not quite so many in one car as the Indians contrive to accommodate. The bodywork of the probably ancient vehicle will be at something of an angle to the chassis and the chances are that it will be belching exhaust which gives off that particular petrol or diesel smell so symptomatic of Africa, or for that matter anywhere East of Suez. And always there is the backdrop of mountains many miles distant though looking relatively near in the clear atmosphere of high altitude.

All this and more is for me the real Africa, but equally so are some of the smaller towns of which Grahamstown is a stereotype. Much of it could easily be Beaconsfield or Witney or any quiet English market town transplanted into Africa, the tree-lined streets with carbon copies of mid-19th century English cottages. Though not necessarily terraced, they will be uniform in their green painted front doors and the type of door knocker so familiar in England. The shop fronts, their window displays, and often their interiors, are redolent of counterparts familiar to me as a schoolboy, such as the last surviving examples of those fascinating mechanical devices which took your bill and your money overhead at speed to a kiosk where the cashier in her turn pulled the trigger and sent the receipt and change back to you.

Grahamstown is full of schools where you see, as at Bishop's in Rondesbosch and at Michaelhouse, teenage boys in shorts wearing straw boaters and carrying old-fashioned satchels, while the girls wear the same style of uniform you see in many an English private school. The public school is very much a part of the South African educational scene, and how refreshing it is to be the recipient of politeness and manners not always the hallmark of English schools today. And to complete the transplanted Englishness of the scene there is the sound of church bells ringing before Sunday Evensong, while even more reminiscent for me was the Salvation Army band playing in the gardens opposite the Town Hall in Durban.

Perhaps one of the most nostalgic features of South Africa is the continuing existence of steam locomotives, still to be found there in some profusion, though not for long. To see a great engine belching out smoke as it slowly hauls a large load up one of the many steep gradients is a sight and sound of great power, almost frightening at times. If you happen to catch a whiff of the smell of the smoke that is even more nostalgic—and delectable. No less nostalgic, and certainly anticipatory, is seeing the familiar blue and orange livery of South African Airways as proudly displayed by name on one side of the aircraft as is the Afrikaans translation on the other. And how those early morning flights retain their place in my memory for they seem to be so inevitable a part of one's mobility and to encapsulate so many of the most penetrating memories.

But again and again it is the awareness of smell, that most evocative of all the senses, to which I find one reverts, for this conjures up such vivid pictures: the brown earth, the dry murram of the roads and the long clouds of dust which cars throw up in their wake. All these, and more, while at night there is the warm, benevolent air and the night smells, with the croaking of frogs and crickets and the barking of dogs which always seem to be in the far distance, and these the only intrusion on what otherwise would be total silence. Whether this, or the bitterly cold nights of the High Veld in winter, there is always in the crystal clear night sky the myriad stars, many more than we ever see in Europe, and in different positions, but always with the bonus of the Southern Cross. But—most welcome of all for me is the well nigh predictable weather of Southern Africa which guarantees in the Transvaal virtually never a cloud in the sky between April and October.

In the overall spectrum of my overseas journeyings there is firmly implanted in my mind the ever predictable as well as repetitive formula of the ritual of flying. The seemingly slow trundling down the runway of the mighty 747 and its equally slow rise at take-off, often in the middle of the night, when you hope desperately that you will be airborne before the runway ends, as it so often seems to, in the sea. Then the switching off of the no smoking signs, followed by the click of seat belts being unfastened and passengers starting to talk and to relax, which they seldom seem to do at the moment of take-off, then perhaps a gin and tonic before one's meal. If overnight, there is the unfailing anti-climax not so much of dawn, which is always so fascinating to watch, but of the always predictable breakfast. On the African, Australian and Far East routes, crews seem so much more attentive and friendly than when crossing the Atlantic which invariably seems to be such a clinical process and where you feel you are but one of an endless shuttle service of human cargo, which exactly sums it up.

But, in all this globe-trotting saga, the sound I find more nostalgic than all others is that of *Lillibulero* prefacing the news on the BBC World Service.

CHAPTER TWENTY

Farewell to the Palace

As the day of my retirement as Director drew near, I frequently found myself reflecting on what after all had been a fairly long and certainly varied working life, most of it linked in one way or another with the Church and its music. But I instinctively knew the timing was ripe for a change and that retirement at 65 was right and proper. After sixteen years as Director I knew I had done virtually all I could and, even more to the point, that I was as a consequence beginning to run out of fresh impetus, as I had similarly felt at the end of my fifteen years at Exeter.

I knew I now ran the risk of not only marking time but, worse still, that the momentum I had been at pains to project over the years could not be indefinitely sustained by me. The fact that I had seen these things happen in others made me the more determined not to make the same mistakes. I had no illusions but that the time had come for me to hand over to someone younger, with new ideas and concepts, a parallel to the situation I inherited when taking up my two major tasks over the years.

In a strange way I had few regrets, the very opposite in fact, and I found the prospect for the imminent future to be rather exciting, for I was about to embark on something uniquely novel for me. So, with both eyes firmly fixed on the future, I began to think out what I might do, and equally what I would not do. In the event the future was to work out rather differently than envisaged. But more of this later.

My final year at the RSCM was at times tinged with some sadness that I was now doing certain things probably for the last time ever. But there were other aspects I could not shed quickly enough. I was also saddened that the expectations of earlier years had not always materialised. One such was my visits to the theological colleges on which I had initially set such high hopes, for I felt this to be a priority. During the earlier years I regularly visited most of the colleges, a task as exhilarating as it could in some instances be frustrating. There were few problems with those who understood and subscribed to the role of music with its power to enrich worship which it was my task to relay over a broad spectrum. As time went on I became all too increasingly aware of the growing number of way-out rebels who at all costs wished to be difficult and who viewed me with suspicion, even hostility. I found myself in contact with those whose priorities were for ever inconsistent, confused or illogical, and who jumped on to the popular bandwagon which dictated the preaching *in excelsis* of a predominantly social gospel with music to match it, in other words the *Honest to God* syndrome. Playing to the gallery, being gimmicky, drawing in the crowds through *ad hoc* free for all unstructured services, with music at its lowest common denominator of quality and performance, were all part of what many were bent on pursuing as the be all and end all, and in defiance of the established and proven traditions and values they so readily spurned.

I obviously spoke as much a foreign language to them as they to me, the more so when I was confronted, as in certain areas of the Church today, with no small measure of the arrogance which proclaims the 'I'm right, you're wrong' syndrome. Such unbending certainty can surely have frightening implications.

How encouraging then it was to find those whose vision and ministry was rooted in the best of the past, spiritually, liturgically and musically, increasingly in the minority though their numbers were to become, but who were open-minded in pursuing the best of the present, of which there is so much, and whose thinking was receptive to *all* valid aspects. Nevertheless, overall I realised how dismally I was failing in the very area where I knew I should have been helping the most, for there were those who did not want to know and I suspect resented me because I was, on the face of it, 'establishment'.

Most depressing of all was the attitude of some of the staff who openly supported and even promoted these attitudes all but exclusively. All of this in one way or another added up to the fact that the theological colleges then, as now, gave scant musical training to their students.

But there were also many joys and causes for rejoicing during these latter years, not least the one-off occasions such as in 1979 when the Archbishop of Canterbury awarded me a Lambeth Doctorate in Music. The ceremony of receiving the degree took place in the chapel of Lambeth Palace, most of it in Latin with the ancient links between Church and State emphasised in the handsome parchment I received, one part from the Queen and the other from the Archbishop, with both indissolubly bound together by the Great Seal of the Realm and the archiepiscopal Seal of Canterbury. For these degrees, which rank as real and not honorary, recipients take the university of the Archbishop awarding them, in my instance Cambridge.

During Holy Week in 1981 we were invited by the Queen and the Duke of Edinburgh to dinner at Windsor Castle as part of a smallish house party after which we stayed overnight, a further occasion for reminiscence and reawakened memories of our early months of married life in the Castle.

Some aspects of music had by now become a casual hobby for me. I seldom played the organ apart from simple services in the chapel at Addington, for there was little time to practise, and somehow neither the inclination nor the same need was there as in the earlier years. On leaving Exeter a chapter had closed and an entirely new era had emerged, with very different preoccupations which claimed my attention and focus in other ways. In exchange for being a cathedral organist came more and more conducting of choral festivals, frequently with some hundreds of singers taking part. Making music on this scale in our great cathedrals was certainly inspiring for me and, I hope, for the singers. Sharing this experience with them and knowing that they went back to the necessary week by week routine of their work recharged and with new incentives was reward in itself.

One year I sent a letter to the Editor of *The Times* bemoaning the increasing number of Christmas cards we received signed merely with a first name, and how difficult—sometimes even impossible—it was to discover who some of them were from. I signed my letter 'Lionel' and it was duly published. This brought a considerable spate of correspondence both to the paper and to me. While much of it was light-hearted and amusing, some people were abusive, even vicious. Those with similar experiences to ours came up with some interesting comments, such as the Head Master of Ampleforth who said 'I have thousands of parents who take it for granted that they are my most intimate friends. It is only when they happen to be called Ichabod or Horatio that I have any hope of identifying them'. The author Jilly Cooper, who had long experience of receiving similarly unidentifiable cards, sent me one of her books which contained a most amusing chapter on the subject, and on the appalling doggerel which can be encountered on Christmas cards, such as

> 'Noel' the festive Robin cried,
> When he the heavenly babe espied.
> But Santa said 'Enough of that'
> And with a yule log squashed him flat.

As far as *The Times* is concerned I felt I had really 'arrived' when my birthday appeared for the first time on the Court Circular page.

At home I increasingly enjoyed my gramophone records, especially when late in the evening I could settle down to a book, a whisky, and whatever might take my musical fancy. Often it would be Elgar's *Sea Pictures*, the *Four Last Songs* of Richard Strauss, maybe some Wagner, Bach or other Baroque music, though seldom church music which at that hour could hardly be termed a relaxing contrast to the rigours of the day.

Holidays now tended to be few and far between and consequently the more enjoyable, although I found my overseas tours on the whole fulfilling and unexpectedly relaxing in many respects despite the demands they made. It was sad that Elisabeth was often prevented from being with me because of her commitments at Addington. Even so, in 1981 we went to the Holy Land on a pilgrimage led by John Kirkham, the Bishop of Sherborne. This was basically a Salisbury Diocese affair although we knew many of our fellow pilgrims, for whom I became 'the minstrel', armed with a pitch-pipe and detailed to rehearse the group for the hymn singing which became an integral part of visits to the holy places. We began in Amman and on the first day were driven up to Mount Nebo from where Moses looked across to the promised land. 'Could we but climb where Moses stood / And view the landscape o'er' became very much a reality, for that is exactly what we did, though the hymn writer's prospect was marred on that particular morning by the heat haze and it would be some years later before I would see the distant vista of the thin green strip of the Jordan valley with the Jerusalem hills in the distance. The tour also included the amazing hill fortress of Masada, also Azrak where T. E. Lawrence had his head-quarters at one time during the first world war.

With my father's death in 1978, my mother having died the previous year, our financial situation changed and we were able to purchase a small house in the country. Merryam Cottage at Ticehurst in East Sussex became the first home we owned, always having lived in a tied cottage which went with the job. We loved Ticehurst which was an attractive and friendly village only an hour's drive from Addington. The cottage had great character with attractive 17th century beams in most of the rooms and an open fireplace in the sitting room.

In 1985 Elisabeth suddenly developed cancer. She was im-mediately operated on and, with the sheer force of perseverance and faith which have always been so much a part of her life, her determination to fight and the many prayers being said, she was in the fullness of time completely cured, for which we all uttered— and continue to utter—a fervent *Deo gratias*. Her illness meant our abandoning the 'Music of Bach' tour I was to lead to East Germany for Inter-Church Travel, though we were later able to do this in the first year of retirement. Lower Saxony, where Bach was virtually the Lutheran Church's organ adviser, has more than a score of Silbermann organs virtually unaltered since his time and many of these we visited with Peter Hurford playing them and talking about Bach and his music. The additional thrill of visiting Bach-associated places culminated in the Thomaskirche in Leipzig, where, as one's eye roamed round, you could not but fail to marvel that this was the very building in which the St Matthew Passion and the B minor Mass were heard for the first time. If only the very stones could speak!

This final year became something of a non-stop round of farewells with virtually every Saturday given over to conducting Diocesan Choral Festivals and my invariably arriving home with gifts ranging from books, prints and paintings to silver and engraved glass. These occasions included St George's Chapel, Windsor Castle and Exeter Cathedral, with an especially memorable festival in King's College Chapel, Cambridge, such a wonderful building for making music in and where, as someone once remarked in terms of its unique acoustics, 'even a sneeze sounds musical'. The final festival was in Romsey Abbey with Colin James, now Bishop of Winchester and an old friend since the Exeter days when he was the BBC's director of religious broadcasting at Bristol, presenting me with a handsomely engraved glass bowl.

There was also the last of the annual round of Christmas carols in the Great Hall at Addington, an informal afternoon which had taken place every year since my arrival and which I always enjoyed conducting with Elisabeth as my accompanist. And finally, to crown it all, Queen Elizabeth The Queen Mother very kindly invited us to a small farewell lunch party which she hosted for Elisabeth and me at Clarence House. This was a most happy and relaxed occasion full of good talk and fun, so much so that we all went on chatting much longer into the afternoon than I suspect was intended.

We moved to Salisbury early in January of 1989, though two days later we returned to Addington for the farewell dinner which the Council had arranged for us and at which both the Archbishop of Canterbury and Lord Coggan together with Lady Coggan were present. There were speeches and generous gifts for us both, with Elisabeth being made an Associate of the RSCM, an entirely unexpected bonus.

CHAPTER TWENTY-ONE

Sarum – Close and City

After a longish and at times frustratingly non-productive search during my final years at the RSCM we eventually found our retirement home. On first seeing it we both immediately sensed that this was the right house even though it was somewhat different from our original idea of either being in the Close or in one of the nearby villages. What we had in fact opted for was a nicely proportioned, if predictable, mid-Victorian house of three storeys, only four minutes walking distance from the cathedral in one direction and the railway station in the other. We have a view of the water-meadows just west of the cathedral which were the haunt of George Herbert when he walked in from Bemerton to the cathedral. So extensive is this view that we might well be in the depths of the country.

Soon after settling in we took a short holiday to Crete to visit the ruined palaces and other architectural delights. We enjoyed the company, most of whom were also retired, though we did wonder why two Cockney couples had opted for this particular tour. They seemed singularly disinterested in either architecture or history and on one occasion when our guide had a lot to say about St Paul one of them was heard to proclaim in a loud voice 'Who the bloody hell was St Paul?'

In my last months at the RSCM I made it quite clear that when retired I had no intention of actively continuing with church music. Having said this rather forcefully and frequently I began to wonder if I had perhaps overstated my case and would be left on the shelf. I genuinely wanted to pursue new interests without the pressures and responsibilities I had previously been subject to.

In the event the business of retiring would all too soon become the busyness of retirement. This was triggered off by my approaching the Bishop of Salisbury and saying that if there was any small task I could do I would be glad to help the Diocese—but not in church music. Swiftly came the invitation to be his representative on the board of governors of the Godolphin School. This I did for a couple of years but I did not feel it was quite my scene and that consequently I contributed less than expected.

For more than twenty years I have been chairman of the Organs Advisory Committee of the Council for the Care of Churches where we give advice on work needing to be done to historic organs. In addition we are able to provide some financial assistance when an application merits this. This prompted the Bishop to ask me to become chairman of the Salisbury Diocesan Advisory Committee, a statutory body which in every diocese seeks to ensure that only the best and most worthy in artistic endeavour is allowed in churches. This was a challenging proposition which, though I warmed to it, made me seriously question whether I had the necessary expertise to guide so high powered a group of specialists who comprise the most unloved committee in any diocese when advice goes counter to what a parish wants, feels it has a right to, and resents the legality of the Faculty Jurisdiction Measure.

I asked to sit in on the monthly meetings for some time; this reassured me and I agreed to take on the task though with some foreboding for, apart from the two organ advisers, I was ill informed by contrast with the expertise all around me, let alone guide them as their chairman. In the event this has proved to be work I greatly enjoy and from which I have learned much about all manner of ecclesiastical needs from the technicalities of lighting, heating and drainage systems to stained glass, memorials, bells, the multifarious work of architects and the reordering of churches to meet current liturgical and worship needs. This last is something I particularly relish for the often exciting opportunities it affords to open up spaces within a church and get rid of so much *bric a brac*, especially Victorian pitch pine pews.

As a committee we advise the Chancellor of the Diocese who is a judge; he then either allows or not proposals put forward by parishes. This process is as much part of the law of the land as is local planning permission in the secular field. This absorbing task demands my regularly visiting parishes in Wiltshire and Dorset in company with members of the committee to give on the spot guidance and advice.

What proved to be the Bishop's hat trick was then to invite me to become one of the four lay canons of the cathedral who, in Salisbury, play a uniquely important role as part of the Dean and Chapter. This has brought me in close contact with the day to day business and decision making of a major cathedral, not least in the ever present constraints of finance with the huge sums involved not only in respect of maintaining the day to day worship and ministry but, especially relevant to Salisbury, the far greater sums needed for the major task of restoring and maintaining the fabric—at the moment the cloisters and the west front of the building. All of this, and more, is in such marked contrast to my years as a cathedral organist, for I now look down the other end of the telescope.

Other interesting new tasks have also come my way or been widened since retirement. Being President of the Incorporated Society of Musicians is a case in point. This is something of a benevolent trades union for the profession, dealing with the interests and concerns of performers, composers, teachers, and music in education. During my term of office the National Curriculum and its many ramifications claimed much time as did broadcasting fee negotiations and the role in many areas of the Musicians' Union.

I continue to be a member of the five-man board of directors of Hymns Ancient and Modern, whose work in recent years has been greatly widened through our acquiring a number of publishing concerns, not least *Church Times*. I enjoyed being part of the Editorial Committee preparing *Worship Songs Ancient and Modern*. This was an entirely new departure for us, involving the gathering together and editing of what we believed to be the best examples of popular choruses, folk songs and the like, many of which had up to then appeared in a conglomeration of publications, with many distinctly suspect or unworthy examples sandwiched between material we considered worthy of retention and promotion.

When Oxford University Press felt the time was ripe to update their popular *Church Anthem Book* they asked me to be General Editor for this project. The original collection of a hundred examples had first appeared in 1933 and I suggested that about one-third of its contents were for one reason or another not now acceptable. I brought in new material both old and especially contemporary, and as much of the editing in the parent book was either sketchy or inaccurate we asked leading scholars to prepare new editions of 16th, 17th and 18th century examples. It was a considerable encouragement to me in compiling a collection of this size for the first time to see the favourable reception it received in the press as well as the resultant sales. I also wrote an accompanying handbook with general hints for choir directors, as well as relevant information hopefully of interest to congregations.

For some time I continued to be fairly heavily involved as part of the Archbishops' Commission in Church Music where, as with most other committees I sit on, I worked with discerning colleagues whose viewpoints I respected and learned from, though there are always those who would drive anyone to despair. New committees and with them new-found responsibilities such as the working party arising from the report of the Archbishops' Commission continue to provide fresh incentives and new challenges, a great deal of which, because it is innovatory for me, is the more stimulating.

These concerns increasingly take me to London, with The Athenaeum being for me more and more a haven of peace and relaxation. I have never ceased in my affection for the spell of London as for club life. For some, the gracious living, good cuisine and wine cellar, together with a degree of politeness not by any means easy to encounter in many areas of life today, might seem élitist—whatever that much quoted word means today—but I do find the club a most rewarding setting where no one disturbs your wish to read, write, or merely cogitate in one of its deep leather armchairs, even if some of them are not all that comfortable. That same element of quietness applies equally to being able to read *The Times* over a silent breakfast. I am all in unashamed favour of gracious living and, as for élitism, I suspect

215

that some who shout the loudest in condemning it are often guilty of an inverted snobbery which smacks of jealousy, if the truth were known.

Living in Salisbury is in every respect the antithesis of all this, a privilege we never cease to be grateful for, especially when perhaps after a long day of meetings in London I am at Waterloo Station and hear the train announcer reel off those magical station names so redolent of the Atlantic Coast Express of old. And then, ninety minutes later, the welcoming spire of Salisbury Cathedral comes into sight, keeping watch over the city, whether it be on a summer evening or on a winter night when the floodlighting makes it more majestic than ever, swathed in the steel scaffolding which envelops its extensive restoration work.

Weekday Evensongs and early morning weekday Eucharists in the cathedral are an especial joy, yet best of all is the centrality of the Sunday Eucharist with its spendidly ordered liturgical awareness, musical excellence, and the care taken in doing all things well and with unfussy dignity, the ongoing reliability of impressive preaching and, perhaps most important of all, the moments of silence, a rare commodity in much of today's worship. With clatter and chatter a feature of so much contemporary churchgoing, surely St Denis had his priorities right when he suggested that 'Man rises to contemplation of the divine through the senses'.

The daily round of the cathedral's prayer life is something very precious to us both. This is particularly so in Holy Week services with the intensely moving Liturgy of Good Friday. As I grow older I invariably find such services more spiritually fulfilling than the great paeans of praise on festival occasions, though there is always here in Salisbury the enriching power of music so beautifully presented and performed. What a privilege this is— and such an aid to worship.

In a wider context, another reason for wanting to live in Salisbury was the countryside of Wiltshire, and especially Dorset with its Thomas Hardy and T. E. Lawrence associations, the magnificent coastline south of Dorchester stretching on westwards into Devon with the unusual rise and fall of the hills.

And how good to the eye is the immensity of the broad sweep of Salisbury Plain and the Downs above Marlborough.

Salisbury itself is inhabited by interesting people many of whom are similarly in retirement. At Addington we may have lived in a rather special house in the midst of the Surrey hills, but we seldom came into contact with many people other than through our work, whereas here it is all so different, with not a little entertaining the enjoyable order of many a day.

And then in 1992 Exeter, of blessed memory, awarded me from its university an honorary doctorate in music, a distinction I greatly cherish.

The Associated Board of the Royal Schools of Music for whom I have been an examiner for many years quickly pounced on my new-found freedom with tempting invitations to examine in many parts of the world. With my love of travel I put up little or no resistance and in the five remaining years before reaching the age limit of 70 I was sent to South Africa, Mauritius, Namibia, New Zealand, Malta, Bermuda, the United States, Canada and Switzerland. I also experienced for the first time the extraordinary opulence of the Gulf States and with it the bid of each state to produce hotels excelling in grandeur and luxury those of their neighbouring counterparts. I particularly enjoyed sorties into the desert even if many of the Bedouin tents now proudly sport a television aerial, a far cry from the desert T. E. Lawrence knew. I found Bahrain and Dubai especially fascinating in their history, as in driving over the mountains into Oman and coming down to the Straits of Hormuz incessantly plied by giant oil tankers. As the British Empire has disintegrated and receded into history so the Gulf in many respects has taken over, not least in its virile international cities which remain the great trading emporiums they have been for centuries. The fabulous wealth of the Gulf States created by vast oil revenues have rapidly made them without parallel the 20th century growth areas.

And how good it was to be in Cairo once again after so many years' absence, even if much had inevitably changed. All Saints' Cathedral no longer nestles in its nostalgically English-style Close, for it was demolished to make way for yet another six-lane bridge over the Nile. Its replacement in Zamalek was wisely conceived on a much smaller scale, for the post-war congregation is greatly diminished. Gone in all but name is Groppi, while the Gezira Sporting Club has become a sort of free for all Macdonalds. Most of the familiar war-time haunts are no more, nor are most of the street names one knew, even if they smacked of empire. No trace remains of Music for All, while the Semiramis Hotel which was so full of character, even though its former splendour had already become somewhat faded during the war years, has been replaced by a monotonous carbon copy of so many present day hotels the world over, a predictable bedroom layout with outsize table lamp and reproductions of contemporary paintings which as you lie in bed keep you guessing as to what, if anything, they are meant to represent.

If we thought Cairo dirty in the 1940s, it would seem orderly as compared with today when people, buildings, rubbish and vehicles are in such profusion. Some of the past still lingers on nostalgically in Alexandria which, with its French Mediterranean ambience, architecture and relative peacefulness, is in marked contrast to the noise, bustle and uniquely distinctive odours which are so much a feature of Cairo, and which have not changed.

Retirement has also provided Elisabeth and me with opportunities for holiday travel as never before. Short visits to Prague and Florence have been complemented by one to St Petersburg. This fulfilled our wish to see what in the event was architecture even more magnificent in its scale, beauty and colour than we had ever envisaged.

During the Mozart bicentenary year a leisurely boat ferried us down the Danube from Passau to Budapest, taking in Vienna, Melk and other places en route. Plenty of Mozart was thrown in for good value.

Then, in 1994, we embarked on a two-month round-the-world tour, for the first time ever pure holiday and no work. We began in the Cook Islands in the Southern Pacific before being in New Zealand, Australia and Tasmania for over a month. We stayed for part of the time with friends and visited places where no musical connection had previously claimed me. The Great

Barrier Reef, Ayers Rock, the two-day journey on the Indian Pacific train from Melbourne to Perth, Milford Sound at the bottom of New Zealand and Cape Reinga at the top, were followed by short stays in Singapore, Hong Kong and Bangkok, this last being a first for us both and most rewarding for the architectural splendours of its temples and palaces.

While I continue to be involved with an interestingly varied menu of committees and projects in Salisbury and London, Elisabeth turns her attention to the family, especially so when new babes arrive and she assumes an amalgam of granny, nanny and *au pair*. We are so fortunate in having four happily married daughters and ten grandchildren. Two families are in London and one in Oxfordshire. With Juliet and Giles living in Brussels, their young family is rapidly becoming bi-lingual, while Luke, all of six years old, was disappointed on his first journey through the Channel Tunnel not to see any fish as he hopefully looked out through the window.

While we were at Addington my rapidly expanding collection of books had to be housed wherever I could find space. Consequently it was higgledy-piggledy and in no real order, so at Salisbury I carefully designed shelves and cupboards for my study which were then made up by an artistic local carpenter. Although everything is now potentially in order and catalogued there are still occasions when some of my 7,000 books manage temporarily to elude me, but my study is permeated by the highly individual aroma of books, and how distinctively different American books are in this respect as compared with English ones.

My love of book collecting has grown apace over the years and continues to broaden. I now possess a large collection of T. E. Lawrence and associated material, and have embarked in a similar, though smaller, way on Siegfried Sassoon and Eric Gill, as well as collecting private press books and bibliographies. My delight in book design and in handling beautifully printed and bound editions has become something of an obsession. In this my mentor and guide is Anthony Rota whose father, Bertram Rota, founded what has now become one of the most highly respected firms dealing in modern first editions. Over the years I have got to know Anthony well and respect his utter honesty and his help in our business relationships. He is always guarded in encouraging me not to buy anything I may see which he considers to be unduly excessive in price and not in pristine condition, while he has introduced me to many delights which have helped to widen my literary interests. We have also become good friends into the bargain and, as we both enjoy good food, good wine, and club life, we repair from time to time to the Athenaeum for lunch or else he will take me to the Garrick.

To mark the 50th anniversary of T. E. Lawrence's death Anthony and I jointly produced a little book in a limited edition of 100 copies containing Hugh Walpole's hitherto unpublished review of *Seven Pillars of Wisdom*, the manuscript of which I possess. As a frontispiece we reproduced a drawing of Lawrence sketched by Augustus John at the Versailles Peace Conference in 1919 which I had purchased a few years ago. To complete the book Rupert Hart-Davis wrote an informative introduction. Later, in 1988, when the National Portrait Gallery mounted a comprehensive Lawrence centenary exhibition they included some of my treasures.

Two private presses have especially claimed my interest. Stanbrook Abbey, the Benedictine monastic house near Worcester, was one of the first such presses working in a relatively small way. My introduction to its work was Siegfried Sassoon's *The Path to Peace*, his final collection of poems. This acquisition led to my getting to know Dame Hildelith Cuming, the printer, whose quality of work was exemplary, especially in design. The fact that she had been a student at the Royal Academy of Music and, as it later transpired, was the guiding force behind the Panel of Monastic Musicians which was to work in close liaison with the RSCM, were further contact points. Through the kindness of Dame Hildelith I now have a large collection of interesting ephemera from the Press.

The Whittington Press, under the guidance of John and Rosalind Randle, has embarked on a wide range of books, some of them extremely ambitious, beautifully designed, printed and bound, and many of which I acquire as and when they are published. And then there is always without fail the anticipatory pleasure of opening parcels coming from one or other of the Presses and dealers.

Elisabeth has always been a steadying force, coping over the years with my temperament and moods, though I rejoice that I have now mellowed in this respect. Never having been all that good a listener I seem now to be more vague than ever, all too often tending to switch off, however involuntarily. I also know that I am given to exaggeration in some of the statements I make. 'Never trust his figures; take off two noughts and you'll be much nearer the mark' is a favourite family quip.

Now, in our twilight years, we look forward to the future, hopefully together, for none of us should surely validly hanker for the past other than in reminiscence. I remember reading somewhere that 'the present contains the seeds of the future'.

For me, as I envisage for many others, it is the memory of people which is so potent a factor in looking back to the past, those whose voices ring through crystal clear from earlier days. Yet it is sad to realise how many we lose touch with over the years and the friends who have as it were sunk without trace, especially those who at one time were much in evidence in church music circles and who have disappeared into the woodwork. And then there are those who, having married, cut off many of their links with friends of old, or maintain only a discreetly cautious, token and distant connection. Of others, death has taken its inevitable toll, some well before their allotted span. There are so many ghosts.

Over the years personalities and characters abounded. One such, whom I have already mentioned, was John Sanderson, an eccentric of the first order, and something of an enigma, who, despite my knowing him well, I never really succeeded in fathoming. He was so complicated and unpredictable, not least in his comings and goings. He would disappear for months at a time and then suddenly resurface, expecting conversation to go on as if he had only been away for a few days. But he rejoiced in being a man of mystery and evasiveness, and delighted in shocking all and sundry. I well remember during our early years as students together at the Royal Academy of Music that we shared a great regard for the music of another eccentric, Peter Warlock, and how when we visited his grave at Godalming John urinated on it as a mark of what he regarded as respect. John could be extremely vitriolic which could be either refreshingly delightful or embarrassing in the extreme. If you happened to waver over any matter, you knew his unfailing retort would be 'Damn it all, man, don't be mealy-mouthed. Speak your mind', a maxim which on many occasions landed him in trouble. His attitude could all too easily stretch the bonds of friendship to the limit for those of us who subscribed to more stable and rational relationships. John could certainly be difficult though I never for a moment questioned his integrity and sincerity, nor his deeply held religious beliefs.

In a parallel way I have known cathedral organists who, though exceedingly gifted, were utterly impossible, even to the extent of being infantile, in their relationships and dealings with people. But the course of history is peppered with eccentrics, delightful or otherwise. T. E. Lawrence was reputed to be able to read a book in a matter of minutes, such was his photographic eye and mind, while Peter Warlock, before he turned on the gas to commit suicide, thoughtfully put his cat out into the street. The composer Bernard van Dieren at a crisis in illness had a temperature of 112 degrees. And then there were Edith Sitwell and Oscar Wilde, pre-eminent examples among many intriguing and extremely gifted eccentrics, and such a boon to biographers. Genius often produces strange oddities, not least among those I have known who were 'gay', which invariably meant they were also highly gifted and skilled, and yet by a seemingly strange quirk so gracious towards women.

Although I have never cultivated many lifelong friends with whom I have been in constant touch, a number almost come within this category. Christopher Regan, who since the time that we were students together, was for many years Director of Studies at the Royal Academy of Music; Allan Wicks who was organist of Canterbury Cathedral and who is now a fellow Director with me of Hymns Ancient and Modern; and not least Irvine Watson, for many years Secretary of the British Council, now retired and living in York. He is the most admirable and caring of bachelor hosts, whom Elisabeth and I always look forward to staying with in his elegant house at Fulford. He and I also contrive to meet fairly frequently in London either at his club or mine. It gave me much pleasure to nominate him for membership of Nobody's Friends, the dining club of which I have been a member for some years and which meets three times annually in the Guard Room at Lambeth Palace. I am the only musician member and it is refreshing to be in the company of archbishops, bishops, politicians, judges and headmasters.

One instinctively senses the difference between real friendships and those which are contrived or superficial. I think of some of the church musicians I know in North America and Australia who, although they may have been blessed with pronounced musical gifts, often came across as self-satisfied people, full of their own importance, which can often seem to be linked with questionable sexual proclivities. Bertrand Russell perhaps got it right when he spoke of window dressing as being irresistible to Americans.

CHAPTER TWENTY-TWO

Reflections on reaching 70

In order to arrive at what you are not
You must go through the way in which you are not.
T. S. Eliot: *East Coker*

The passage of time seems to have bleached out men's stains.
T. E. Lawrence: *Seven Pillars of Wisdom*

While it is one thing to be nostalgic, which is certainly indicative of advancing years, I have never hankered to be back in work I have completed and left. I had few real regrets at leaving anywhere or anything, choosing to think less of closed chapters than the anticipation of new tasks, new pastures and, above all, new challenges, which seem to me to be far more of the essence. As a result, I have now settled easily and painlessly into a new way of life which is quite different from anything I have previously known, and I certainly do not have the slightest wish to be involved in any way with the work of the RSCM where there is plenty of new initiative building on the best of the past and expanding into new areas of perceived need, which is exactly what I in my turn had sought to do. The new regime is rightly imposing its new thinking and personalities, even though I may not entirely agree with all of it. In this sort of situation who does?

THE CHURCH AND THE WORLD. It is all too easy, and fashionable, to dwell on the current difficulties confronting the Church where so much of the traditional is questioned, probed or even discarded, and where many are reluctant or unwilling to take eternal truths at their face value any more.

A sizeable part of the Church universal seems obsessed with charismatic, casual and informal worship in which structured liturgy plays little or no part. The fervour this generates, with the urgency to write off as of no consequence those of us who have not experienced this particular brand of renewal, further classifies those of us not of this vocabulary as being second-class Christians. I prefer to think of renewal as an ongoing process affecting most of what I do, in or out of church. How relatively seldom is it the sudden and blinding light on the road to Damascus.

The rejection of awe and reverence, the wholesale matiness, the clatter and chatter of so much contemporary worship is unacceptable, even abhorrent to many, and a far cry from the Warden of Barchester who suggested that 'where there is no music there is no mystery, and where there is no mystery there is no true worship'. Jeremy Taylor, the 17th century divine, spoke of joy as 'the perfectest convoy for religion', though I suspect he meant that *inner* joy which can, and surely should, be the experience of so much worship.

I spoke earlier of the failure of many theological colleges to make their students aware of the power of music as an ingredient of worship and an instrument of evangelism. Music surely should be an inescapable and inevitable constituent in the ministry of every priest.

The fragmentation of what we once conveniently referred to as churchmanship has now mushroomed to a bewilderingly wide spectrum, ranging from high Anglo Catholic to a conglomeration of born again Christian sects, the latter drawing in the crowds. Why is this? Is it a passing fashion, as have been other renewal movements in the past, or is it disenchantment with the *status quo*? Are codes of Christian principles long subscribed to in the process of being eroded away? Is it that adherence to strict discipline is being offloaded and exchanged for an all too easy acceptance of compassion and 'love' being emphasised, come what may?

Here, as in the higher echelons of the established Church, thinking is so confused, with the seeming failure of the House of Bihops to arrive at a consensus on issues such as the ordination of women to the priesthood, the remarriage of divorcees and gay/lesbian issues. In a world where virtually everything is questioned and scrutinised, within the Church some contest, even debunk, aspects of fundamental belief. Is it any wonder that the resulting insecurity and lack of leadership from the Church reflect so adversely, and to the confusion of many of those in the pews whose faith is grounded in simple and unquestioning terms? The apparent certainty and veracity of what fringe sects offer may on the face of it seem to be an attractive alternative for many.

On a personal level I find it no less hard now than ever to pray in a calculated way, and in this I am only too aware of the morning and evening discipline which Elisabeth exerts in this respect and which is in contrast to my all too spasmodic approach, though I tend to rely more and more on what Dick Babington when he was Archdeacon of Exeter referred to as 'arrow' prayers. I invariably find it easier to say my prayers spurred on by the spontaneous inspiration of events as they unfold such as when I see hills, mountains and the eternal snow, or visit great churches and cathedrals and hear lovely music, even in the train going up to London. But perhaps this is me being undisciplined and too simplistic.

Nevertheless, I have all along been only too aware of the guidance of the Holy Spirit at every remove. This is not mere wishful thinking, though I do now realise more than ever before the need to pray in thanksgiving more than in constantly asking for what I want, a shortcoming perhaps too much in evidence in many contemporary approaches to worship. Jill Furze, the poet wife of Laurence Whistler, wrote that 'so often I find myself praying too much in petition and not nearly enough in gratitude'.

In this context I have frequently borne in mind one of Michael Ramsey's comments on religious experience, 'People have asked me if I have ever felt like losing my faith. No: my faith is part of me. But faith isn't a state of easy and calm security. It is an adventure of ceaseless battling with troubles: a peace of mind and serenity indeed, but a costly peace and serenity in the midst of conflict'.

In the wider and non-ecclesiastical sphere, thinking back fifty years is in many respects more vivid and easier to contemplate than five years ago. How relatively peaceful, relaxed, and gentle much of life then was, with crime and violence but a fraction of what they are today. It was a world in which you could with impunity leave your bicycle unchained and your car unlocked. Perhaps by a quirk of human nature it is the best of the past which generally predominates, while time has the habit and convenient knack of eradicating the unpleasant as well as the uncomfortable which we prefer not to remember or contemplate. I do just wonder if life then was in fact really all that halcyon. Certainly the bees in my mother's lavender bushes at Uplands lazily went about their task perhaps even reflecting something of the nature of life at that time. Yet somehow the smell of lavender seems in retrospect evocative of what for me in the 1930s was synonymous with quiet summer days when the sun seemed to be for ever shining—or was it?—for when we experienced thunder-storms they were mightily fierce ones. But, again and again, it is smell which acts as a potent and nostalgic reminder of the past such as when I recently passed someone in the street who was smoking a cigar. It was the smell which immediately transplanted me back to boyhood, to my grandfather's house and with it a momentary picture of those round brass ashtrays attached to a leather strap on the arm of an easy chair permeated by the added aroma of stale tobacco ash.

Today, as you travel worldwide, so much has become commonplace, almost monochrome. Modern hotels are a particularly valid example, having an all but identical bedroom and bathroom layout, even to the same dry air-conditioning smell in the corridors. Everything from bath essence, shampoo sachet and Gideon Bible is predictable. Many of the old style hotels which were full of individual character have either been torn down as with the Semimaris in Cairo, or have been rebuilt and tarted up beyond recognition, which has destroyed the personality and individuality which was previously so attractive a feature. The Imperial at Sliema in Malta, the old part of the Taj Mahal in Bombay, and the Mount Nelson in Cape Town have so far resisted bland modernisation as had Ryall's in Blantyre, though it is all of twenty years since I last stayed there and, who knows, maybe it has now succumbed to an eager development corpora-tion or an international hotel chain. And, as for television aerials, they are now in profusion the world over and have ruined the character of many a once beautiful city roofline.

Overall we seem to inhabit a world afraid of silence. Oh for the joys of life devoid of noise instead of cars revved up and accelerated dangerously by angry young men bent on showing off, with Radio One blaring forth and imposing itself on all and sundry. And then there is the curse of the mobile telephone; how ridiculous people look using it as they walk along the street, the more so when they clutch a half eaten sandwich in the other hand. Even on a train to London I could not avoid hearing a man having a loud telephone argument with his wife. And then, when winners of the National Lottery noisily proclaim the priority social status of having an expensive car, one is left wondering if the prognosis for the future of society in general is all that reassuring.

At my juncture in life I find I have cultivated certain likes and even stronger dislikes. Perhaps I am becoming something of an eccentric. While the late arrival of the postman puts me, perhaps childishly, in a bad mood, I do enjoy expeditions to the graves of famous people, and staying in smart hotels, with unhurried total immersion in a piping hot bath more relaxing than the vagaries of a shower which is invariably either too hot or too cold. I find myself becoming increasingly irritated by television newsreaders and weather forecasters who bid me 'Hallo—and a *very* good evening', television credits which move so quickly that you cannot read them, and being expected to look at friends' holiday photos. My greatest *bête-noir* is men who come into a restaurant with hands buried in trouser pockets and who then proceed to take off their jacket to eat. As a boy I was taught in both instances to do the very opposite for reasons of good manners bred into me by my parents. I see no reason, need or logic to depart from these principles.

Today we so often witness to our detriment thinking which denigrates the past and seeks to devalue our imperial history. There is an almost obsessive cult for promoting the shoddy and the unworthy in so many walks of life, instead of proudly raising our sights high and keeping them there. In a word, there is far too little national pride and aspiration in either the past or the present, linked with a frightening sense of malaise.

Having witnessed the all but universal abandoning of so many values, I can only re-echo what Osbert Sitwell felt in 1914 when he suggested leaving others younger and less resentful to cope with the accelerating onslaught of change in attitudes and values within contemporary society.

On a more cheering note I continue to enjoy meeting and talking to interesting people, which for me is as potent a stimulant as that produced by certain places. One such place is the chapel of King's College, Cambridge, which I first visited as a schoolboy organ enthusiast. I was greatly moved by the beauty of the building, and its spell never ceases to work its magic on me every time I enter it. At the time this spell was so forcefully complemented for me by the 'devout prayer' of the College's founder, King Henry VI:

O Lord Jesus Christ, who has created and redeemed me, and hast brought me hither where I am: thou knowest what thou wouldest do with me; do with me according to thy will, with mercy. Amen.

These words have been with me constantly over the years, not least as a help in times of depression and uncertainty.

I frequently ponder the words of Bunyan's Shepherd-boy's Song: 'I am content with what I have, little it be or much', for I am now really content, not with a little but with so much, and I never cease to be grateful for the good fortunes which have come my way. I am acutely aware of having been immensely lucky and of how different the course of events could have been, and probably would have been, but for my flat feet in my initial army training.

CHAPTER TWENTY-THREE

Towards the future?

Time present and time past
Are both perhaps present in time future,
And time future contained in time past.
    T. S. Eliot: *Burnt Norton*

. . . to make an end is to make a beginning.
    T. S. Eliot: *Little Gidding*

Why quote Eliot again? Because I believe these to be two profound statements, the more so as he is spatial and forward-looking, and this we all must surely be by our very nature. We have to scan new horizons.

       'We cannot revive old factions
       we cannot restore old policies
       or follow an antique drum'.

T. S. Eliot yet again. Everything is conditioned to that of looking forward. It is as unnatural to walk backwards for more than a few paces as it is to drive one's car in reverse gear other than for a few yards. Similarly, a stream moves forward for, if it ceases to do so, it will stagnate. Even so, we all inevitably look back, whether it be in nostalgia or, as we grow older, through an instinctive reluctance to change things, often preferring to remember what we now *think* of as the good days of the distant past, for the passage of time has the knack of glossing over, softening, or even eradicating, the less than pleasant memories, even though Lawrence Durrell may have cynically remarked that 'History is the endless repetition of the wrong way of living', or, as someone once commented, memory is either a delusion or a survival kit. Perhaps it is a bit of both.

    Change, as I suggested earlier, must never be equated with decay, but rather as a challenge which we either cope with or reject. What we must have, and take on in abundance, are vision, imagination and, above all, faith. This last I sometimes find the hardest of all, especially when we experience the death of old people such as Elisabeth's mother who at the age of 92 wanted no more than to slip peacefully away, as she eventually did, though not without a period of much waiting, when we sensed her soul struggling to release itself from the body it was locked into. Perhaps there was something of Gerontius there—'the mind bold and independent, the purpose free'. Whittier contemplated death as 'the covered way that leadeth unto light', for death is surely the most incomprehensible and mysterious of all situations, with life beyond the grave a state which relies utterly on faith. As finite mortals we cannot comprehend immortality or the infinite any more than it has been given us to see beyond the as yet impenetrable veil. Yet, if there were no mystery, there would be less reason for faith.

Even so, whatever that great mystery will reveal to us, I not too naively hope that among 'those who rejoice with us but upon another shore', (as the Bidding Prayer of the Christmas Eve Festival of Nine Lessons and Carols so vividly puts it), I shall have contact again with those I have known and admired, not least perhaps J. S. Bach and T. E. Lawrence, for I cannot conceive of eternity without the music of Bach. But, because we cannot think in other than mortal or finite terms, any such visions, or existence, will obviously not be in the shape or form which are at present the only ways in which we can comprehend, blinkered and limited as our vision is. Dame Felicitas Corrigan, in her book on Siegfried Sassoon, wrote 'Though I pray each night for preparedness of soul for the day of my death, when it will be judged . . . yet there is the unanswered question—how much—if any—of human memory survives? . . . I suppose the best thing to do is to say "I trust you, O my God, and I leave it all to you".'

There are times when I have to admit to some nagging uncertainties. Who does not? Suppose death were the end? Yet, as we look around at the beauty and innate wonder of this planet and universe, my inner faith consolidates itself and reassures me. In this I am so greatly helped and constantly renewed, as I know others are, by the spirituality, the witness and, not least, the beauty of Salisbury Cathedral, especially when I look up and see

231

bold and clear above the High Altar the words 'Though I be lifted up, yet will I draw all men unto me'.

I frequently find now that some chance happening will suddenly take me back to my early days, such as when I was recently walking towards the High Street Gate which leads to the Close and saw the graceful spire half hidden from view by a damp and misty December morning. My thoughts immediately went back to my first sight of the cathedral, when as a young teenager I came to play the organ on just such a winter's day, when cathedral cities somehow seem to take on a special aura. Little did I then envisage, all those years ago, the path on which life would take me, nor did it even remotely occur to me that I should come to live here these many years later, although it was at about that time that I first came across Henry VI's prayer which has seldom been out of my thoughts or utterance since, for I do believe most fervently in the guidance of the Holy Spirit and in what is ordained. The course of events is often the very opposite from what one anticipates or would have. On the wall above my desk are *Ten Rules for the Spiritual Life*, the thoughts of the 5th century Diadochus of Photike. Beautifully printed by the Stanbrook Abbey Press, they are a continuing source of thought and guidance, not least the parting injunction 'merrily to meet the sadness of death'.

But—I hope there is yet time to spare, and a lot of it, time to relax, time to see more of the world, time to be with Elisabeth more, with our daughters and their families, and above all time for more unrestricted and unconditioned joy, but in the rightful sense of that much misused contemporary concept in the Church. Time also to enjoy good health and hopefully for not seeing ourselves becoming increasingly immobile or unable to communicate in a lucid way—and time for quietness, silence, for reading and for repose.

When Robert Runcie retired as Archbishop of Canterbury, his predecessor Donald Coggan wrote in appreciation 'For all that has been—thanks. To all that will be—yes . . . The best is yet to be . . . The last of life for which the first was made'.

And now it really is time for me to end or, as someone once said to an after dinner speaker, 'If you cannot finish, do at least stop'.

Perhaps the last word must again be with T. S. Eliot, that most mystical of 20th century poets, who in *Little Gidding* said
We shall not cease from exploration . . .
And the end of all our exploring
Will be to arrive where we started
And know the place for the first time.

The end is where we start from.

Index

Addington Palace 9, 10
  College of St Nicolas 152-156
Alcock, Sir Walter 26
Alexandra Palace 4, 5
Alexandria 218
Archbishops' Commission on
  Church Music 185, 215
Armytage, Duncan 86
ASB Psalter 161
Associated Board of the Royal
  Schools of Music 74, 75, 123,
  130-134, 138, 146, 196, 217
Association of Anglican Musicians
  172, 183
Aston, Peter 160, 163
Athenaeum, The 165, 215, 216,
  220
Australia 218, 219

Babington, Dick 107, 108, 112,
  226
Bad Homburg 134
Badminton, John 144, 145
Bahrain 198
Baillie, Isobel 81, 95, 169
Bairstow, Sir Edward 39, 43-47,
  50, 51, 66, 70, 73
Baker, Bishop John 213, 214
Baker, Richard 157, 167
Balmforth, Henry 107, 144
Barbirolli, Sir John 96, 116
  Lady Evelyn 167
Barrow, John 161
Bartlett, Donald 98
Battle of Britain 32, 33
Bavin, Bishop Timothy 194
BBC 119, 127, 128, 135, 138, 160,
  161, 165, 184, 186
  Children's Hour 29
  In Town Tonight 29
  ITMA 29
  Monday Night at Eight o'clock
  29
Beccles 33

Beecham, Sir Thomas 47
Bennett, H. A. 26
BET 164, 182
Beverley 40-42
Blantyre 227
Bombay 134, 197
Boston (Mass) 194
Boult, Sir Adrian 121
Bournemouth Symphony Orchestra
  115, 116, 120, 121, 136, 142
Bristol, Lee H. 171
British Army of the Rhine (BAOR)
  170, 172, 175, 195, 196
British Council 59, 74, 85, 126,
  198

Cairo 53-63, 123, 217
  All Saints' Cathedral 57-59,
    123, 217
  Music for All 56-63
  Semiramis Hotel 57, 123, 227
Calcutt, Sir David 137
Calcutta 132, 133
Cambridge, King's College Chapel
  56, 158, 163, 229
Canterbury 15
Cape Town 144, 148, 149, 173
  Mount Nelson Hotel 144,
    148, 199, 227
Cason, Frank 10, 11
Cathedral Organists' Association
  97, 167
Cathedral Peak (Drakensburgs) 195
Cecil, Bishop Lord William Cecil
  109
Churchill, John 191
  Jean 191
Charleston 175, 199
Chatham, Dockyard 30
  Navy Week 30
  Parish Church 26, 38
Chelsea, St Luke's 36
Chicago 192
Childe Okeford 161

Cobham 4
Coggan, Archbishop Donald 165, 182, 211
Collins, Peter 158
Cooper, Janet 158, 159
   Jilly 209
Coronation, The (1953) 89, 90
Corrigan, Dame Felicitas 231
Crystal Cathedral 193, 194
Cuming, Dame Hildelith 220

Dakers, Charles 4, 5
   Dora 4
   Dorothy 4
   Ethel (mother) 4-6, 8-13, 15, 17, 19, 22, 24-31, 33, 34, 38, 50, 64, 78, 126, 210
   Felicity 105, 114, 116, 144
   Geoffrey 3
   Juliet 97, 105, 219
   Lewis (father) 6-10, 12-15, 19, 22, 24-26, 28-34, 36, 38, 49, 50, 64, 78, 85, 126, 210
   Mary 97, 137, 144
   Rachel 85, 105, 137
   William 3, 14
   William Henry 1, 2
Daldry, Sir Leonard 140, 141
Dams, John 107, 108, 143
Darjeeling 133
Dartington String Quartet 115
Delhi 197, 198
Dent, Edward 48, 67
Durham University 51
Durston, Monty 177
Dykes Bower, Sir John 122, 137, 143
   Michael 85, 122, 123

Eastbourne 88
Edmonton (Alberta) 175
Elgar 37
Exeter 103-151
Exeter Cathedral Old Choristers' Association 120
Exeter Chamber Orchestra 115, 116

Exeter Cathedral 84, 102
Exeter Diocesan Choral Association 112, 120, 128, 182
Exeter Musical Society 113-116, 121, 126, 129, 130, 135, 136, 139, 142, 143, 146
Exeter University 217
Europe, Diocese of 196
European Music Year 185

Fellowes, E. H. 74, 75
Fenby, Eric 50
Ferguson, John 195
   Maureen 195
Ferrier, Kathleen 47, 81
Festival Chorus (Exeter) 120, 141, 142
Fiji 177, 198
Finchley, St Mary at 68, 69
Ford, May 77, 79
Frindsbury, All Saints' Church 35

Gate Theatre 4
Germani, Fernando 119
Gibson, Bill and Ethel 49, 71
Gill, Eric 99, 219
Glyndebourne 143
Goddard, Charles 115
Goossens, Leon 169
Graham, Harry 98
Grahamstown 148, 172, 174, 203
Grand Canyon 192
Gravesend County School 31
Greene, Eric 113
Groves, Sir Charles 116, 121, 157, 167
Gulf States 217

Hall, Ted 107
Hanson, Ned 191
Harris, Sir William 72-85, 88, 89, 97
Harrogate String Orchestra 96
Heath, Sir Edward 168, 182
Heath, Mary 141
Henley on Thames 17, 97, 100, 117

Hill, Derek Ingram 164, 165
Hill, Olive 60
Holderness, Winsome 141
Hopkins, Douglas 69, 131, 132
Horsley, Colin 113
Howells, Herbert 157
How, Martin 163, 164, 174, 181
Hong Kong 131, 132, 171, 176, 197
   Mandarin Hotel 131
   Peninsula Hotel 131, 132
   Repulse Bay Hotel 132
   St John's Cathedral 131
Hughes, Frederic 94, 98
Hurford, Peter 158, 210
Hughes, Marian 181
Huntsville in Alabama 192
Hymns Ancient and Modern 168, 214, 222

Incorporated Association of Organists 143, 168
Incorporated Society of Musicians 214
India 132
In Town Tonight 29
ITMA 29

Jackson, Francis 100, 158, 174
James, Bishop Colin 211
Jarrett, Miss 7, 8
Jasper, Ronald 111
Jefferies, Richard 47
Johannesburg 125, 144, 145
Johnson, George and Polly 68, 69
Johnstone, Rupert 19-21

Kennedy's Latin Primer 20
Kenya 147
King's Singers 183
Kiwanis Music Festival 191
Kneller Hall 164
Knight, Gerald 62, 129, 145, 149, 155, 165, 167, 170, 188
Knight, Marcus 106, 107
Knox, Pat 64

Lanzerac Hotel, Stellenbosch 149
Latin for Today 20
Laughton, Dennis 49
Lawrence, T. E. 68, 85, 87, 122, 194, 210, 217, 219
Leighton, Michael 186
Leipzig 210
Levett, Joe 21, 26
Ley, Henry 75-77, 81, 83, 84, 110
Litton, James 177
Llewelyn, Reginald 107
Lloyd, John 35
Lyall, Gordon 194, 199
   Dorothy 194, 199

Macao 132
Madras 133
Malacca 131
Malawi 148
Malta 138
Marchant, Sir Stanley 50, 68
Massey, Roy 161
Mathias, William 183
Matjiesfontein 173
Mauritius 125, 126
Mayrhofen 80, 139
McKie, Sir William 66, 172
Medway Towns 65
'Meet, Eat and Sing' 164
Melbourne 196, 197
Michelmore, Sir Godwin 141
Milton, Alan 124
Mississippi, Diocesan Conference 177
Mitchell, Ena 95, 115
Montgomery, Field Marshal 141
Moody, Charles 93, 94, 97
Moore, Reginald 104
Morgan, Paul 130
Morshead, Mary 86
   Sir Owen 86, 140
Mortimer, Bishop Robert 108, 109, 140
Music for All, Cairo 56, 59-63
Musicians' Benevolent Fund 168

Nairobi 147
Navy Week 30
Nethsingha, Lucian 148
New Mexico 192
Newton, Ivor 169
New Zealand 218, 219
New Orleans 199
Nicholson, Sir Sydney 36
Nicholson House, Addington Palace 146, 179, 180
'Nobody's Friends' 223
Nsubaga, Edward 190

Ootacamund 133, 134, 197
Oram, Bishop Kenneth 174
Organ, The 36
Organs Advisory Committee 143, 187, 213
Oxford University Press 215
Oxley, Harrison 163

Parkinson, John and Joan 198
Patterson, Paul 117, 130, 183
Penang 176
Perth (Western Australia) 176
Peto, Jim and Carice 195
Poole, Joseph 160
Poona 134

Quilter, Roger 71
Quirk, John Shirley 116, 142, 183

Read, Ernest 69
Rediffusion 164, 167, 176, 193
Redlands University 173
Regan, Christopher 222
Rickard, Jeffrey 173
Ridley, Dame Betty 68, 146, 185
    Michael 68
Ripon Cathedral 90, 92-102
    Choral Society 95, 96
Roberts, Bishop Edward 140
Rochester 19-31
    Cathedral Choir School 19-31
    High Street 30
Rose, Reginald 51

Rota, Anthony 219, 220
Routley, Erik 135, 136, 165, 174, 191
Royal Academy of Music 62, 65-70, 90, 101
Royal Army Education Corps 50, 59
Royal Army Pay Corps 42-59
Royal College of Organists 50, 63, 71, 130, 143, 145, 158, 169
RSCM Diamond Jubilee 160, 182, 183
    Golden Jubilee 157, 160, 174
Russell, Lady Dorothea 56, 59, 61
Rutter, John 157, 168

Salisbury DAC 213, 214
    Lay Canonry 214
    (Zimbabwe) 124
Salzburg 101
Sanderson, John 67, 69, 70, 81, 88, 99, 100, 118, 123, 191, 221, 222
    Marjorie 191
Sassoon, Siegfried 61, 62, 64, 219, 220, 231
Scaitcliffe School 77, 81
Scandinavia 196
Secker, Martin 64
Sellick, Phyllis 116, 143
Shaw, Allan 171
Shaw, Martin 4
Shephard, Richard 163, 183
Sherborne, Bishop of 209
Shewring, Walter 99
Singapore 130, 131, 176, 197
Slough, St Mary's 80
Smith, Barry 148, 199
South Africa 124, 125, 144, 145, 147, 148, 172-175
Southern Cathedrals Festival 157, 184
Southern Rhodesia (Zimbabwe) 124, 148, 171
Sowerby, Leo 123
St George's School, Windsor Castle 77

St Michael's College, Tenbury 165
St Peter's Singers 121
Stanbrook Abbey Press 220, 232
Steinitz, Paul 70
Stonor, Francis 60, 67
Strood 1
    Gordon Road School 7, 8
    High Street 13, 14
Swann, Donald 135, 167

Tasmania 171
Taylor, Cyril 161, 165
Tenbury, St Michael's College 59
Thornhill, Miss 19
Ticehurst (Merryam Cottage) 210
Toronto 172, 174, 191
Torquay Philharmonic Society 115
Tribe, Clarke, Darton and Pollock
    33, 34
Turner, Philip and Margaret 46, 64

Uganda 147, 190

Venables, Malcolm 86
Vidler, Alec 86

Wallace, Ian 167
Wallace, Ross 106, 112
Washington, DC 123
Waterhouse, Vincent 146, 156,
    175, 177
Watson, Irvine 222, 223

Watson, Sydney 76, 81-83, 95, 102
Weir, Gillian 158
Welch, Henry 22
Werry, Nigel 176
Westminster Abbey 36, 145, 161,
    167, 183
Westall, Bishop Wilfrid 22,
    105-107, 141
Whittington Press 220
Wicks, Allan 175, 188, 222
    Elizabeth 188
Wilkinson, Canon 98
Willan, Healey 100
Willcocks, Sir David 156-158
    167, 183, 187
Williams, Claude 79, 80
    Mary 231
Williamson, Henry 47, 61, 64
    122, 130
Wills, Arthur 160
Wilson, J. G. 87
Windsor and Eton Choral Society
    82
Windsor, St George's School 77
Wisconsin, University of 192
Wyton, Alec 175

Yeoman, Dorothy 96
York 43-52, 63, 222, 223

Zimbabwe 195